KT-469-993

Contents

Foreword

C ongratulations on your engagement! The following months will be a
busy and exciting time for the bride and everyone involved in the
wedding preparations. There are many things to consider, numerous
details to plan and decisions to make. This may involve booking the
church and the reception venue, buying clothes and accessories,
interviewing caterers and choosing menus, selecting cars — and keeping
everyone happy at the same time. A look at the Contents pages of this book
may seem a little daunting and no one would deny that there will be
plenty to do, but if preparations are made carefully, the wedding day
should go smoothly without any hitches. The Complete Wedding
Organiser and Record *is designed to assist in the preparations for every
aspect of the wedding day. It is based on etiquette and the experience of
brides who really know what it is like to plan a wedding. There are many
useful charts including timetables, fact files, infill/check lists for use when
making decisions, planning the arrangements with the various service
suppliers, and for record purposes. Consequently the book is the complete
organiser for the special day. Planning should start well in advance so
that the actual organising becomes an enjoyable part of the wedding
preparations and ensures a perfect wedding day.*
*For those marrying for a second time, the last chapter details the subtle
differences according to tradition and what is acceptable today. All
weddings are special and should be celebrated with joy, symbolising hope
and happiness. A new marriage marks a new beginning so there is every
reason to celebrate.*

The Complete Wedding Organiser and Record

Carole Chapman

foulsham

LONDON • NEW YORK • TORONTO • SYDNEY

foulsham

The Publishing House, Bennetts Close, Cippenham, Slough
Berks SL1 5AP, England.

Illustrations by Sarah Sliwinska

While every effort has been made to ensure the accuracy of all the information contained within this book, neither the author nor the publisher can be liable for any errors. In particular, since laws change from time to time, it is vital that each individual checks relevant legal details for themselves.

ISBN: 0-572-02338-3

Typeset in Great Britain by Ann Buchan (Typesetters), Shepperton, Middlesex
Printed in Great Britain by Creative Print and Design (Wales), Ebbw Vale

⁓ Introduction ⁓

F or most couples, their wedding day marks the start of their new life together. The ceremony and celebrations are a public announcement and a private commitment, something to be remembered for the rest of their lives. It is an exciting and perhaps daunting prospect. Involvement in the arrangements for a sister's or brother's wedding may have already provided lots of ideas, but many couples will be starting from scratch. The cost of services and supplies, the suppliers and scheduling may all be a mystery. One thing is certain, the couple will want a wonderful day to mark the start of their married life. So what kind of wedding will be chosen? How much will it cost? Where is the advice on planning that very special day? The answers are all here in The Complete Wedding Organiser and Record.

This book is designed to provide as much information as possible about as many options as possible so that informed decisions can be made on the kind of wedding to be planned. There is a wealth of practical information on how to organise the day and check lists at each stage to help ensure that nothing is forgotten. The book includes not only the etiquette and basic information, it also details what to expect on the day. The aim is to avoid any problems.

There are many things to consider and some will be mentioned in several chapters so the advice is to read through the whole book first, and then study it in more detail. In some areas, such as the catering for the reception for example, it is prudent to seek professional advice. The experts will have handled many similar celebrations and will be aware of what is available and how economies can be made.

Setting an overall budget at an early stage is extremely important since weddings can be very expensive occasions. Keeping to a fixed budget automatically provides a sense of priorities where expenses are concerned and is a good starting point. After all, it is not how much is spent, but how it is spent which is important.

Where etiquette is concerned, it is the couple's decision as to how much they wish to conform. The relevant information is included, but weddings are more flexible these days so the details should be considered and choices made on how the day should be organised. Convention need not be the rule. For example, if a veil seems inappropriate, then this can be omitted; if a garden buffet is more appealing than a formal meal, then this choice should be made. The important thing is that the day is arranged to suit the couple, and that guests are made to feel welcome and able to enjoy themselves.

It may be that the couple's ideas do not fit exactly with those of their parents and they may feel torn between choosing exactly what they want and following the family traditions. There are no easy solutions to this, except to listen tactfully, talk problems through and compromise. It is an emotional time for everyone and a little forethought and understanding will go a long way to making the arrangements easier. Well-meant advice should be received diplomatically!

Now to the actual planning. All available time should be used to best advantage. An early start means plenty of time for making the right decisions. If left too late, preferred suppliers may already be booked, forcing rushed decisions and these of course may not be the best ones. A diary based on the check lists in this book needs to be devised and ample time allowed for 'shopping around'. Magazines are a good source of useful information where ideas may be jotted down and considered before commitments are made. Hence, the style of the wedding will emerge in the mind and it will be easier when making final choices. The couple will want to make all the important decisions themselves. The bride should not forget that the groom will have his own opinions, even though he may not be as interested in the details. Recording wedding plans, keeping up-to-date at every stage and having this book to hand will ensure order and structure to the proceedings.

It is inevitable that at some stage during the preparations, the 'planners' will feel despondent at the very thought of the wedding and when this happens the book should be closed for a few days and any thoughts about marriage erased from the mind; the return to it will induce fresh enthusiasm. It is no surprise that a couple's relationship may suffer during the hectic planning stages. After all, it is probably their first experience of scheduling a major event together, and the excitement is bound to affect their relationship in some way. It does not help to get upset because things are not going as well as hoped; seeking advice and support at a time like this will do wonders.

Everyone enjoys a wedding but the essential extensive planning and preparations can seem unduly daunting for the unwary bride and her family. Spontaneous weddings, spur of the moment flings with all the family organising the celebration a few weeks prior to the big event, have declined and generally today's wedding is often planned and arranged twelve or more months in advance. This book will help you to plan, prepare and decide on the options available, and provides practical guidance about all that a wedding entails.

Everyone dreads things going wrong on the important day and obviously everything will be done to avoid problems, but in the case of minor accidents, for example, a torn seam in the bride's gown, it is important to maintain a sense of proportion. It will no doubt be disappointing but it makes no difference to the real purpose of the day, and probably no one else will even notice.

TRADITION

Joining couples in marriage is a tradition which dates back thousands of years, and is a custom which is immersed in ritualistic significance. Nowadays, not much attention is paid to traditions, customs and superstitions, and it is often difficult to establish why things are done in a particular way. The origins of many of the customs which survive today are very ancient and were originally introduced not merely for enjoyment or convenience, but with a specific purpose, usually associated with warding off evil and bringing good luck, prosperity and children to the newly-married couple. Here are some old traditions concerning marriage in general which are perhaps interesting and amusing.

Originally, 'marriage' was often more like kidnap in that an Anglo-Saxon man would seize his chosen woman from her family and carry her off to keep house and bear children for him. It made no difference whether she was willing or not.

A wife, of course, was a valuable working member of the family as she could cook, clean and bring up a family. When fathers began to realise that their unmarried daughters were a valuable asset, they became more protective and introduced the 'bride price' where women were regarded as their father's 'chattel' or property and in order to acquire this 'chattel', prospective husbands had to show that they could be good providers and began to offer valuable gifts to the family or work off the price of the daughter's hand in marriage. The most famous example of this, of course, is Jacob in the Bible who worked for seven years in order to marry Rachael. Rather than marry off his youngest daughter first, the father substituted her sister Leah, and Jacob had to work a further seven years in order to marry his chosen wife.

Centuries later, the situation was reversed in that fathers began to offer a dowry (payment) to their daughter's prospective husband. This was an insurance against divorce, as the woman now brought something of her own into the marriage, and the husband could only control the dowry as long as they stayed married.

In some societies, children were engaged to one another when they were very young. Contracts were drawn up detailing all the arrangements, and these were considered legally binding. If one family backed out of the arrangements, they could forfeit half their property.

Arranged marriages still take place in some cultures.

1

Preparing For Life Together

Every bride spares some thought for what married life will be like: how she will get on when living with her partner; whether she is making the right decision; whether both partners will change as time goes by; the gravity of her decision to marry. Considering the importance of marriage, it is not surprising that everyone has some apprehensions.

Living With Each Other

Preparing for a life together does not simply mean making plans for the wedding, buying clothes and booking service suppliers. It is true that the wedding marks the start of married life together but there are many issues to be considered beforehand such as compatibility and how lives will be affected by the union. Consequently, it is vital that time is spent learning to communicate about both important and everyday issues.

It is not easy to imagine how marriage will alter a relationship but there can be no doubt that there will be some degree of change. This does not mean that it will take place overnight just because of marriage and neither does it mean that each partner will be magically transformed into the perfect married couple just because they have made their vows.

Everyone has parts of their make-up which will not change; the influence of parents and upbringing shape early life to form the basis of an individual's character but opinions and ideas are developed in the maturing process and are constantly restructured by new experiences and increasing awareness throughout life. On-going and inevitable

maturity subjects opinions and principles to constant adjustment and when living together each partner becomes part of that developing process even though the basis of the character is already established. As people continue to mature and share experiences, characters and relationships develop resulting in a change in the way the partners see each other. This should not be a source of concern but something to welcome. Life would become very boring without change! It may be apparent that other couples no longer seem 'head over heels' in love but their relationship may be different in that they have grown comfortable with each other. This does not mean that their love is any less, it is just different.

A good marriage does not just evolve, it demands commitment, love and the desire to be together. Starting life together is a new experience and will involve a period of getting to know each other by sharing experiences and learning about each other. This may involve a few eye-openers if one partner discovers things about the other that have never been apparent before. Odd habits which were at one time endearing may become annoying when experienced every day. This happens to everyone and is all part of readjustment to life as a married person. Irritations with each other inevitably arise in any relationship and can become a problem if not acknowledged and checked at an early stage. It takes time to get used to each other and a relaxed attitude to the new life helps to keep things in perspective. The role of families may also change in that they can be very supportive and helpful or they can create a nuisance. If the latter happens the problem must be addressed.

As well as being in love and looking forward to spending every day together, there are many practical necessities to consider including work, preparing meals, housework, paying bills — all of which can tarnish expectations if partners are unrealistic about the future.

If both partners understand each other's beliefs and ambitions and know how to talk about such feelings, then this is the best way of starting out together. Each partner needs the ability to respect the other's opinions, even in times of disagreement, and learn to compromise, then there is already a strong relationship on which to build. Compromise is vital in every marriage.

It can be a mistake to think that marriage means doing everything together. Each partner may have their own interests and it may be advisable to retain such individual interests for the future. But at the same time it is important to develop some mutual interests never ceasing to communicate with each other about thoughts, experiences and feelings, recognising each other's strengths and weaknesses.

Love may change and develop and the only way to maintain its strength is to resolve difficulties as they arise by listening and understanding. Even the best marriages suffer stress, doubt and difficult situations. The engagement period may be used to consider how to cope with and resolve such situations. Good communication in any marriage is vital and is the key to keeping a developing relationship fresh and every effort needs to be made during married life to keep such channels open. Talking things through will smooth out the bad times and enable the good times to be enjoyed to the full. Communication must be honest, without anger and recriminations. Problems will not just disappear, they need to be discussed and compromises reached.

Whatever the scale of wedding, the bride is the centre of attention and she may find that after the excitement is over there is an overwhelming feeling of anti-climax. This is only natural after the build up of anticipation and the excitement of the day itself. She should be well prepared for this eventuality by thinking about the commitments being made so that marriage is entered into seriously and with a determination to make it work.

What is a Wedding?

A wedding is a serious ceremony at which life-long commitments are made. It is a celebration, a public performance and a personal experience not to be entered into lightly. Love, romance and ritual make this mysterious and magical event one of the most exciting and memorable experiences of life.

Who gets Married?

The three hundred and fifty thousand or so weddings that take place in England and Wales each year confirm its continued popularity.

Why get Married?

Reasons for marriage are love, togetherness, companionship, sharing a home, social acceptance, joint income benefits, a family. There may be other reasons and it is important to identify such expectations as entry into marriage must be a serious and conscious step towards a life-long stable commitment.

Legal considerations are noted at the end of Chapter 3.

What Does the Future Hold?

When trying to realise expectations, it may be difficult to look beyond the wedding day but it should be remembered that this is only the start of a married life together.

Here are some practicalities:

Accommodation

It is vital that a decision is made concerning accommodation well before the marriage takes place.

Buying a Home

Buying a home provides a starting point in the property market and a residence that feels owned, but of course it is an expensive commitment. Mortgages generally span twenty to twenty-five years and can be obtained from building societies, banks and other organisations, most of which demand a deposit of around ten per cent. Additional expenses include: legal fees, such as solicitors' fees and search fees; survey costs; land registry fees; and furniture removals. It is vital therefore to take good advice about the amount of money that can be realistically loaned as a mortgage, to shop around to obtain the best offer and to borrow only that which can be repaid comfortably at the stipulated time.

There are many bills to pay in addition to paying a mortgage. If a loan is in joint names, each is personally responsible for its repayment if the other fails to make payment. A mortgage will, most likely, be the largest loan for any couple and a joint arrangement can avoid any dispute over ownership of the home should a divorce ever ensue. Lenders will require evidence of ability to repay their loan. This may be a statement of income or they may require some collateral. In particular, any lender granting a mortgage will take a charge on the couple's property which entitles them to sell the home should the couple default on repayments. In the case of inability to make the repayments — whether mortgage, rent, hire purchase or other credit — it is advisable to explain the situation to the lender and request that the terms of the loan be discussed and altered to allow lower repayments for a time.

Renting a Home

Rented accommodation provides independence without the financial strains of owning and upkeeping a purchased property. If rates are reasonable, renting can provide the opportunity to save enough capital for a substantial deposit on a subsequent house purchase which can be an effective way of reducing mortgage payments.

If renting a council house, the conditions and obligations will be clearly identified. If renting privately, it is important that the parties concerned are clear about their rights by entering into signed agreements detailing obligations concerning: the payment of rent, amount, frequency, methods of payment, and the likelihood of increases; what the rent includes, such as heating, electricity, gas, water, telephone; responsibility for repairs and the notice required to terminate the tenancy. If possible, it is advisable to consult the previous tenant and present occupants to ascertain whether the landlord is approachable and whether he or she has a reputation for dealing with problems swiftly and efficiently. It is obviously important to maintain a good working relationship with the landlord.

Sharing a Home

Sharing a home with friends, colleagues or other acquaintances has both advantages and disadvantages. Good communication is essential for any such arrangement to work and many considerations need to be discussed and agreed upon from the outset.

Living with relatives has the obvious advantages of less financial responsibility, shared chores and companionship; the disadvantages include a feeling of marrying the whole family. It is vital to be realistic about how the arrangement is likely to work and to establish conditions early, for instance, housekeeping, division of chores and responsibility for the payment of bills. It is advisable to set a definite time limit on the arrangement after which the couple will move into other accommodation.

Joint Finances

As a married couple it may be advisable to change certain financial arrangements but the decision must suit both partners and both incomes. Competition between banks and building societies means that new types of accounts are becoming available all the time so it is prudent to shop around before making commitments.

It may be preferable to keep separate bank accounts if one partner travels a great deal or it may feel important to retain a personal fund where each takes responsibility for different financial obligations. On the other hand, it can be beneficial to use a mutual fund which is easier to administer as there is only one set of statements. If two cheque books are used for the one account, a record of the balance needs to be kept. Having one account may mean that there will be no arguments over who pays the bills. Similarly, building societies offer a choice of single or joint accounts. Credit agreements can remain in individual names or change to joint names after marriage.

Consideration should also be given to a savings account of which there are many types offered by banks and building societies.

Pensions

Pension and insurance schemes are designed so that by making relatively small regular contributions, claims may be made on the fund at some future date when specified eventualities dictate.

It is important to provide for retirement. Pension plan choices include employer's, government's or private plans and if the employer's plan is not attractive or non-existent, it is prudent to take out an affordable savings plan spread over a stated number of years. Marriage may make a difference to payments and returns.

Insurance

Life

Life insurance is a safeguard for dependants and is especially important if there is a family. The couple may be already covered for personal insurance under mortgage arrangement but if this is not the case, it is advisable to arrange life insurance in each other's favour. If depending on two incomes and one is suddenly terminated, the working part-

ner could be left in financial difficulties especially if caring for children.

Cover should include enough to replace income for as long as possible, take care of children and pay many of the bills. Advice about a suitable policy should be sought from a reputable firm.

Buildings

Home buildings insurance is obligatory when buying a home.

Home Contents

Home contents should be insured against possible loss such as from theft and fire. The policy should cover the replacement value as new and the coverage should be upgraded every year to keep pace with inflation.

Most companies offer a 'new for old' policy which means that for a damaged carpet for instance, payment will be equivalent to the cost of a comparable new carpet even though the damaged one was several years old. All policies differ and it is wise to be aware of any exceptions or penalty clauses, such as paying the first £50 of any claim. It is easy to underestimate the value of possessions so it is wise to keep the list and values up-to-date. Many policies require the applicant to list any items over a certain value, or items which are to be insured whether they are in or out of the home, such as jewellery. Photographs of particularly valuable items and the use of security markers provide good means of identification in the event of loss. The wedding gift list will be a guide when listing the contents and value of possessions for insurance purposes.

Financial Planning

Money problems can be one of the major causes of disagreements in any relationship. A sense and an understanding of how much will be left for savings and leisure activities after the bills are paid can go a long way towards preventing disputes. All couples should discuss how they intend to manage their financial affairs.

It is essential that finances are organised carefully so that there are no disagreements about money and no financial difficulties. Priorities need to be established and a simple budget set for the first year to allow for revision as circumstances change and to provide rough guidelines for assessing realistic spending power. Income and outgoings should be realistic and an assessment made of the money left over for leisure and savings. Being realistic in advance prevents disappointments later. If income and outgoings do not balance, some adjustments will be necessary.

	BRIDE	GROOM
Do you expect to share all your debts and assets?		
Will you have separate or joint bank accounts?		
Will you have a joint mortgage or rent agreement?		
Will you take the responsibility for making all the financial decisions or will these be made together?		
Do you ever worry about your partner's attitude towards money?		
How do you feel about using credit or credit cards?		
How important is it to you that bills are paid on time?		
Who will be responsible for their actual payment?		
Do you plan to save?		
Do you plan to make long-term investments?		
If so, will they be separately or jointly held?		
Have you considered separate pension plans, life insurance and death benefits?		
Will you have a household budget?		
If you regularly overspend, would you be prepared to transfer the budgeting to your partner?		
Do you manage your day-to-day finances efficiently?		
Do your cheques often bounce?		
Are you the right one to manage the finances?		
How do you feel about a wife having a larger income than her husband?		
Would you consider writing a legal contract outlining your financial arrangements?		
How would you cope with redundancy?		
How would you cope with disability and its impact on your income?		

INFILL LIST	FINANCES			
	£ per annum	£ per quarter	£ per month	£ per week
INCOME (net)				
Husband				
Wife				
Interest, etc.				
Other				
TOTAL INCOME				
OUTGOINGS				

Home
  Mortgage/Rent
  Council Tax
  Home insurance
  Hire purchase repayments
  Loan repayments
  Water rates
  Gas
  Electricity
  Telephone
  Television licence
  Home maintenance
  Home improvements
  Household items				

Housekeeping
  Food
  Cleaning				

Travelling/motoring
  Loan repayments
  Insurance
  Tax
  MOT
  Maintenance
  Fuel
  Other travelling				

Clothes, Accessories and Personal
  Wife
  Husband				

Medical
  Doctors
  Dentist				

Leisure
  Sport
  Entertainment
  Gifts
  Holidays				

Savings				
Pensions				
Other				
TOTALS				

2

Engagement

*E*ngagements began in the sixth century when King Ethelbert deemed it
illegal for a man to 'steal' the woman of his choice from her family,
thereby protecting her father from losing a useful pair of hands.
The penalty for stealing a woman was a fine of fifty shillings to com-
pensate lost 'manpower'. The 'wed', as it was known, sealed an agreement
between the groom and the bride's father that a marriage would take place.
In Victorian times, a man would first obtain the permission of his
prospective bride's father by formally requesting 'her hand in marriage'.
The prospective groom had a legal obligation to marry his betrothed and
if he jilted her, she could sue her former fiancé for 'breach of promise'.

Today an engagement has no legal standing and a proposal of marriage could as
easily come from the woman as from the
man, but usually it is the man who poses
the all-important question. When the
woman has accepted the proposal she
then has the right to name the day.

Announcements

Informal

Family and Friends

Announcing an engagement is much less
formal today but it is still worth bearing
in mind a few pointers.

Although these days it is the exception rather than the rule, taking the
trouble to ask or discuss intentions with
the woman's father is still one of the best
ways of establishing an amicable son-in-
law/father-in-law relationship. However,
more often the couple usually tell their
parents that they have decided to get
married and ask for their 'blessing'. It is
important to ensure that there are no
absolute objections to the marriage and
that the bride's parents are satisfied that
the prospective son-in-law can provide
the happiness and support their daughter is expecting.

> **TRADITION AND SUPERSTITION**
>
> *The prospective groom made his proposal
> of marriage in a romantic setting and by
> appealing humbly on bended knee. In the
> past it was thought that to be engaged more
> than once meant positive damnation!
> If the groom's representatives saw a monk,
> a blind man or a pregnant woman when
> visiting the prospective bride or her family,
> these were bad omens and indicated that
> they should abandon their visit. Nanny
> goats, a pigeon or a wolf were good omens
> and meant that they should proceed.
> The first letter of the bride's surname:
> Change the name and not the letter —
> You'll marry for worse and not for better.*

Both sets of parents should be informed as soon as possible and should
be the first to learn of the news. It is
traditional for the bride's parents to be
informed first. Face-to-face communication is always desirable but if this is
impossible, a telephone call is the next
best option.

It is only natural that when a couple
become engaged, they want everyone to
know and of course family and friends
want to share the news and convey best
wishes. Most people like to inform close

relatives and friends personally or by telephone, and many people write to other relations and friends announcing their engagement and giving a few details about their fiancé/fiancée and their future plans. If letters are to be sent, it is advisable to post them all at the same time so that no one feels excluded from the news. A list of all those to be informed is a good idea.

If both sets of parents are unacquain-ted, arrangements should be made for them to meet and socialise at, perhaps, a family dinner which is traditionally paid for by the groom's parents if the bride's parents will be paying for the wedding. If a meeting of both sets of parents is impossible because of distance, it is a thoughtful gesture if they exchange letters mentioning their happiness at the news and that they are looking forward to meeting one another at the wedding. Traditionally the groom's mother writes the first letter but it is perfectly acceptable for the bride's mother to make the first approach. Many couples these days prefer the informal announcement with or without the date of the wedding.

Formal

Party

Some couples like to announce their engagement officially and as a surprise at a party given by parents who already know the news.

The bride's mother issues the invitations. For a formal seated dinner party, the wording for invitations might be:

> *Mr and Mrs Nancy North request the pleasure of the company of . . . at an engagement party to celebrate the engagement of Nel North and Samuel South on Saturday . . . at 8 pm at The Homestead,*
> *Northton*
>
> *Mrs N. North*
> *(Address)*   *RSVP*

For a less formal setting, the wording might be:

> *Nel North and Samuel South*
> *invite you/Ann Other*
> *to a party*
> *to celebrate our engagement*
> *on . . .*
> *at . . .*
>   *RSVP*

or

> *To: . . .*
> *Please join us to celebrate*
> *our engagement.*
> *Time . . .*
> *Place . . .*
> *From . . .*
>   *RSVP*

The bride's father makes the announcement at the celebration and toasts the happy couple. The prospective groom replies by proposing the health of both sets of parents.

Guests will usually bring gifts but it is not usual for the couple to distribute a list as they might for wedding gifts. Whatever is offered must be acknow-ledged formally and immediately with a handwritten thank-you note.

Some couples prefer a party purely for friends when they make their own announcement.

The engagement ring is not usually worn in public until the engagement has been officially announced.

Newspapers

Some couples choose to announce their engagement in the national newspapers, but for most an announcement in their local paper is a good way of informing neighbours and casual friends of their engagement. Conventionally, it is the bride's parents who announce the engagement of their daughter in the press unless the couple are older or marrying for the second time. The parents (usually the mother) of the bride-to-be, or the bride, is responsible for sending the announcement to the editor of the chosen newspaper (national or local) a week or so beforehand, stating the date on which the announcement is to appear and including a daytime telephone number in case of queries. Many papers have a standard form for obtaining this information. Whether hand-writing the announcement or filling in a form, the script must be clearly legible and spelled correctly.

Example wording for the press:
Formal

> *Mr S South and Miss/Ms N North*
> *The engagement is announced between Samuel, only son of Mr and Mrs Sidney South of Southton and Nel, youngest daughter of Mr and Mrs Nigel North of Northton.*

or

> *The marriage has been arranged (and will shortly take place) between Mr Samuel South, son of . . . of . . . and Nel, daughter of . . . of . . .*

or

> *Mr and Mrs Nigel North are pleased to announce the engagement of their daughter Nel to Mr Samuel South, son of Mr and Mrs . . . of . . .*

If the groom's father is dead and his mother re-married:

> *Samuel, son of the late Mr Sidney South, stepson of Mr John James*

If the groom's mother was still married to the groom's father at the time of his death:

> *Samuel, son of the late Mr Sidney South and Mrs South*

If the groom's mother was already divorced from the groom's father when he died:

> *Samuel, son of the late Mr Sidney South and Mrs Sandy South*

If the groom's mother had re-married before the groom's father died:

> *Samuel, son of the late Mr Sidney South and Mrs Sandy West*

Less formal

> *Nigel and Nancy North are delighted to announce the engagement of their daughter Nel to Samuel, son of . . .*

> *Nel North*
> *Samuel South*
> *Nel and Sam together with their families are delighted to announce their engagement*

'Son/daughter of' implies the only son/daughter. 'Younger/elder' implies younger/elder of two. 'Youngest/eldest' implies youngest/eldest of three or more.

It is unwise to include a full home address in the press as this may alert burglars to the prospect of engagement and wedding gifts!

. . . .
TRADITION AND SUPERSTITION
On country farms where bees are kept it is customary to tell the bees of the forthcoming marriage and to give them some of the wedding cake!
. . . .

Well-wishers

Well-wishers should congratulate the groom; women are not to be congratulated but wished every future happiness.

Engagement Ring

. . . .
TRADITION
The Romans introduced the engagement ring and after they converted to Christianity, a ninth-century Pope deemed that engagement rings must be worn.
It is worn on the third finger of her left hand because the Greeks considered that this finger was connected to the heart.
. . . .

An engagement ring is offered by the groom to his prospective bride as a token of the promise made. There is no necessity for the bride-to-be to have an engagement ring but if desired, its design can take any form — it does not have to be a diamond.

In return for the engagement ring, it is usual for the bride-to-be to give her fiancé an engagement gift, such as a gold signet ring, chain, or a tie clip.

More information about engagement rings is contained in Chapter 16.

INFILL/CHECK LIST **INFORMAL ANNOUNCEMENTS**

Name	Address	Telephone	Visit ✓	Letter ✓	Tel Call ✓	Done ✓

INFILL/CHECK LIST

Press	Newspaper	Address	Telephone	Wording
National				
Local				

When to Marry

There are a number of considerations when deciding when to marry and setting the exact date may require some manoeuvering so that arrangements suit the diaries of the couple (work/examination commitments for instance) and special guests, and the bookings for the service, reception and honeymoon. It is virtually impossible to arrange a formal wedding in less than six weeks, and probably the minimum realistic length of an engagement should be three months. Some religious denominations forbid marriage on certain dates and at certain times. The minister will be able to advise about such restrictions.

Day and Time

Legally marriages may take place on any day of the week but not at any hour of the day. The law specifies that marriages have to take place between 8 am and 6 pm. The only exceptions are Jewish and Quaker ceremonies and weddings per-formed under Special Licence or a Register General's Licence.

Weddings are generally not allowed in churches on Sundays and in synagogues on the Jewish Sabbath (sundown Friday to sundown Saturday). Register offices are closed on Saturday afternoons and on Sundays. The day of the week on which the marriage takes place has superstition surrounding it but despite this, most people marry on Saturday and this is certainly more convenient for working guests. However, it is quite acceptable to have a weekday wedding if this suits those concerned.

SUPERSTITION

It is considered unlucky to marry on a Friday especially on Friday 13th. To marry earlier in the week is meant to be more fortunate.
Married on a:

Monday	*brides will be healthy*
Tuesday	*brides will be wealthy*
Wednesday	*brides do best of all*
Thursday	*brides will suffer losses*
Friday	*brides will suffer crosses*
Saturday	*brides will have no luck at all*

FORMAL ANNOUNCEMENTS					
Photo				Publication	Deadline
Can we have one?	If so, black and white/colour	Size required	Is it returned?	Day and Date	Date

Date

Legally marriages may take place on any date, except Christmas Day and Good Friday. Many brides favour a specific season but particularly for a large or formal wedding, it is very important to allow enough time for preparations. The bride will also need to consider the convenience of the guests and avoid times when many are likely to be on holiday or when the weather may make travel difficult; it would be unfair to inflict long winter journeys on elderly or infirm relatives if this can be avoided.

It is also worth considering the health aspect. Hay fever or bronchitis sufferers may wish to avoid certain months. If the bride suffers great discomfort at some particular time in every month, it would be advisable to plan a date in between these events.

> **SUPERSTITION**
> *The month of May is considered unlucky because it was the month in which the Romans celebrated the feast of the dead and the festival of the goddess of chastity.*
> *Marry in May, rue the day!*
> *Marry in May, unhappy for Aye!*
> *A June wedding was considered to guarantee a happy marriage.*
> *June became popular because the ancient Greeks and Romans honoured Juno, the goddess of love and marriage.*

Spring and summer weddings are generally the most popular because of the likelihood of good weather and the fact that there is more opportunity to take a holiday as a honeymoon. Anyone booking a winter wedding can expect a dark afternoon.

When the date has been roughly decided upon, it is necessary to ascertain the dates on which the ceremony and reception venues are available.

> **SUPERSTITION**
> *Marry when the year is new;*
> *Always loving, kind and true;*
> *When February birds do mate,*
> *You may wed or dread your fate.*
> *If you wed when March winds blow*
> *Joy and sorrow both you'll know.*
> *Marry in April when you can,*
> *Joy for maiden and for man.*
> *Marry in the month of May,*
> *You will surely rue the day.*
> *Marry when June roses blow,*
> *Over land and sea you'll go.*
> *They who in July do wed,*
> *Must labour always for their bread.*
> *Whoever wed in August be,*
> *Many a change are sure to see.*
> *Marry in September's shine,*
> *Your living will be rich and fine.*
> *If in October you do marry,*
> *Love will come, but riches tarry.*
> *If you wed in bleak November,*
> *Only joy will come, remember.*
> *When December snows fall fast,*
> *Marry and true love will last.*

Type and Style of Wedding

An early consideration before starting the wedding planning is the type of wedding — whether it will be a church or civil ceremony. This largely depends on religious beliefs. If a traditional wedding is chosen there are many variations of style to consider.

Military

If one or both of the couple is in the Forces, it may be desirable to have a military-style wedding. If the groom is in the Forces, he may wear his regulation uniform, but a bride in the Forces may prefer to wear a traditional dress. Attending military personnel may also wear uniform.

Clergy

If the groom is a minister, the couple may choose to be married at his church rather than at the bride's parish church. The groom may wear his vestments. It is customary to invite the entire congregation to attend the wedding ceremony, although they do not have to be invited to the reception.

INFILL/CHECK LIST			SETTING THE DATE
Year	Season		Month

Wedding
Possible dates

Dates to be avoided	Bride		Groom
Decided date Day		Time	
Availability: Best Man			
Chief Bridesmaid			
Bridesmaid			
Bridesmaid			
Bridesmaid			
Flower Girl			
Page			
Page			
Page			
Usher			
Usher			
Usher			
Bride's Parents			
Groom's Parents			
Church/Register Office			
Reception Venue			

Notes

Honeymoon Dates From To

Notes

If a minister's son or daughter is to be married, he may conduct the ceremony in the chosen church if the resident minister agrees. The bride's father could give the address.

Double and Mass Weddings

Double weddings which usually involve twins, siblings or close friends are not uncommon but ceremonies involving the simultaneous marriage of three couples are rare. There is no restriction on mass weddings linking together any number of couples at the same time.

Double and mass weddings can be economical in terms of reception and attendant expenses, especially for weddings of twins or sisters. In the procedures, the elder or eldest sister takes precedence. If they are not twins or sisters, then the elder groom and his bride are attended first.

Breaking off the Engagement

Admitting a mistake takes courage and can be painful but a broken engagement is much less painful than a broken marriage. It is far better to offend the family than enter into a life-long commitment about which there are uncertainties.

Relatives and friends can be informed quietly and they should not expect an explanation. A simple note to relatives and friends should suffice; something along the following lines:

> *Nel North and Samuel South regret to inform you that the wedding, arranged for (day, date, time and place) will not now take place. Thank you very much for your kindness.*

However, if the engagement was announced in the press, the bride's family should place a brief notice in the same newspaper:

> *The marriage arranged between Nel North and Samuel South will not now take place.*

or

> *Mr and Mrs Nigel North announce that the marriage of their daughter Nel to Mr Samuel South will not now take place.*

If an engagement is broken by the bride-to-be, etiquette demands that she offers to return the ring immediately together with any gifts she has received from her fiancé. However, if the groom-to-be breaks off the engagement, his betrothed is entitled to keep the ring, although she may decide that it would be more reasonable to return it.

The couple must offer to return engagement and early wedding gifts which they may have received prior to the wedding.

INFILL/CHECK LIST		ENGAGEMENT
	Notes	Date done
Inform everyone		
Arrange press announcements		
Select engagement ring		
Plan engagement party		
Write thank-you notes to gift-donors		
Set the wedding date		

3

Legal Requirements

This chapter deals with the legal requirements that must be fulfilled and seems long and complicated for the simple reason that there are many rules which must be observed. The Marriage Act 1994 changed the law in two ways; firstly, local authorities may license 'suitable premises' for the solemnization of marriage, and secondly, there is no need to live in the district in which marriage is to take place. Ministers and local registrars should be consulted with queries or doubts as they are able to explain the simplest and best solution for each individual. The word 'wedding' originates from the Anglo-Saxon word 'wed' meaning pledge and it is this that constitutes a marriage.

Public Declaration

For a marriage to be legal in Britain, it has to be a public declaration before at least two adult witnesses and the couple must fulfil the legal requirements. As the wedding cannot be private, the doors must not be locked while the ceremony is in progress.

Who can Conduct the Ceremony?

In England and Wales, a marriage must be solemnized by an uthorised person(s). These include:
• Superintendent Registrars and registrars (civil ceremony)
• ordained ministers of the Church of England (in a ceremony performed according to the rites of the Church of England)
• ministers of other religious denominations who have been legally authorised to register marriages.

If marrying in accordance with the rites of a religious denomination other than the Church of England, a licence has to be obtained from the authorised registrar for the area. The building in which the marriage takes place must normally be registered for marriages. The minister, or if he is not authorised, the registrar, must be present to register the marriage.

Sex

In the United Kingdom, it is a legal condition that one partner must have been born male and the other female.

Consent

Both people to be married must be acting by their own consent.

Sound Mind

Both people to be married must be of sufficiently sound mind to understand the nature of the marriage contract.

Minimum Age

Both partners must be over the age of sixteen. If either is under eighteen and previously unmarried, a parent or guardian's legal consent is needed. If parental consent is unreasonably with-held, it is possible to apply for a court order. However, someone between the ages of sixteen and eighteen who has been divorced or widowed does not need parental consent.

Relations Who May Not Marry

The prohibited marriages are those of close family or blood relatives. Marriage solemnized between persons within these degrees of relationship is void:

For men	For women
Mother	Father
Adoptive mother or former adoptive mother	Adoptive father or former adoptive father
Daughter	Son
Adoptive daughter or former adoptive daughter	Adoptive son or former adoptive son
Father's mother	Father's father
Mother's mother	Mother's father
Son's daughter	Son's son
Daughter's daughter	Daughter's son
Sister	Brother
Father's sister	Father's brother
Mother's sister	Mother's brother
Brother's daughter	Brother's son
Sister's daughter	Sister's son
Wife's mother	Husband's father
Wife's daughter	Husband's son
Father's wife	Mother's husband
Son's wife	Daughter's husband
Father's father's wife	Father's mother's husband
Mother's father's wife	Mother's mother's husband
Wife's father's mother	Husband's father's father
Wife's mother's mother	Husband's mother's father
Wife's son's daughter	Husband's son's son
Wife's daughter's daughter	Husband's daughter's son
Son's son's wife	Son's daughter's husband
Daughter's son's wife	Daughter's daughter's husband

Note: 'brother' and 'sister' include half-brothers and half-sisters. If there is any doubt, the minister or superintendent registrar should be consulted.

Certain Degrees of Affinity

Marriage is prohibited between persons within certain degrees of affinity, unless certain conditions are met.

The conditions under which a marriage within the below degrees of affinity is permissible are that both parties to the marriage have attained the age of twenty-one at the time of the marriage and that the younger party has not at any time before attaining the age of eighteen been a child of the family (i.e. a child who has lived in the same household as that person and been treated by that person as child of the family) in relation to the other party.

For men	For women
Daughter of former wife	Son of former husband
Former wife of father	Former husband of mother
Former wife of father's father	Former husband of father's mother
Former wife of mother's father	Former husband of mother's mother
Daughter of son of former wife	Son of son of former husband
Daughter of daughter of former wife	Son of daughter of former husband

In addition, marriage to the parent of a former spouse is prohibited unless both parties to the marriage have attained the age of twenty-one and both the former spouse and the other parent of the former spouse are dead when the marriage is solemnized. Marriage to the former spouse of a son or daughter is similarly prohibited unless both parties to the marriage have attained the age of twenty-one and both the son or daughter and other parent of the son or daughter are dead when the marriage is solemnized.

A valid marriage may be contracted between a man and a woman who is the sister, aunt, or niece of a former wife of his (whether living or not), or was formerly the wife of his brother, uncle, or nephew (whether living or not). This applies also where the kinship is of the half-blood. However, a marriage is not valid if either party is at the time of the marriage domiciled in a country outside Great Britain which does not recognise its validity.

The following notes outline the legal requirements for marriage in England or Wales. Further information may be obtained from any Superintendent Registrar (addresses and telephone numbers can be found in the telephone directory under Registration of Births, Marriages and Deaths) or from the General Register Office for England and Wales (see page 39).

Before a marriage may take place in England or Wales, there are certain preliminary formalities that the law required to be observed. These fall into two categories.

Civil

These must precede every marriage in a register office or on approved premises or according to any religious faith other than the Church of England (see paragraphs 1–7).

Ecclesiastical

A marriage in the Church of England may take place after certain civil preliminaries (see paragraphs 1–4), but it is more usual for the marriage to follow banns or a licence by the Church authorities (see paragraphs 14–16).

Superintendent Registrar's Certificate without Licence

The official will fill in a form giving the bride's and groom's names and addresses, ages and the location of the ceremony. A declaration has to be signed which states that there is no legal objection to the marriage.

1. If both parties reside in the same registration district, each party must have lived within that district seven days immediately preceding the giving of the notice. Notice must be given to the Superintendent Registrar of that district and may be given by either party.

2. If the parties reside in different districts notice must be given to the Superintendent Registrar of each district. Each party may give notice in his/her district or either party may give both notices. However, notice cannot be accepted until both parties have lived in their respective districts for the seven days immediately preceding.

3. The building in which the marriage is to take place must be specified in every notice of marriage.

4. Twenty-one clear days must intervene between the day on which the Superintendent Registrar enters the notice in his notice book and the day on which he issues his certificate. The marriage may then take place at any time within three months from the day on which the notice was entered.

Superintendent Registrar's Certificate and Licence

As with the Certificate without Licence, the relevant information is included on the appropriate form and a declaration is completed, but the residence qualifications are different.

5. Both parties must be in England or Wales or must have their usual residence in England or Wales on the day the notice is given. Only one notice is required whether the parties reside in the same or different registration districts and the notice may be given by either party. One of the parties must have resided in the registration district in which notice is to be given for fifteen days immediately preceding the giving of the notice. If both parties have resided for fifteen days in different districts, the notice may be given to the Superintendent Registrar of either district.

6. The building in which the marriage is to take place must be specified in the notice.

7. One clear day, other than a Sunday, Christmas Day or Good Friday, must intervene between the day on which the Superintendent Registrar enters the notice in his notice book and the day on which he issues his certificate and licence. The marriage may then take place at any time within three months from the day on which the notice was entered.

Marriage in Special Circumstances

Marriage of House-bound and Detained Persons

8. Marriage between parties, of whom one is either house-bound or a person detained as a prisoner or mental patient, may be solemnized on the authority of a Superintendent Registrar's Certificate Without Licence at the residence of the party who is house-bound or detained.

9. Notice of marriage must be given as set out in paragraphs 1–4. Further information can be obtained from the Superintendent Registrar who will also explain what evidence is required to meet the statutory conditions.

10. The marriage may be solemnized according to the rites of the Church of England, by such other religious ceremony as the parties choose (other than according to the usages of the Jews or the Society of Friends), or by civil ceremony.

Registrar General's Licence

This method was introduced in 1970 and is reserved for cases of extreme illness where it would be impossible for the marriage to take place in a register office or other registered building. The licence permits the marriage to be solemnized in any place and at any time within three months from the date of entry in the notice book. There is no residence qualification and the licence can be issued immediately.

11. Where a person who is seriously ill and not expected to recover and is too ill to be moved to a register office or registered building, the Registrar General may grant a licence for the marriage to be solemnized in the place where the patient is lying.

12. Notice of marriage must be given personally by one of the parties to the Superintendent Registrar of the district in which the marriage is to be solemnized, who will explain what evidence is required. There is no waiting period before the licence may be issued.

13. The marriage may be solemnized by civil ceremony or according to the rites of a denomination other than the Church of England, or according to the usages of the Jews or the Society of Friends. (For marriage in such circumstances according to the rites of the Church of England see paragraph 16.)

Marriage According to the Rites of the Church of England

14. A Church of England marriage may be solemnized after any of the following four preliminaries:

i the publication of banns;

ii the issue of an ecclesiastical licence (in these notes referred to as a common licence);

iii the issue of a special licence granted by or on behalf of the Archbishop of Canterbury;

iv the issue of a Superintendent Registrar's certificate.

15. Questions relating to marriage according to the rites of the Church of England are a matter for the Ecclesiastical Authorities. Further information is available upon application to the clergyman of the church in which it is desired that the marriage shall take place.

Generally, both parties will be expected to be members of the Church of England and at least one of them should live in the parish of the church where the marriage is to take place, although exceptions are made, for example, if marrying by Special Licence or if an established member of a church outside the home parish.

Banns

16. This is the most popular and cheapest method. The minister of the parish in which it is proposed that the marriage should take place needs to be visited. If it is proposed that another minister officiates at the wedding, for example, an old friend of the family, this should be discussed. The couple may be expected to meet the minister several times as he or she needs to be sure that the implications of the commitment are fully understood. When all of the preliminaries have been completed, the minister will publish the banns. If known generally by another name which is not on the birth certificate, the banns should give that name, or both. This is because the purpose of publishing banns is to publicise the forthcoming marriage, and to substitute a misleading name is fraudulent.

Application for the publication of banns should be made to the clergyman of the parish in which each party resides; a small fee is payable. Banns must be published on three Sundays before the marriage can take place. This practice dates from the fourteenth century when cousins were forbidden to marry and three weeks was allowed for objectors to come forward.

The banns are published by being read aloud in church on three successive Sundays preceding the ceremony.

They are normally read at the main service and the couple usually attend church on at least one of these three occasions. When the couple do not live in the same parish, the banns must be read in both parishes and a certificate confirming this must be obtained from the minister whose church is not being used for the ceremony to give to the officiating minister. Once the banns have been published, the wedding can take place on any day within the following three months. If there is a delay the banns will have to be called again.

The church authorities advise that a marriage in a church of the Church of England between two foreigners or between a foreigner and a British subject should be by licence and not after banns.

Common Licence

This exempts the parties from the necessity of banns and is a much quicker procedure. There need only be one clear day's notice before the licence is issued. A Common Licence may be obtained from the Faculty Office in London, or from the Bishop's Register Office (in any cathedral town) or from one of the Surrogates for granting licences in the diocese. If the local minister does not hold this title himself, he will be able to advise on how and where the licence may be obtained in the particular area.

To obtain the licence, one of the couple must appear in person and sign a declaration that there is no legal reason why the marriage cannot properly take place and that one or both of them have lived for at least fifteen days prior to the application in the parish of the church where they can be married.

Special Licence

This is issued only by the Archbishop of Canterbury at the Faculty Office and is granted only in grave emergencies or very exceptional circumstances, for example, when there is some particular reason why normal methods are unsuitable, and enable a marriage to be solemnized according to the rites of the Church of England at any time and place without restrictions but within three months of the date of issue.

Superintendent Registrar's Certificate

This method is very rarely used. A marriage according to the rites of the Church of England may be solemnized on the authority of a certificate of a Superintendent Registrar instead of after the publication of banns. In such cases:

i the conditions set out in paragraphs 1–4 apply. In addition, note that, with certain exceptions, one of the parties must have the required residence in the parish or ecclesiastical district in which the church or chapel where the marriage is to take place is situated. Further, the place of residence and the church or chapel must be within the registration district of the Superintendent Registrar to whom notice is given;

ii the marriage may not be solemnized without the consent of the clergyman of the church or chapel in which it is desired it shall take place or by any person other than a clergyman of the Church of England;

iii the notice to the Superintendent Registrar takes the place of the publication of banns – there cannot be publication of banns in respect of one party and the issue of a Superintendent Registrar's certificate for the other party.

General Information

Fees

17. Civil preliminaries – details are available from Superintendent Registrars.

18. All parishes in the provinces of Canterbury and York – derived from the table of fees issued by the Church Commissioners. Details are available from ministers.

Giving Notice

19. Where notice of marriage has to be given to a Superintendent Registrar it should, whenever possible, be given to that officer direct. For the convenience of the parties, however, notice may usually be attested on personal attendance before any Registrar of Births, Deaths and Marriages for the district in which the party giving the notice resides. The notice so attested may then be sent by post or otherwise to the Superintendent Registrar but the party giving the notice is responsible for the cost of transmission and must take the risk of delay or loss in transit. The notice is held not to have been duly 'given' until it has been received by the Superintendent Registrar and entered in his notice book.

Consent to the Marriage of a Minor

20. The consent of parents or other lawful guardians/guardian of a person under eighteen years of age must first be obtained and it should be produced in writing when notice of marriage is given to a Superintendent Registrar. The fact that such consent has been obtained forms a part of the declarations which are made when the notice of marriage is given or when application is made for a common or special licence. If the parents or guardians are abroad, their signatures to the consent should be properly witnessed, preferably by a notary or a Consular Officer. When the marriage is to be solemnized after the publication of banns and the parent or other lawful guardian openly declares in the church or chapel, at the time of the publication, his dissent from the marriage, the publication of banns will be void. A marriage may not take place between persons either of whom is under the age of sixteen.

Objections to a Marriage

21. If any circumstances are alleged which, if true, would invalidate a notice of marriage, or if any caveat has been entered, the issue of the licence or certificate may be delayed until the allegation has been satisfactorily met by the party who gave the notice.

Production of Documents

22. If the birth certificates of the persons getting married are readily available it is helpful to the Superintendent Registrar if they can be produced when notice of marriage is given. In the case of a marriage involving a person from abroad, an official travel or identity document for that person should be produced.

All persons who have been previously

married should also produce documentary evidence of the death of the former spouse or of the dissolution or annulment of the marriage. Photocopies of the documents are not acceptable without certification. All relevant certificates or licences must be handed to the minister or registrar before the ceremony.

Witnesses

23. The parties to the marriage must arrange for the attendance of two witnesses to be present at the marriage and to sign the marriage register.

Marriage Certificate

24. A certified copy of the entry recording the marriage may be obtained at the time of marriage.

Scotland

The rules governing weddings are slightly different under Scottish law and are governed by The Marriage (Scotland) Act 1977. Gretna Green was associated with runaway marriages and elopements because it is the first place over the Scottish border and Scotland's marriage regulations are not as restrictive as those of England and Wales and at one time it was possible to marry in Scotland simply by a declaration before two witnesses. However, Scottish laws have now been tightened. The minister still has wider discretionary powers than he does in England and Wales. Banns are unnecessary and it may be possible to marry at a chosen venue.

A couple may be married by a registrar, or assistant registrar, and the wedding will normally be held in his office. Alternatively, a couple may be married by any clergyman who is entitled to undertake marriages under the Act. The minimum age for marriage in Scotland is sixteen and those under eighteen do not need the permission of parents and guardians. There must be two witnesses present who are at least sixteen years of age.

A marriage notice form must be obtained from a registrar of births, marriages and deaths in Scotland whose address will be in the telephone directory. Both parties must fill in their names, addresses, sex and marital status. They must confirm that they are not closely related in any way that forbids marriage. The forms must be signed and if any of the information given is incorrect, the marriage will not be valid.

If either of the parties has been married before, the forms must be completed at least six weeks before the ceremony. Otherwise they should be completed about a month before (fifteen days is the minimum). The forms must be returned to the registrar for the district where the ceremony is to take place. He will also require birth certificates. If either of the parties has been married before, it is necessary to produce a death certificate of former spouse or the divorce decree. If either party lives outside the United Kingdom, they must produce documentation, in a certified translation if necessary, that there are no reasons in their own country why they should not be married.

The registrar will then prepare a marriage schedule. If the ceremony is to be in his office, he will keep this until the wedding. If it is to be held elsewhere, one party must collect it in person not more than a week before the wedding. After the ceremony, the schedule must be signed by the bride and groom, two witnesses and the minister who conducted the wedding. This needs to be returned to the registrar within three days. Arrangements must also be made with the church or register office where the ceremony is to take place.

One Party Resident in Scotland

25. If one of the parties lives in Scotland and the other in England or Wales, the one in Scotland should give notice in the normal way. The one in England should give notice to the Superintendent Registrar where he or she lives. Notices issued in England and Wales are valid in Scotland and vice versa, as long as only one of the parties lives in Scotland. Marriage by licence in a register office in England or Wales, however, is not possible in this case. A marriage may take place in England or Wales in a registered building, a register office or according to the usages of the Society of Friends or the Jews, on production of a Superintendent Registrar's certificate in respect of the party living in England or Wales and a Scottish registrar's certificate of no impediment in respect of the party living in Scotland. For information about the procedure to be followed by the party resident in Scotland, application should be made to the Registrar General, General Register Office for Scotland (see page 39).

26. A marriage in England or Wales in a church or chapel of the Church of England or the Church in Wales may be solemnized after banns or by common licence or, with the consent of the officiating clergyman, on production of a Superintendent Registrar's certificate in respect of the party living in England or Wales and a Scottish registrar's certificate of no impediment in respect of the party in Scotland.

Marriage in Scotland

27. The party resident in England or Wales may obtain a Superintendent Registrar's certificate for production to the registrar in Scotland, or may give notice to the registrar in Scotland, either in person or by post. It is recommended that, about six weeks before the date of marriage, enquiry should be made of the Scottish registrar in whose district the marriage is to take place.

28. Further information may be obtained from the Registrar General (see page 39).

One Party Resident in Ireland

29. Where one of the parties lives in Northern Ireland or the Irish Republic and the other in England or Wales, a marriage may take place in England or Wales in a church or chapel of the Church of England or the Church in Wales after the banns or by common licence.

30. If the residence of one of the parties is in Northern Ireland a marriage may be solemnized in England or Wales in a non-conformist registered building, a register office, according to the usages of the Society of Friends or the Jews or, with the consent of the clergyman, in a church or chapel of the Church of England on the authority of a Superintendent Registrar's certificate in respect of the party living in England or Wales and a certificate issued by a District Registrar of Marriages in Northern Ireland in respect of the party living there. For information as to the procedure to be followed by the party resident in Northern Ireland, application should be made to the Registrar General, General Register Office for Northern Ireland (see page 39).

31. If, however, one of the parties lives in the Irish Republic and the marriage is to take place in England or Wales, notice cannot be given to a Superintendent Registrar until that party arrives in England or Wales and has acquired the necessary residential qualification.

Northern Ireland

In order to marry in Northern Ireland notice must be given to the District Registrar of Marriages for the district of residence for the last seven days. The marriage can then take place by licence, special licence, certificate from a registrar, licence from a District Registrar of Marriages or the publication of banns. Notices issued in Northern Ireland are valid in England and Wales and vice versa, but as in Scotland, the couple cannot marry in a register office in England or Wales if one of them lives in Northern Ireland (or Scotland).

Marriage in Ireland

32. The party living in England or Wales may give notice to the Superintendent Registrar of the district in which he or she has resided for the preceding seven days and obtain his certificate for production to the District Registrar in Ireland. If the marriage is to be solemnized in a church or chapel of the Church of Ireland or in accordance with the usages of the Society of Friends or the Jews, notice may be given for marriage by certificate. In the case of a marriage in a registered building or the office of a District Registrar of Marriages, notice may be given for marriage either by certificate or by certificate and licence. In any case seven days must elapse between the date on which notice is given and the date on which the Superintendent Registrar's certificate is issued. After this has been issued, a period of seven days must elapse before the certificate becomes effective for production to the District Registrar in Ireland and if the marriage is to be solemnized without licence, the ceremony cannot take place until after the expiration of twenty-one days after the date of entry of the notice. Notice cannot be accepted by a Superintendent Registrar in England or Wales for a marriage in Ireland in any Roman Catholic Church or certified Presbyterian meeting house.

33. If the party giving notice in England and Wales for a marriage in the Irish Republic has not reached the age of twenty-one years, enquiries should be made of the registrar in the Irish Republic to ascertain what evidence of consent to the marriage it will be necessary to produce.

34. Further information about marriage in Northern Ireland may be obtained from the Registrar General, General Register Office. For marriages in the Irish Republic, from the General Register Office (see page 39).

Marriage of Persons Living outside England and Wales

35. If either of the parties to a marriage in England or Wales has a foreign domicile, the marriage, if performed in accordance with the requirements of English law, although valid throughout the British Commonwealth (subject to reservations in regard to any part of the Commonwealth where there may be particular requirements, for example, Cyprus), may not be valid in any other country unless the legal requirements of the country or countries of domicile are also complied with. The parties to the proposed marriage should, therefore, take steps to obtain satisfactory assurance upon this point by reference to the nearest Consul or other representative of the foreign state in this country. No Registration Officer in England or Wales can accept responsibility with regard to such legal requirements.

36. Foreigners wishing to be married in England or Wales are warned against marriage agents and interpreters who claim that they are able to procure marriages quickly without the necessary statutory residence indicated above. Any person making a false statement as to

residence or any other particular contained in a notice of marriage is liable to prosecution for perjury.

Marriage on Ships

It is not possible to marry on British ships on the high seas but Royal Navy personnel can give notice of their intention to marry and do so when they are on land. The Superintendent Registrar will be able to provide details.

Roman Catholic Faith

As with all marriages outside of the Church of England, the couple will require a licence; parties must give notice of their intention to marry to the local Superintendent Registrar as detailed in this chapter. Usually, the priest is authorised to register the marriage, otherwise a registrar will need to be present. Where both parties are Catholic, the ceremony usually takes place at a Nuptial Mass, although it can be conducted outside Mass, and this is most likely if one of the parties is not Roman Catholic.

Jewish Faith

Notice to marry must be given to the Superintendent Registrar, but a Jewish wedding may take place in a synagogue, a private house, or even out of doors. Wherever the ceremony is held, the secretary of the female's synagogue must detail all the necessary particulars. The couple must obtain the permission of the chief rabbi. Both parties must be Jews and produce evidence that their parents were married according to Jewish rites. If either of the couple is not of Jewish birth, evidence of proselytization is necessary.

Quaker Faith

The ceremony may take place in the Quaker meeting house which is the usual place of worship and at any time of the day, or it can be held elsewhere such as in a private house or public hall providing the legal requirements are met.

Other Denominations

If a couple wish to be married according to a religious denomination other than the Church of England, a licence must be obtained from the Superintendent Registrar as described above.

Mixed Denominations

Some religions forbid the marriage of members to members of other religions. It is important to check this at an early stage by consulting respective authorities and if both refuse, it may be necessary to have a civil ceremony.

In the case of a Roman Catholic marrying a non-Catholic, it is necessary to obtain special dispensation from the priest and also from a bishop if the marriage is to take place in a non-Catholic church. For marriage in a Catholic church, the priest may need six month's notice and the couple may be required to attend a course of instruction on marriage, its significance, responsibilities, including a promise to bring up any children in the Roman Catholic faith.

In the case of a member of the Jewish faith marrying someone who is non-Jewish, then he or she must be proselytized into the Jewish faith before the marriage.

Canada

The legal requirements and procedures for marriage differ from one province to another. It is therefore very important to establish exactly how to make the correct arrangements by consulting the Registry Office at the local Town Hall.

United States of America

The law relating to marriage varies from state to state. It is very important to ascertain the correct requirements and procedures by consulting the office of the Clerk of the Circuit Court. Every state requires a licence before the marriage can take place and in most cases this must be obtained at least one to five days before the date set for the wedding, and will expire thirty days after issue. The licence must be signed by two witnesses, and it must be kept safely after marriage.

All states now require both parties to have a blood test before they can marry, and some make further stipulations as to medical testing. Sufficient time must be allowed for these procedures to be carried out.

The building where the marriage is to take place must be registered for marriages and the minister must be authorised to register the marriage. If he or she is not, the registrar must be present.

The Merits of Marriage

Being married gives certain rights and protection to the husband and wife in the event of separation, divorce or the death of one partner, but for unmarried couples (whose relationship holds no legal validity), there is no clearly defined legislation.

Property

There is no statute law governing the division of property upon the separation of unmarried couples. It is essential for them to consult a solicitor so that a written agreement can be drawn up that will cater for separation and make legally valid and up-to-date wills leaving property and possessions to each other if this is their wish. Otherwise the estate of the partner who dies will pass to the next of kin, namely parents or other family members. In addition to making wills, it is advisable to take out an insurance policy and to put forward the dependent partner's name for pension rights in the event of death. Inheritance tax may be avoided by making gifts during lifetime, for anything left to a cohabitee – unlike a spouse – will be liable to tax.

Children

When a married couple separate or divorce, the law attempts to deal with custody and access to children in a civilised and fair way. For separated unmarried couples, there is no legislation. Couples with dependent children are certainly very well advised to consider marriage.

Useful Addresses

The authorities listed below supply information on remarriage, civil and religious, mixed religion and interdenominational weddings, and divorce.

The Dean or Provost of a Cathedral should be addressed as The Very Reverend in a letter. The Enquiry Centre of the Church of England or The Book of Common Prayer will provide more information.

Enquiry Centre, General Synod of the Church of England, Church House, Great Smith Street, London, SW1P 3NZ. 020 7898 1000

Church of Scotland, Department of Communication, 121 George Street, Edinburgh, EH2 4YN. 0131 225 5722

Scottish Executive, St Andrews House, Regent Road, Edinburgh, EH1 3DG. 0131 556 8400

Methodist Church Press Office, 25 Marylebone Road, London, NW1 5JR. 020 7486 5502

Baptist Union, Baptist House, 129 Broadway, Didcot, Oxon, OX11 8RT. 01235 517700

Religious Society of Friends (Quakers), Friends House, 173-177 Euston Road, London, NW1 2BJ. 020 7387 3601

United Reformed Church, 86 Tavistock Place, London, WC1H 9RT. 020 7916 2020

Catholic Care, Clitherow House, 1 Blythe Mews, Blythe Road, London, W14 0NW. 020 7371 1341

Jewish Marriage Council, 23 Ravenshurst Avenue, London, NW4 4EE. 020 8203 6311

General Register Office for England and Wales, Marriages Section, Room C201, Smedley Hydro, Trafalgar Road, Southport, PR8 2HH. 0151 471 4803

General Register Office for Scotland, New Register House, 3 West Register Street, Edinburgh, EH1 3YT. 0131 334 0380

General Register Office for Northern Ireland, Oxford House, 49-55 Chichester Street, Belfast, BT1 4HL. 02890 252000

General Register Office for the Irish Republic, Joyce House, 8-11 Lombard Street East, Dublin 2. 00 353 1671 1863

Presbyterian Church in Ireland, Church House, Fisherwick Place, Belfast, BT1 6DW. 02890 322284

General Register Office for the Isle of Man, The Civil Registry, Deemster's Walk, Bucks Road, Douglas, Isle of Man, IM1 3AR. 01624 685265

Registrar General for Guernsey, The Greffe, Royal Court House, St Peter Port, Guernsey, GY1 2PB. 01481 725 277

Superintendent Registrar for Jersey, 10 Royal Square, St Helier, Jersey, JE2 4WA. 01534 502335

4

Civil Ceremony

It is not essential for a marriage to be solemnized either by a minister or in a place of worship. It is only the civil law which needs to be satisfied and so a marriage conducted by a Superintendent Registrar is as completely lawful as any conducted through any religious body. Superintendent Registrars are duty bound to perform marriage ceremonies so long as the necessary legal requirements have been met. Many couples choose to marry at a register office or on approved premises for a variety of reasons; they may not share the same religious beliefs, preferring to marry under a neutral authority; religious convictions may have no significance for them; they may feel that because they are not active in a particular faith and do not attend a place of worship, it would be hypocritical to be married there; family objections may encourage them to take the civil ceremony option; or one or both of them may be divorced and unable to remarry in church.

In addition, some religious marriage ceremonies are not legally recognised — Sikh and Hindu religions. So partners of such faiths who wish their marriage to have legal recognition, are required to marry according to civil law.

The Ceremony

The Marriage Ceremony (Prescribed Words) Act 1996 offers alternative shorter wording.

The Statement

The bride and groom stand. The Superintendent Register states: 'This place in which you are now met has been duly sanctioned according to law for the celebration of marriages. Before you are joined in matrimony I have to remind you of the solemn and binding character of the vows you are about to make. A marriage according to the law of this country is the union of one man with one woman voluntarily entered into for life to the exclusion of all others.'

The Declaration

The groom, and then the bride, repeat after the Superintendent Registrar:

Old Version:
'I do solemnly declare that I know not of any lawful impediment why I (name) may not be joined in matrimony to (name)'.

'I call upon these persons here present to witness that I (name) do take thee (husband's name) to be my lawful wedded wife'.

The Registrar then says, 'You are now man and wife'.

New Version 1:
'I declare that I know of no legal reason why I (name) may not be joined in marriage to (name).'
'I (name) take you (name) to be my wedded wife/husband.'

New Version 2:
'Are you free lawfully to marry (name)?'
The couple answer: 'I am'.
The couple need not 'call upon these persons here present to witness . . . .'.

The two witnesses are conventionally the best man and the bride's father but they can be complete strangers.

As with religious ceremonies, it is common practice for the groom to place the wedding ring on the bride's third finger of her left hand but this has no legal significance under civil law. The marriage register is then signed by each of the newly-weds, the two witnesses, the Superintendent Registrar and the Registrar.

The Register Office

Register offices are civic departments and usually form part of Town Halls or other municipal buildings. Some register offices have more than one room for marriages, so it is advisable to ask about this before making a firm booking. Many rooms are specially decorated with soft furnishings, attractive surroundings and fresh flowers.

A civil ceremony at a register office is a shorter and much less formal affair than a religious wedding lasting between ten and fifteen minutes and entails no religious service. The bride and groom are free to travel to the reception either separately or together. The groom may arrive first but the bride should not be late.

The Superintendent Registrar attends the ceremony but it is the Registrar who conducts the wedding and at the appropriate time, he or she calls the names of the partners for a private interview to check the accuracy of details, collect the attendance fee, enter the marriage into the register and onto one copy of the marriage certificate. The rest of the wedding party and guests then enter. The couple and the witnesses approach the table while the guests sit or stand behind; arrangements are very informal. The groom or best man hands the certificate of marriage or licence to the registrar and the ceremony begins.

Photographs

A photographic session outside the register office should be brief; the reception venue will provide more opportunity.

Guests

Although technically the ceremony must take place 'with open doors' (anyone who wants to witness the marriage can do so), a register office cannot accommodate too many people possibly holding only thirty including the wedding party, so the number of guests is likely to be limited to the couple's immediate family and closest friends. Most people will appreciate the restrictions on numbers and additional guests could be invited to the reception celebrations afterwards, in which case they should receive 'reception only' invitations.

Timing

As the civil ceremony takes approximately ten minutes and there are likely to be several bookings one after the other, particularly on a Saturday, it is essential that the wedding party arrives on time or ideally five minutes before the ceremony is due to start. Being earlier or late may cause confusion with other parties.

Preparations

As for a church wedding, it is usual for the marriage to take place near to the bride's home. The Superintendent Registrar should be consulted as soon as possible about obtaining a licence and to check the times that the Superintendent Registrar is in attendance before setting a date for the wedding. Some offices are not open all the time.

Register offices may be booked well in advance for Saturdays and other popular times and they do not take bookings more than three months in advance.

Although it is not necessary for both partners to attend the interview, it is advisable so that the Superintendent Registrar is able to elicit all the details at one meeting. He or she will establish eligibility and the best method for authorising the marriage. At this time, the Superintendent Registrar will post the marriage notice for which payment will be necessary.

Best Man's Role

The best man's role at a civil ceremony is to ensure that he gets the groom or the couple to the register office on time and produces the ring(s) when requested.

Attire

Brides may dress traditionally but more often they wear special dresses or early cocktail attire and carry a small bouquet. Veils are unnecessary, a hat may be more appropriate. Very often there are no bridesmaids or page boys. Grooms may also dress traditionally but generally they wear dark suits. Guests dress smartly as they would for a religious wedding.

Approved Premises

It is the intention of the new legislation (The Marriage [Approved Premises] Regulations 1995) to allow civil marriages to take place regularly in hotels, stately homes, civic halls and similar suitable premises without compromising the fundamental principles of English marriage law and to maintain the solemnity of the occasion. A private dwelling house is unlikely to be an appropriate building as it would not be known to the public as a marriage venue or regularly available for their use. The Regulations preclude marriages from taking place in the open air, a marquee or any other temporary structure and in most forms of transport. A directory of registered premises in England and Wales is kept by The General Register Office for England and Wales (see page 39).

If opting for approved premises, most couples would probably want to marry at the reception venue since this is much more convenient for the wedding party and guests.

The setting must not resemble a church in anyway, for example prayerbooks would probably not be allowed. The marriage room must be separate from any other activity on the premises and accessible to the public and without charge so that they may witness the marriage and be able to make any objections. No food or drink may be sold or consumed in the marriage room for one hour prior to or during the ceremony.

As for a register office, the ceremony held on approved premises must not include any religious elements. Any reading, words, music or performance which forms part of a civil ceremony of marriage must be secular. Any material used by way of introduction to, in any interval, or by way of conclusion to the ceremony forms part of the ceremony. Not only must the material not be religious, it must also not be blasphemous. It is for this reason that many Superintendent Registrars insist on confining the ceremony to include only the legal elements, with perhaps one or two very minor additions, and conduct the proceedings in registered premises rooms in the same way as they do in register offices.

On arrival at the approved premises, the Superintendent Registrar meets the couple privately to explain the procedure. Meanwhile the guests gather in the marriage room. The Superintendent Registrar, the bride and groom then enter and the ceremony takes place. After the register is signed and the ceremony is concluded, the Superintendent Registrar leaves the premises.

INFILL LIST		CIVIL CEREMONY
Register office/approved premises address		
Telephone		
Superintendent Registrar Registrar		
Interview		
Take to interview: Birth Certificates Death Certificate Decree Absolute Marriage Notice Fees See Ceremony Room		
Ceremony Date		
Time	From	To
Number of guests		
Witnesses (minimum two over 18 years)		
FEES	NOTES	£
Marriage Notice Posting Certificate/Licence		
Attending Approved Premises		
Certified copy of entry of marriage		
Music		
Flowers		
Photographs		
Confetti		
Other		
TOTAL		

If two districts are involved:
Collect certificate of marriage from second district when issued (21 days after notice of marriage is posted). Remember to take this with you on the day.
Date for collection
If marrying by licence:
Collect and pay for it one day after notice is posted.
Date for collection

5

Church Wedding

A church wedding ceremony is, firstly, a civil ceremony in that it has to be recognised by law and performed by a minister who is legally registered to do so. It is the minister's duty to check the couple's eligibility before the marriage can legally take place.

The Church

Although there is no reason why a couple should not marry in any church (as long as the minister is in agreement), it is traditional for the wedding to take place in the bride's parish church. The tradition of banns was introduced in the fourteenth century by the Archbishop of Canterbury whereby the public are invited to come forward if they know of a just cause or impediment preventing the marriage. At one time it was thought unlucky for the bride and groom to hear the reading of the banns, but today it is expected that they will attend church.

These days many ministers will officiate only if the couple have religious commitments and some may insist on the couple attending the church every week until the wedding day.

If the couple wish to marry in a different church, then the minister must be consulted. If the couple are of different faiths, open discussion should lead to an amicable decision. If the bride is Church of England and the groom is Catholic for example and they decide to marry in the bride's church, an arrangement may be made for the groom's priest to attend and give the bride his blessing. Whatever the circumstances, the minister should be approached as soon as possible so that he may advise accordingly and a mutually convenient wedding date and time can be organised well in advance. Many churches are 'booked' well in advance, especially during the spring and summer, and some churches discourage weddings during Lent (the time of denial).

The minister will instruct about procedures, including the publishing of banns, as well as discussing the ceremony itself. The couple should take with them to the meeting with the minister their birth certificates and, if appropriate, a certified copy of a former spouse's death certificate, or an original Decree Absolute or Decree Nisi. The couple should find out about other aspects of the service, for example, choir, soloist, photographs and music and the exact order in which the elements of the service will occur. The marriage itself is generally near to the beginning of the service as most other elements such as prayer, blessing and address relate to the couple as man and wife.

If any key people do not speak English, it is tactful to employ a fluent interpreter so that everyone may partake fully in the activities of the day.

The minister may advise on a parish magazine entry to share the news of the wedding with members of the congregation.

Marriage Preparation Sessions

The minister may ask to see the couple nearer to the wedding date to discuss the significance of the vows and religious implications. He may suggest or request attendance at several meetings either with himself or a member of the Church to explain in detail the ceremony and discuss the implications of the commitments being made to each other.

If given the chance, it is good advice to attend the sessions as thinking through the issues before the wedding can provide invaluable guidance. The sessions will also aid understanding of the vows to be taken in church and the views of the Church concerning the marriage bond.

Giver-away

The giver-away is usually the father of the bride but it is acceptable for others to perform this function, for example, the bride's mother. Alternatively, it is not necessary to have the 'giving-away ceremony' in the service at all.

Service

Order

When the wedding party is assembled at the front of the church, the minister gives an introduction followed by a hymn. The marriage usually takes place after this first hymn. The minister will elaborate on the significance of marriage, check the intentions of the bride and groom and ask if there are any legal impediments to the marriage and then supervise the exchange of vows and rings before declaring the couple to be husband and wife. The order of elements in the service may then be arranged according to preference but usually the minister offers some prayers for the couple, he may give a short address which normally includes advice and well-wishing and then there are often one or two bible readings and one or two more hymns to conclude the religious part of the service before the party enters the vestry for the signing of the register.

When all the details of the service are agreed with the minister, the bride (or her mother) may like to arrange for the printing of order of service sheets for distribution to the guests as they enter church on the day.

Vows

The couple have the option to repeat short phrases after the minister or learn phrases by rote and perhaps stand facing each other so that family and friends can see and hear more clearly.

Prayer Service

Marriage services currently authorised for use in the Church of England are as follows:

> The 1662 Solemnization of Matrimony (from the *Book of Common Prayer*) in which the bride promises to obey her husband;
> The 1966 Solemnization of Matrimony (*Alternative Services, Series 1*) in which reference to obedience is excluded;
> The 2000 Marriage Service (*Common Worship*) in which there is a choice.

A full timetable for the day's procedures at church is included in Chapter 19.

Music

Music adds dignity and a special air to the occasion; its role is to:

- set the scene and fill time before arrival;
- herald the arrival of the bride;
- accompany the walk down the aisle;
- occupy and interest the congregation to take an active part;
- provide the couple with a chance to choose one or two pieces that are special to them.

The choice of music helps to create the desired atmosphere, whether it is something traditional or favourite. In any case, the minister should be asked for his views. It may have to be religious or it could be modestly secular. However, a rock band may not be such a good idea! The music will need to be chosen before a decision is made concerning the wording for the order of service sheets as the couple will probably want to include the titles of the musical pieces on the sheets themselves.

Any proposal to use any sort of recording equipment inside the church must be agreed by the minister and in advance of the wedding day.

With all music in church, personal favourites can be included as long as the organist has time to learn them if they are not well known.

Music played at weddings is considered to be 'private' and is therefore exempt from copyright fees.

Organ

The music chosen should be suitable for playing on the church organ. There are good and bad organs and good and bad musicians but the experienced church organist will be able to advise on the best pieces to be played on a particular organ.

Most church weddings are accompanies by organ music as this is the most available instrument in a church setting and is powerful enough to fill the whole church with music, whereas a violin, an oboe, a soloist or a tape recording may not be so effective. To fill time before the bride arrives, the organist should have a repertoire that will last for at least twenty minutes before she is due to arrive. This creates the mood and aids relaxation of the guests while they wait. Classical music would be most appropriate unless a specific piece particularly suits the style of wedding.

A selection of popular wedding music

Arrival of the Bride

The music should be positive and joyous.

Theme from the *St Anthony Chorale*, BRAHMS.
Prelude to a Te Deum, CHARPENTIER.
Prince of Denmark's March, CLARKE.
Nimrod from the *Enigma Variations*, ELGAR.
March on Lift up your Heads, GUILMANT.
Hornpipe in D from the *Water Music*, HANDEL.
Hornpipe in F from the *Water Music*, HANDEL.
March from *Scipio*, HANDEL.
Coro from the *Water Music*, HANDEL.
Minuet No 2 from the *Water Music*, HANDEL.
Arrival of the Queen of Sheba, HANDEL.
March from the *Occasional Oratorio*, HANDEL.
Wedding Processional, HARRIS.

A Trumpet Minuet, HOLLINS.
Bridal March, PARRY.
Trumpet Tune, PURCELL.
Rondeau from *Abdelazar*, PURCELL.
Grand March from *Aida*, VERDI.
Wedding March/Bridal Chorus from *Lohengrin*, WAGNER.
March from *Richard III*, WALTON.
Crown Imperial, WALTON.

Entrance (or Processional) of the Bride

This is usually something relatively stately, stirring and exciting to mark the significance of what is about to happen.

Hallelujah Chorus from *The Mount of Olives*, BEETHOVEN.
A Wedding Fanfare, BLISS.
Trumpet Voluntary, BOYCE.
Theme from the *St Anthony Chorale*, BRAHMS.
Allegro Marzialle, BRIDE.
Allegro from *Sonata in D minor*, GUILMANT.
Arrival of the Queen of Sheba, HANDEL.
Praise the Lord O My Soul, KARGELERT.
Sonata No. 3 (first movement), MENDELSSOHN.
Wedding March from *The Marriage of Figaro*, MOZART.
Fanfare, PURCELL.
Trumpet Voluntary from *Suite in D*, STANLEY.
Wedding March, SUTTLE.
Choral Song, WESLEY.

Signing of the Register

The time during the signing of the register can be boring for the wedding guests and is the traditional time for a friend(s) of the bride and groom to play or sing, or both, or for a choir to use this time for their major contribution. The music should be restful and melodious. Details should be printed on the order of service sheets so that guests know what to expect and whether they are expected to join in.

Adagio in G Minor, ALBINONI.
Air on a G String, BACH.
Ave Maria, BACH.
Jesu, Joy of Man's Desiring, BACH.
Adagio from *Toccata Adagio and Fugue*, BACH.
Behold, A Rose is Blooming, BRAHMS.
Minuet from *Berenice*, HANDEL.
Air from the *Water Music*, HANDEL.
To a Wild Rose, MACDOWELL.
Allegretto from *Sonata No 4*, MENDELSSOHN.

Romanze from *Eine Kleine Nachtmusik,*
MOZART.
Benediction Nuptiale, SAINT-SAENS.
Ave Maria, SCHUBERT.
Traumerei, SCHUMANN.
Chorale Prelude on Rhosymedre,
VAUGHAN-WILLIAMS.
Air from *Three Pieces,* WESLEY.

Exit of Bride and Groom from Church

Recessional music is usually something
classical or modern that is triumphant,
joyful and celebratory.

Toccata in G, DUBOIS.
Pomp and Circumstance March No. 4,
ELGAR.
Festive Toccata, FLETCHER.
Grand Choeur in D, GUILMANT.
Bridal March, HOLLINS.
Now Thank We All Our God, KARGELERT.
Wedding March from *A Midsummer
Night's Dream,* MENDELSSOHN.
Carrilon-Sortie, MENDELSSOHN.
Postlude in D, SMART.
Carrilon in B Flat, VIERNE.
Final from *Symphony No. 1,* VIERNE.
Wedding March from *Lohengrin,*
WAGNER.
Crown Imperial, WALTON.
Fanfare, WHITLOCK.
Toccata from *Symphony No. 5,* WIDOR.

Hymns

There are usually three hymns: on
arrival when standing before the
chancel steps; after the marriage
ceremony; and after the blessing.

*Love Divine All Loves Excelling.
Praise My Soul, The King of Heaven.
Now Thank We All Our God.
The Kind of Love My Shepherd Is.*

Hymns

A standard Church of England service
includes three hymns, four if communion is included, but there can be more
(depending on the time available) or
fewer. The minister will advise on suitable hymns.

Choir and Bell-ringers

If there is to be a choir, it is advisable to
check that it is strong enough to sing
the chosen hymns and if not, the more
popular hymns should be selected.

Choir members and bell-ringers tend
to disband during the month of August
and many churches do not permit bell-
ringing during church festivals such as
Lent (between Shrove Tuesday and
Easter) and Advent (about a month before Christmas).

The minister must be consulted in
advance with any special requests
regarding singer(s), soloist(s) and rela-
tive(s) reading the lessons.

Flowers

The couple should offer to pay for the
flowers which are bought by those who
usually decorate the church. For those
who wish to acquire and arrange their
own flowers, they will need to check on
a convenient delivery time. If there is
more than one wedding in the church
on the particular day, the minister may
rule against private flowers.

Many churches do not permit flowers
to decorate the church during church
festivals such as Lent (between Shrove
Tuesday and Easter) and Advent (about
a month before Christmas).

Confetti

Tossing paper confetti at the bride and
groom is a relatively new idea and since
it can make such a mess of the church-
yard it is often not allowed for this
reason. Modern practice is to revert to
the tossing of rice, grain, fresh flower or
rose petals, or confetti of the type which
birds will eat such as wild bird food. It is
wise to avoid the 'litter' type but rice is a
good deal heavier than paper confetti
and should be thrown into the air and
allowed to fall gently! If the throwing of

paper confetti is allowed, there may be a charge for this. Local litter laws should be checked beforehand and observed at all times and if the church door opens directly on to the street, paper confetti will not be allowed.

· ·
· **TRADITION** ·
· *Before the introduction of paper confetti, it* ·
· *was customary to toss and throw rice or* ·
· *grain, both of which are symbols of food* ·
· *and children.* ·
· ·

Collection

The minister may stipulate that a collection is to be taken following the ceremony. Usually a plate is left at the door so that guests can contribute as they leave.

Photographs and Videos

Photographs and videos may be allowed in church if flash is not used, but there may be restrictions in the vestry.

Rehearsal

Although not all ministers feel that it is necessary, there is usually a rehearsal at the church a week or so before the event so that the principal members (the bride, groom, best man, chief bridesmaid and perhaps parents) can have a final check on their duties so that they are clear about procedures thereby minimising the risk of confusion on the day. This is an excellent opportunity for the principal members to get together not only to check on the procedure but to make any last minute adjustments to arrangements. Most people find it a useful way of allaying any worries and reassuring everyone that things will go well on the day. If the rehearsal is held shortly before the wedding, the procedures are less likely to be forgotten.

The rehearsal also provides the opportunity to invite the minister to the reception. Very often he or she will decline unless he or she knows the family very well.

Sometimes the bride and groom arrange a small dinner or other celebration for the wedding party after the rehearsal to thank them for their support. This would be a suitable time for the wedding party to present the couple with their wedding gifts so that these may be unwrapped at leisure, and likewise for the couple to present their gifts to the attendants. This occasion also gives the best man a chance to get to know the close members of both families, ask any outstanding questions and finalise arrangements.

Going through everything in detail at the rehearsal will be time well spent and may save some frantic moments later on. The date and time for the rehearsal should be agreed with the minister.

Charges

Certain fees, for example, the reading of the banns, are set by the Church Commissioners. Other charges might include a sum to cover the organist, choir and bell-ringers.

It is advisable to pay church fees in advance rather than burden the best man with an additional task immediately after the ceremony. Since the minister puts in so much effort it may be appropriate to consider a special personal donation to his church.

INFILL/CHECK LIST			CHURCH ARRANGEMENTS
Church	Name		Fees £
	Address		
	Telephone		
	Minister		
	Verger		
	Organist		
	Choir		
	Bell-ringers		
Availability	Dates	Times	

Interview
Date of Interview with Minister
Take to the interview:
  Birth Certificates
  Death Certificate
  Decree Absolute/Decree Nisi			

Number of Guests			
Type of Service			
Dates when banns will be read 1			
2			
3			
Licence/certificate obtained			
Flowers			
Photography			
Videography			
Confetti			
Collection			
Personal donation			
Marriage preparation sessions	Dates	Times	
Rehearsal	Date	Time	
Agreed payment time for fees			
Agreed payer of fees			
TOTAL			

INFILL/CHECK LIST	CHURCH — ORDER OF SERVICE NOTES
Before the bride arrives Music	
Bell-ringers	
As the bride arrives Music	
Entry of the bride Music	
Minister's introduction	
Hymn 1	
Marriage ceremony, including vows and rings	
Hymn 2	
Prayers/Sermon/Holy Communion/Nuptial Mass	
Short address	
Bible readings	
Blessing	
Hymn 3	
Special readings/performances	
Signing of the register Music	
Leaving church Music	
Bell-ringers	

INFILL LIST	CHURCH — ORDER OF SERVICE SHEET

The Procession: (Title and Composer)
Introduction

Hymn: (Title and Composer followed by full text)
The Marriage between
(Miss . . .)
and
(Mr . . .)
Hymn: (Title and Composer followed by full text)
The Sermon
Hymn: (Title and Composer followed by full text)
The Signing of the Register: (Title and Composer)
The Recession: (Title and Composer)
(time)
(date)
(Church)

(Minister's name)

6

Finance

Traditionally the burden has fallen heavily on the bride's father who inherits the dowry tradition whereby the groom confers an honour on the bride's family by marrying their daughter, and he has to be rewarded.

Responsibility for Payment

This age-old dowry custom is not always relevant today and since a wedding can be and usually is, a very expensive event, it is somewhat unreasonable to expect the bride's father to bear responsibility for the entire cost especially if both the bride and groom are in full-time employment. Besides, the cost of a large wedding would be well beyond the means of many families, especially if they had to pay for every part of it. So more often today both families tend to share the financial responsibility by dividing the cost between them and the couple themselves. Some brides' parents pay for most of the wedding, with the bride and groom and the groom's parents opting to pay specific expenses such as the clothes and drinks at the reception. Discussions concerning the division of expenses need not be limited to parents alone. There may be a generous relation who would like to pay for something or contribute in one way or another. A grandparent, godparent, or an aunt might like to bake and ice, or purchase, the cake for example or an uncle might provide a case of Champagne! Some couples wait until they are financially secure before marrying so that they are in a position to pay for it all by which time some are able and willing to spend a fortune on the day, others (although financially able) are happy to economise, and others have no option but to economise. If the couple are older than the traditional age for first marriages, it may be inappropriate for the bride's par-

ents, or either set of parents to pay. They may be retired in which case it might be better for the couple to take over all of the expenses and the administration.

If the two sets of parents are contributing and are unacquainted or do not know each other well, they may be embarrassed to talk about costs but it is important that everyone knows where they stand and that the bride and groom negotiate with both families to calculate an honest estimate, so getting them together early is good advice. When the wedding date is fixed, the bride's father should arrange a meeting with the groom's parents to discuss arrangements. Shared responsibility for the costs may already have been assumed, but the bride's father should not expect this of the groom's parents, nor should he be offended if they do not offer to contribute.

Whoever is paying for the wedding or however the expenses are divided, it is prudent to establish a detailed budget and to do this well beforehand to ensure that the style of wedding chosen can be ultimately afforded and so that there is no confusion over financial responsibility. It may be helpful to know who traditionally pays for the various expenses and this is indicated in a column on the Budget List at the end of this chapter.

Financial Arrangements

Agreements and Contracts

It is prudent to deal with reputable companies and obtain written agreements for the supplies and services to be provided as such evidence will be vital should an expected supply or service not be rendered. Any agreements must be scrutinised thoroughly before signature so that commitments are perfectly clear to both parties.

It would be careless to skip over the small print contained in any contract as important terms are frequently detailed in this way, for instance: 'subject to price fluctuation'; 'price payable shall be that prevailing at delivery time'.

Estimates and Quotations

As estimates provide only a general idea of final cost, subsequent invoices are likely to be in excess of the original figures. A quotation is usually a fixed price for a specified job and for this reason it is advisable to obtain quotations in preference to estimates although delivery charges and the possibility of price increases should be checked.

Deposits

A supplier will want some advance payment as confirmation of the authenticity of a booking and to cover the cost of any work undertaken should there be a cancellation and it is for this reason that a deposit may be non-returnable, or a deposit may be part-payment of the final bill.

Methods of payment vary depending on the type of goods or services supplied and need to be agreed in advance of any commitment.

Insurance

Insurance cover provides compensation for unforeseen circumstances and in view of the considerable expenses involved, couples are well advised to take out a policy of the value which reflects their planned event.

Public Liability

Most policies will automatically cover the insured for public liability, for example, in the event that a guest sustains injury or damage to their property and there is a prosecution or suit for damages.

Cancellation

Compensation will normally be paid if the wedding is cancelled as a result of death, accident, illness, jury service, court summons or redundancy (in some cases) after the policy was taken out.

It might be possible to claim for the cost of re-booking the whole day's services if the original reception venue cannot accommodate the function due to sudden closure of the premises, or to claim for the cost of re-booking the reception elsewhere if there is time.

On the other hand, it is unlikely that compensation will be paid for a wedding which has been cancelled because of bad weather!

Non-cancellation

It might be possible to claim if the wedding attire is damaged. Even when such damage does not result in cancellation, it should still be possible to insure and receive compensation for its replacement.

Photography cover might include non-attendance of the photographer, damage to or loss of photographs.

Gifts kept overnight at the reception venue should be covered.

The Insurer

An insurance broker will be able to advise on those firms which offer wedding cover.

Budget

After reading this book, talking to friends and generally shopping around, the bride will be able to establish the type of wedding she would most like and compile a draft of estimates in order to ascertain the likely total cost involved.

Priorities

Everyone has their own personal opinions about how things should be done at a wedding. To one person, good food may be the most important consideration, yet to another the choice of entertainment may be more significant. When compiling the draft budget it is clear that the bride needs to have an idea of her priorities. The Priorities List

INFILL LIST			PRIORITIES
	Order	Item	Rough Estimate £
Reception venue	1		
Food	2		
Cake	3		
Drink	4		
Entertainment	5		
Honeymoon	6		
Wedding dress	7		
Groom's attire	8		
Photographs/Video	9		
Flowers	10		
Stationery	11		
Transport	12		
Ceremony	13		
TOTAL			

can be reorganised to create the most suitable option for the needs of the bride and groom.

Draft (Estimated) Budget

The bride and groom need to agree on their high priorities at the start of the planning. Once the decision has been made as to which items will receive the most expenditure, the remaining items may be budgeted. The draft budget will highlight any particular costs which could be prohibitive and out of proportion with the total funds available for the wedding. Seemingly insignificant expenses should not be omitted as the cost of these can accumulate to a surprisingly high total.

When comparing estimates or quotations from suppliers it is important to compare like with like. For example when comparing the cost of two bouquets, figures should reflect the cost of similar flowers otherwise the comparisons will be irrelevant and misleading. If estimates do not match the funds available, the costs will need to be modified until the wedding budget is affordable.

Final Budget

When the overall draft budget has been calculated and modified to suit priorities and available funds, it will be possible to finalise the budget plans. As actual costs become evident, these should be entered on the Budget List and any deposits paid noted so that the Budget List represents a full, accurate and up-to-date record of how the fin-ances stand at any particular time. If it transpires that an item costs less than anticipated, the 'saving' may be transferred to another area. It is wise to add between five and ten per cent on to the budget to allow for contingencies.

The numerous expenses involved in acquiring and equipping a new home should not be forgotten.

Budget Records

The following pages may be used to compile a detailed budget and show who traditionally pays for the various expenses. Regardless of responsibility for payment, it is necessary to compile a detailed budget to ensure that the celebration can be ultimately afforded.

INFILL/CHECK LIST					BUDGET LIST
Contingency — Allow an additional 5–10%					
Attire	Bride	Wedding	Dress	Itself	
				Train	
			Headdress	Veil/Hat	
			Shoes		
			Underwear	Slip	
				Bra	
				Pants	
			Hosiery	Stockings/tights	
				Garter	
			Something	Old	
				New	
				Borrowed	
				Blue	
			Jewellery		
			Perfume		
		Going-away	Outfit		
			Shoes		
	Bridesmaids		Dress		
			Dress		
			Dress		
			Headdress		
			Headdress		
			Headdress		
			Shoes		
			Shoes		
			Shoes		
			Hosiery		
			Hosiery		
			Hosiery		

Costs								
Estimate	Quotation	Final (showing traditional payers)		Deposit	Paid	Balance	Due date	Paid
		Bride	Groom					
£	£	£	£	£	✓	£		✓
		✓						
		✓						
		✓						
		✓						
		✓						
		✓						
		✓						
		✓						
		✓						
		✓						
		✓						
		✓						
		✓						
		✓						
		✓						
		✓						
		✓						
		✓						
		✓						
		✓						
		✓						

INFILL/CHECK LIST			BUDGET LIST	
Contingency — Allow an additional 5–10%				
Attire	Pages		Outfit	
			Outfit	
			Outfit	
			Shoes	
			Shoes	
			Shoes	
	Ushers		Outfit	
			Outfit	
			Outfit	
			Shoes	
			Shoes	
			Shoes	
	Groom	Wedding	Morning Dress	hire/purchase
			Shoes	
			Shirt	
			Tie	
		Going-away	Outfit	
			Shoes	
	Best Man	Wedding	Attire	
			Shoes	
			Shirt	
			Tie	
			Umbrella	
	Bride's Father		Morning dress	hire/purchase
Transport	to ceremony	for	Bride and Bride's Father	
			Bride's mother and Bridesmaids	
			Groom and Best Man	
	to reception	for	Bride's Father and Bride's Mother	
			Bride and Groom	
	from reception	for	Bride and Groom	

COSTS								
Estimate	Quotation	Final (showing traditional payers)		Deposit	Paid	Balance	Due date	Paid
		Bride	Groom					
£	£	£	£	£	✓	£		✓
		✓						
		✓						
			✓ (if hired)					
			✓ (if hired)					
			✓					
			✓					
			✓					
			✓					
			✓					
			✓					
		✓(if hired)						
		✓(if hired)						
		✓(if hired)						
		✓(if hired)						
		✓(if hired)						
		✓						
		✓						
			✓					
		✓						
			✓					
			✓					

INFILL/CHECK LIST			BUDGET LIST
Contingency — Allow an additional 5–10%			
Transport	decoration	for	Wedding cars (ribbons)
			Leaving car (tins, foam, etc.)
Photographs/ Video	Wedding package		
	Album	for	Bride and Groom
	Album	for	Bride's Parents
	Album	for	Groom's Parents
	Prints		
Flowers	Church		
	Reception		
	Bride	Bouquet	
		Other	
	Bridesmaids	Bouquets	
	Mothers	Corsages	
		Sprays	
	Groom	Buttonhole	
	Fathers	Buttonholes	
	Best Man	Buttonhole	
	Ushers	Buttonholes	
	Special guests for example Grandparents	Buttonholes	
	Collages for keepsake		
Church/ Register Office Fees	Minister's/Registrar's fees		
	Banns Certificate (fixed by Church Commissioners)		
	Marriage Licence/Registrar's Certificate		
	Marriage Certificate		
	Verger		
	Organist		
	Soloist/singers		
	Choir		

COSTS								
Estimate	Quotation	Final (showing traditional payers)		Deposit	Paid	Balance	Due date	Paid
		Bride	Groom					
£	£	£	£	£	✓	£		✓
			✓					
		✓						
		✓						
		✓						
			✓					
			✓					
			✓					
			✓					
			✓					
			✓					
			✓					
			✓					
			✓					
			✓					
			✓					
			✓					
			✓					
			✓					
			✓					
			✓					
			✓					
			✓					
			✓					
			✓					
			✓					

INFILL/CHECK LIST			BUDGET LIST	
Contingency — Allow an additional 5–10%				
Church/ Register Office Fees	Bell-ringers			
	Collection/Personal donation			
Medical	Blood tests	Bride		
		Groom		
Accommodation	for out-of-town	attendance	— Female	
			— Male	
		guests		
Reception	Hire of rooms			
	Decorations			
	Furniture			
	Caterer			
	Servers	Waiters		
		Waitresses		
	Equipment	Crockery		
		Cutlery		
		Glasses		
	Insurance			
	Food	Menus		
		Cake		
	Drink	with	meal	
			toasts	
			other	
		Barman		
	Entertainment			
	Service charge			
	Tips			
Honeymoon	Travel			
	Accommodation			
	Clothes			

COSTS								
Estimate	Quotation	Final (showing traditional payers)		Deposit	Paid	Balance	Due date	Paid
		Bride	Groom					
£	£	£	£	£	✓	£		✓
			✓					
			✓					
		✓						
			✓					
		✓						
			✓					
			✓					
		✓						
		✓						
		✓						
		✓						
		✓						
		✓						
		✓						
		✓						
		✓						
		✓						
		✓						
		✓						
		✓						
		✓						
		✓						
		✓						
		✓						
		✓						
			✓					
			✓					
			✓					

INFILL/CHECK LIST		BUDGET LIST
Contingency — Allow an additional 5–10%		
Honeymoon	Luggage	
	Spending money	Foreign currency
		Travellers cheques
	Documentation	Passports/Visas
		Maps
		Guide books
	Medical	Inoculations
		First aid kit
	Insurance	
Press Announcements	Before the wedding — including photograph	
	After the wedding — including photograph	
Stationery	Invitations	Cards
		Envelopes
		Maps
		Postage
	Order of Service	Sheets
	Menus	
	Place-name cards	
	Seating plan chart	
	Cake boxes	
	Miscellaneous	Napkins
		Napkin rings
		Drink mats
		Matchboxes
	Bridal notepaper	
	Confetti	
	Thank-you	Letters
		Envelopes
		Postage

COSTS								
Estimate	Quotation	Final (showing traditional payers)		Deposit	Paid	Balance	Due date	Paid
		Bride	Groom					
£	£	£	£	£	✓	£		✓
			✓					
			✓					
			✓					
			✓					
			✓					
			✓					
			✓					
			✓					
			✓					
		✓						
		✓						
		✓						
		✓						
		✓						
		✓						
		✓						
		✓						
		✓						
		✓						
		✓						
		✓						
		✓						
		✓						
		✓						
		✓						
		✓						
		✓						
		✓						
		✓						
		✓						

INFILL/CHECK LIST				BUDGET LIST
Contingency — Allow an additional 5–10%				
Stationery	Diary			
	Keepsake album			
	Guest book			
Beauty treatments	Bride	Hairdresser		
		Make-up		
		Beauty generally		
		Fitness		
	Groom	Barber		
Gifts	to Groom	Ring		
		Wedding gift		
	to Bride	Rings	Engagement	
			Wedding	
		Wedding gift		
	to Bridesmaids			
	to Pages			
	to Best Man			
	to Ushers			
Pre-wedding parties	Engagement			
	Shower			
	Rehearsal			
	Hen			
	Stag			
Petty cash	for Best Man to use on the day			
Special services				
TOTAL				

Costs								
Estimate	Quotation	Final (showing traditional payers)		Deposit	Paid	Balance	Due date	Paid
		Bride	Groom					
£	£	£	£	£	✓	£		✓
		✓						
		✓						
		✓						
		✓						
		✓						
		✓						
		✓						
			✓					
		✓						
		✓						
			✓					
			✓					
			✓					
			✓					
			✓					
			✓					
			✓					
			✓					
		✓						
		✓						
			✓					
			✓					

INFILL/CHECK LIST	BUDGET SUMMARY
	£
Attire	
Transport	
Photographs	
Video	
Flowers	
Church/Register Office/Approved Premises	
Medical	
Accommodation for Guests	
Reception	
Honeymoon	
Press	
Stationery	
Beauty Treatments	
Gifts	
Parties	
Petty Cash	
Special Services	
TOTAL	

7

Reception

*W*hen the ceremony is over the bride and groom will be able to relax and enjoy themselves with their guests. Feasts are a traditional way of celebrating and at most modern-day receptions there is a meal and entertainment. A good party allows the families to join in the festivities and get to know one another.

Style

The purposes of today's reception after the wedding ceremony, are to allow wedding guests to congratulate the newly-weds, join in toasts to the health and happiness of the couple, witness the cutting of the cake, meet families and wish the couple well as they leave for honeymoon.

The choice of reception is the bride's and groom's in consultation with parents if they are contributing, and if ample time is allowed to consider all possibilities and plan, it should be easy to organise.

Reception style could be categorised as follows but there are no absolute rules.

Degree of Formality	No. of Guests	Meal	Drinks	Entertainment	Invitations
ULTRA-FORMAL Grand Hotel	200+	Elaborate Sit-down 5-course dinner	Champagne throughout	Live orchestra	Engraved or printed
FORMAL Reputable Large Hotel or Marquee with caterers	150–200	Elegant Sit-down dinner or Sit-down buffet	Champagne throughout	Live band	Engraved or printed
SEMI-FORMAL Hotel	100–150	Sit-down dinner or Sit-down buffet	Champagne for the toasts	Dance music/ Disco	Printed
INFORMAL Hotel or Hired hall with caterers or relatives and friends providing the food	Up to 100	Stand-up finger-buffet	Wine	Disco	Pre-printed or handwritten
VERY INFORMAL Home	Up to 30	Sit-down fork-buffet or stand-up finger-buffet Home cooked	Champagne and/or wine	CDs or taped music	Handwritten

The couple may choose a formal dinner (wedding breakfast), a buffet or a small lunch for close relatives and friends with perhaps a party in the evening. Whatever the choice, the reception is the culmination of the wedding day when happiness can be shared with others. The major considerations are the number of guests, the budget and the type of reception desired. The choice of venue may then be made accordingly. It is important to spend only that which the budget allows. Catering is a vital consideration in any reception and choosing the right time, atmosphere or theme, and venue helps to ensure that the cele-brations are a success.

Timing

Some couples select a ceremony time that will allow for a luncheon buffet, others prefer a more formal meal or cocktails and hors d'oeuvres. It should be borne in mind that guests will not enjoy a three hour midday party without lunch, or a meal served too early in the reception if people will have just eaten before the ceremony.

Themes

Ideas for receptions based on specific themes include medieval banquet, country and western barbecue and Valentines.

Venues

Ideally the reception venue should be reasonably close to the church or register office or within a short and easy car journey but if it happens to be more than half an hour away, it may be appropriate to hire a coach to transport the guests.

Hotels

If finance is no problem, a hotel or restaurant will be the likely choice, whereby all the catering arrangements, including catering staff, choice of menus and wines, can be organised and supplied by the management as part of their wedding service. A hotel would be able to offer accommodation for overnight guests, facilities for displaying the wedding gifts, a comfortable place where the bride and groom can change and prepare themselves for their honeymoon, and should also be able to cope with the parking of guests' cars. When considering several hotel options, meals could be eaten at the venues to check the standard of the food.

As soon as the venue is selected, a firm booking should be made and written confirmation obtained. Most hotels deal with only one wedding a day and consequently they may be booked well in advance even as far ahead as one year.

Property which will remain on the reception premises overnight may be insured against fire, theft and accidental damage. Items may include gifts, china, cutlery, glassware and a cake.

Hotels	
Advantages	**Disadvantages**
Organised food, cake, drink	Possibly the most expensive
Maximum facilities	Possibly impersonal
Minimal work	Numbers may be limited
Delegation of responsibility	Mass-produced production line
Predictable cost	Need for advance booking
Range of prices	Times may be restricted, particularly on
Range of menus	Saturdays
General comfort	VAT is payable
Car parking	
Comfortable changing facilities	
Overnight accommodation	
Entertainment facilities	

Halls

For a medium-sized budget and not too many guests, it should be possible to hire a local church, village or school hall or a function room in a public house, but these options will probably require outside caterers.

For around a hundred guests, the couple should consider halls which are designed specifically for holding receptions as they are more likely to have the necessary facilities such as cloakrooms; toilets; parking; side rooms for receiving guests, displaying gifts, and for the bride and groom to change clothes.

It is necessary to check the rules that apply to halls or rooms concerning the consumption of alcohol on the premises. Any such rules and regulations must be observed. It is advisable to secure a written agreement for the booking which includes details of all services to be provided. Hired halls may need to be booked about six months in advance and the booking confirmed nearer the date.

Home

For a modest budget it may be preferable to hold the reception at the bride's parents' home or the home of a generous relative or friend. In this case, a buffet meal would probably be preferable, unless the number of guests is very small. Home receptions can have a pleasant, comfortable and informal atmosphere, but the house would need to be sufficiently large to cater for the number of guests. The garden will provide extra room but as the weather is so unpredictable, the best solution might be to hire a marquee, but this will be expensive.

Professional caterers need to be booked well in advance.

Although it is usual to serve food and drink to a number of guests at the celebration after a wedding ceremony, it is not absolutely necessary; a meal with the wedding party may suffice with perhaps a larger party later on.

HALLS	
Advantages	**Disadvantages**
Accommodation of large numbers	Often bare and functional
Choice of sit-down meal or buffet	Limited catering facilities, for example,
Freedom	cooker, fridge
Car parking	Shortage of electric points
Less expensive than a hotel	Doubtful heating
Disco/dance probability	Inadequate water supply
	Insufficient chairs, tables, etc.
	Need to hire equipment: crockery,
	cutlery, glassware, cake stand
	and knife
	Problem of matching caterers with
	facilities
	Cleanliness must be checked thoroughly
	Inadequate toilet facilities, soap, towels,
	coat hangers
	Poor cloakroom facilities
	Absence of changing room for bride and
	groom
	Cleaning up/refuse disposal
	Inadequate washing up facilities
	No licence for alcohol
	Time restrictions
	Decoration of hall
	Smoking may invalidate insurance cover

HOME	
Advantages	**Disadvantages**
Personal, intimate, friendly and informal	Numbers are generally limited
Freedom	Hard work if self-catering
Timing is flexible	Requires organisation in great detail
Cheap unpaid labour	Clearing up
	Inadequate cloakroom and toilet facilities
	Hire/borrow: chairs, tables, china,
	cutlery, glasses
	Hire wine waiter
	Organise wine
	Parking

INFILL/CHECK LIST			HOTELS
Hotel	Venue		
	Address		
	Telephone	Fax	
	Contact		
	Availability Dates		Times
Function	No. of Guests: adults	children	
	Times: Arrival	Meal	
	Speeches	Cake-cutting	
	Entertainment		
	Date booked	With whom?	
Facilities	Room size	Decorations	
	Heating	Seating arrangements	
	Accommodation	Cake table	
	Cloakroom and toilet facilities	Storing glasses table	
	Changing room	Gifts display	
	Car parking	Disabled guests	
Flowers	Supplier	Displays	
Food	Supplier	Cake	
	Menu options	£ per guest	Selected
	Children		
	Printed menus	No. of servers	
	Special dietary requirements		
Drinks	Barman	Glassware	
	Close 'Open' bar at . . .	Last orders at . . .	

INFILL/CHECK LIST		HOTELS	
Equipment	Linen	China	
	Napkins	Candles	
Photographs			
Confetti policy			
Entertainment		Licence to serve drinks late	
Insurance	Liability	Gifts	
Clearing Away			
Costs	Overall cost (so that cost per person may be calculated)		£
	Service charge		
	Tips		
	VAT		
	Deposit/cancellation fee		
	TOTAL		
	Payment date(s)		

Other Venues

A marquee or garden party is always an option and allows plenty of freedom and flexibility of timing but the weather is always unpredictable and the cost of marquee hire is not insignificant. Considerations also include its size, style, colour, heating, lighting, electricity, floor, doors, windows, furniture, stands, portaloos and awnings from the marquee to the house. Another important point is parking space and the neighbours!

The choice of venue need not be restricted to hotels, halls or home with or without a marquee: possibilities include restaurants, barns, art galleries, museums, gardens, railway carriages, buses and boats.

If the budget is extremely low and to ask friends to pay for their own meal seems an imposition, the answer might be to have a register office wedding somewhere remote and far from home and celebrate alone in a hotel with a restaurant meal, a bottle of champagne and stay overnight.

Food

· ·
TRADITION
The bride and groom sharing a meal after the wedding ceremony has always been seen as confirmation of their new status. In fact, in Ancient Rome, the marriage contract was not legally binding until a couple had shared bread together.
The ritual of drinking and sharing wine and communion is part of many Christian ceremonies today and also features in Jewish ceremonies.
Traditionally the wedding breakfast is a sit-down five-course meal of a starter, soup, main course, dessert, petits fours and tea and coffee.
· ·

Meal Types

Options include sit-down hot; sit-down cold (fork buffet); and stand (finger buffet). Good food is vital to the success of a reception, but it need not be exotic or extravagant; a selection of well chosen dishes to suit various tastes and served attractively will be much enjoyed.

A formal meal provided by caterers will be generally more expensive per

INFILL/CHECK LIST		HALLS
Hall	Venue	
	Address	
	Telephone	
	Contact	
Function	No. of Guests: adults	Children
	Times: Arrival	Meal
	Speeches	Cake-cutting
	Entertainment	
	Date booked	With whom?
Facilities	Hall size	Decorations
	Heating	Seating arrangements
	Changing room	Disabled guests
	Cloakroom and toilet facilities	
	Gifts display	Car parking
	Tables: Cake Storing glasses	Food preparation location
Confetti policy		
Entertainment		Licence to serve drinks late
Insurance		
Clearing away		
Costs		£
	Overall cost	
	VAT	
	Deposit/cancellation fee	
	TOTAL	
	Payment date(s)	

INFILL/CHECK LIST			HOME	
Function	No. of guests: Adults		Children	
	Times: Arrival		Meal	
	Speeches		Cake-cutting	
	Entertainment			
Facilities	Room space		Decorations	
	Freezer space		Larder space	

	Tables: Cake
	            Storing glasses
	            Displaying gifts
			Heating	

	Chairs		Parking	
	Disabled guests			
	Accommodation for overnight guests			
	Cloakroom with hangers and toilet facilities			
	Location signs in the house			
Meal equipment	Crockery	Plates: Dinner	Cutlery: Knives	
		Side	Forks	
		Cake	Spoons – Soup	
		Cups and saucers		Dessert
		Serving dishes		Serving
		Salad bowls		
	Glassware	Sherry	Napkins	
		Wine	Candles	
		Champagne	Doilies	
		Beer	Table linen	
	Cake-cutting stand and knife			
	Ashtrays		Matches	
	Tea and coffee pots		Milk jugs	
	Trays		Heated trolley	
	Salt and pepper shakers		Water tumblers	
	Ice cubes			
Flower arrangements				
Food	Cake		Menu	
	Servers		Uniforms	

INFILL/CHECK LIST		HOME
Food	Special dietary requirements	
Drinks	Barman	Wine waiter
Clearing away		
Entertainment		
Costs	Overall £	

head than a buffet because of the cost of staff preparing food on the spot, serving the meal and clearing the tables.

For sit-down meals where everyone eats the same food, it is wise to choose 'safe' dishes that the majority will like, for example, chicken, turkey or beef for the main course. Dishes such as liver, seafood and curry should be avoided. A sit-down meal does provide the opportunity to serve dishes such as soups and hot desserts.

If guests are to stand, a finger-buffet is advisable as it is difficult for guests to control food, a plate, a fork, a glass and a napkin while standing.

Guests may have special diets such as vegetarian or vegan or they may need to avoid eating certain foods because of health reasons or religious beliefs. The variety of a buffet will cater for these circumstances but for a sit-down meal it may be necessary to have alternative menus available.

Choice of Menu

The food should be delicious, attractive and practical. A firm of caterers specialising in wedding receptions will suggest a variety of menus to suit most budgets.

A buffet provides the most scope. A finger-buffet enables guests to eat while standing while a fork-buffet requires guests to use cutlery and sit down to eat and if specific places are laid out, each guest will be assured of a seat.

A finger or fork-buffet allows the guests more choice where a range of tastes, including both popular and unusual, may be included for variety. Canapés should be designed so that they do not disinte-

grate when lifted from the plate. A buffet meal could include: meats, sausage rolls, cheeses, cottage cheese, quiches; sandwiches, rolls; salads with dressings; celery boats; crisps and nuts; crudites (raw vegetables) with dips.

A formal meal offers less choice and has to appeal to most, so it is safer to opt for standard fare.

Starters should whet the appetite for the main course to follow, so something light and delicate would be appropriate, especially for a summer luncheon. A simple hors-d'oeuvre – a prawn, melon or grapefruit dish – are good ideas. For a winter luncheon, a delicious simple soup is a good warming alternative.

The main course should not be too unusual as it needs to please most guests and should be easy to consume. Roast meats are a good choice, served with a suitable gravy or sauce, or perhaps braised cutlets or a pie. A good selection of vegetables of the most popular varieties is preferable to something more unusual. Colour and presentation are important too; white meat with cauliflower and boiled potatoes will look colourless whereas green beans and carrots will add attractive colour. For a summer wedding, a salad may be appropriate, with vegetables to complement the main dish in taste and preparation.

Cold desserts are a popular choice for caterers since it is difficult to calculate the likely time when they will be served. Something light and refreshing would complement a rich main course, for example, a fruit salad, a sorbet or a mousse. To follow a lighter main course, a heavier dessert such as a gateau, pie or a fruit tart may be more appropriate. The dessert selections, whether finger, fork, knife and fork types, must be considered carefully since they can make quite a difference to the choice of menu. Nuts and mints placed in small bowls add a finishing touch.

Caterers

Outside Caterer

A firm of caterers will suggest suitable menus, provide the linen, crockery, cutlery, silver, serve food and drinks and clear up. Standards and prices vary enormously and it is therefore advisable to make a choice from personal recommendation or from past experience. Most people consider that hiring a professional caterer is preferable to self-catering, since they can do all the hard work and clear up afterwards. It is important for parents, the bride and groom and other family members to be able to relax and not have to work hard after what will be undoubtedly an exhausting day.

Selecting a Caterer

Care should be taken when selecting a caterer to suit particular needs. Printed brochures will state their services and terms and if possible it is wise to taste their food. Most caterers will offer a choice of menus for wedding meals or buffets to suit various budgets. A comparison of menus and services offered will check value for money. Discussions with the caterer need to take place well in advance.

Having made a decision, the selected caterer will need all the necessary details of the venue, the time for setting up, the time that the wedding party is expected and when the meal should be served. Most caterers charge a flat fee based on the number of guests attending and the chosen menu. This may include service, clearing up, crockery, cutlery, napkins and so on.

Estimating the number of servers or waitresses required will depend on the sort of food being offered. For stand up meals or hors-d'oeuvres, one skilled server to fifteen guests is reasonable. For more formal meals, one server for every ten guests may be required.

Self-catering

As self-catering demands considerable effort and total commitment, there needs to be total certainty that this is the right choice. Ample time and appropriate temperament are essential. Capabilities and facilities must be realistically assessed as it is very easy to underestimate the amount of hard work involved. The self-caterer should cater for no more than thirty guests, keep things simple by not being too ambitious and accept offers of help. Chores will need to be allocated for which job lists should be drawn up and the assistance of close competent friends will be necessary for the day itself. When organising the preparations it is important to keep written records of who does what and ensure that prompt payment is made to those buying items on behalf of the organiser. A comprehensive timetable will help. Carriage and transport to and from the venue is another important consideration.

To economise, cocktails and hors-d'oeuvres could be served in the afternoon as an alternative to a sit-down luncheon or dinner. At a buffet meal, guests may be left to find their own seats and then rise at the appropriate time to serve themselves, starting with the top table. When self-catering, a buffet is the simplest solution as much of the preparation can be done in advance of the wedding day and is ideal for entertaining a large group, especially a finger-buffet. A familiar menu and items that are not complicated to make are wise choices. Food may be prepared and frozen in advance so that it is possible to concentrate on the fresh foods on the day before or on the morning of the wedding. If unsure of preparation time, it makes good sense to avoid too large a choice of dishes. Recipes will specify the number of servings but the size of servings will vary and not all guests will choose every dish, so quantities should be assessed carefully so that there is enough but not too much left over. If there is a choice of three cold meats, for example, it may be assumed that most people will have one slice of two meats when determining quantities. Professional caterers generally calculate on the assumption of fifteen to twenty items per person for a buffet but there should be some reserves in case of emergencies.

It is important to lay out a buffet in a logical order so that guests make their way along the table as easily and as quickly as possible. This avoids the tedium of standing in long queues. A typical buffet line-up (working from right to left) would be:

The table needs to be long and laid in such a way that guests have freedom to move and access to food. Decorations should be kept to a minimum. A separate table for water and other drinks will provide more space on the food table. The home caterer will need sufficient cutlery, crockery and glassware for all guests. These items may be hired from specialist firms.

For a sit-down meal, a simple table style is the best advice.

A formal place setting is set from the

Napkins ← Cutlery ← Desserts ← Condiments ← Bread ← Vegetables ← Salads ← Meats ← Plates

---

outside in, so the cutlery for the first course is on the outside. Knife blades should be placed towards the plate. Dessert forks or spoons are supplied later. A maximum of three of any one piece of cutlery should be on the table

(unless oysters are being served in which case the oyster fork is placed to the right of the soup spoon).

For an informal place setting the dessert fork and spoon are included.

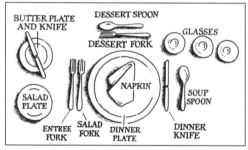

INFORMAL PLACE SETTING

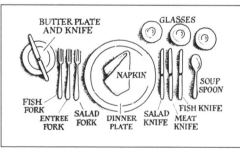

FORMAL PLACE SETTING

INFILL/CHECK LIST		CATERER
Caterer	Name	
	Address	
	Telephone	Fax
	Qualifications	Experience
	References	
	Ability to cope with number of guests	
	When do they need final numbers?	
Function	No. of guests: Adults	Children
	Times: Arrival	Meal
	Speeches	Cake-cutting
	Entertainment	Department
	Date booked with caterer	
Facilities	Room size	Furniture: tables and chairs
	Decorations incl. flowers	Heating
	Seating arrangements	Parking
	Food preparation location:	
	Cooking/storage/serving/clearing up/towels	
	Cloakroom/toilet facilities:	
	Toilet rolls, soap, staff changing	
Equipment	Cutlery	Crockery China
	Glassware	Cake stand and knife
	Table linen	Napkins
	Candles	Menu cards
	Ashtrays	Tea and coffee pots
	Flowers and table decorations	
Food	Menu options	

	Starter	Main	Dessert	Prepared in advance/on day
1				
2				
3				
Children				
Cooking location				

INFILL/CHECK LIST			CATERER
Food	Cake-cutting		
	Special dietary requirements		
	Leftovers		
Drink	Alcoholic		
	Non-alcoholic		
	Is there a charge for bottles not opened?		
Staff	Waiters	Waitresses	
	Wine servers	Barman	
	Uniforms	Bar arrangements	
Insurance	Policy for damage/breakages		
Costs	Overall	£	
	Service	£	
	Tips	£	
	VAT	£	
	Deposit/cancellation fee	£	
	Payment date(s)		

Cake

The cake traditionally has pride of place on the top table where it stands in the centre at a sit-down reception or in the centre of the plates of food at a buffet or on a special display stand set apart from other tables. Until the moment of cutting it should not be directly in front of the newly-weds as it could obscure them from sight of some of the guests.

Cutting the Cake

The cake-cutting ceremony is traditionally the concluding part of the formalities and follows the toasts, although in some cases it takes place before the speeches and toasts so that it may be taken away and cut by the professionals behind the scenes whilst the speeches are in progress. If the meal is at lunchtime, the cake may be served with coffee at teatime. The first slice is ceremonially cut by the bride and groom with the groom's hand covering the bride's. The point of the knife should be placed in the centre of the bottom tier. If the icing is particularly hard, the cake may be cut beforehand and the incision disguised by decoration until the cake-cutting ceremony for which a sharp knife, damp cloth and a cake server are essential. Small slices are handed round on paper napkins so that they may be taken away by anyone not wishing to eat the cake at that time. If any part of the cake is to be preserved, it should be wrapped in greaseproof paper and stored in an airtight tin. The fruit will gradually seep through, discolouring the icing, but the cake can be re-iced when necessary.

Cake Makers

Cakes may be ordered from a confectionery, a cake specialist, a wedding caterer, the hotel, or made by an experienced relative or friend, or the bride may wish to make the cake herself. The cake itself is not too difficult to make but the icing is best left to the experts. Many people run home businesses making wedding cakes and they may be excellent and very reasonably priced. It can be economical for the bride, her mother, a relative or friend to make the cake themselves in which case, cake tops can be borrowed or fresh flowers may be used for decoration.

Before making a decision on an outside cake maker, it is wise to visit several suppliers to look at their portfolio (usually a photograph album featuring cakes made by the firm), ascertain costs and taste their products before ordering. This is a common request and most are willing to comply. Many people choose to make their own cake because home-made cake can be tastier and there is the pride of achievement together with economy reasons. A traditional cake with many tiers will take months to make and must be ordered at least three months in advance of the wedding. Smaller cakes or cakes of a different type may take less time but ample time should still be allowed. Ideally the cake should stand for six to nine weeks before it is iced. Traditional cakes really improve with age.

The finished cake is usually delivered to the caterers the day before the wedding. On the morning of the wedding they will assemble and decorate it for display.

Recipe

Traditionally a wedding cake is a classic rich fruit cake with white royal icing piped and decorated. The supplier will offer a selection of designs and decorations. Most people have a special decoration on the top, perhaps a vase of fresh flowers or a bride and groom embellishment. It may be possible to buy or rent these from the confectioner or they may be acquired elsewhere.

Alternative recipes include: plain white cake with top frosting; plain or frosted sponge; chocolate cake; biscuit wheatsheaf; white frosted Swiss roll stuffed with glace cherries; or a French pyramid of profiteroles bound together with spun sugar.

For the icing of a traditional style cake, there is no reason why a colour or colours other than white should not be chosen. Shades which echo the colours of the bridesmaids' dresses or the flowers would be complementary to the overall visual effect.

Style

There are many styles of wedding cake available. The bride may choose a single cake or a design with several tiers. The latter is generally made up of cakes of diminishing size. The bottom or lower (largest) cakes are cut at the reception and the top layer kept for some future celebration such as a christening.
Cake styles include:
- round cake with round pillars
- square cake with square pillars
- non-pillared
- stacked with tiers sitting directly on top of each other.

Shape

There are many shapes from which to choose but the most popular are round or square. For home baking, shaped tins can be bought or hired from specialist cake shops.

Shape options include simple round, simple square, rectangular, heart, flower, butterfly, hexagonal, octagonal, stars, clover leaves and horseshoes.

Cake Shape	Cake Size		No. of Cake Servings	
Square	cm	inches	Fruit	Sponge
	13	5	17	9
	15	6	28	14
	18	7	41	21
	20	8	56	28
	23	9	73	37
	25	10	92	46
Round	cm	inches	Fruit	Sponge
	13	5	14	7
	15	6	20	10
	18	7	29	15
	20	8	40	20
	23	9	53	27
	25	10	68	34

Iɴғɪʟʟ/Cʜᴇᴄᴋ Lɪsᴛ **Cᴀᴋᴇ**

Supplier	Name
	Address
	Telephone
	Contact

Recipe

Style	No. of guests
	Those unable to attend
	Neighbours
Shape	Colleagues
	House warming
	First anniversary
Size No. of tiers	Christening
	TOTAL

Icing colour   Icing flavour

Decorations

Delivery/Collection:	Date	Time

Delivery address

Insurance   Written confirmation received

Deposit due date   Balance due date

Cost	£

Size

The size of the cake is the bride's choice but the confectioner will be able to advise on an appropriate size for the number of guests (taking into account extra for those people unable to attend the reception to whom small slices are sent following the wedding), colleagues and neighbours, a tier for the house-warming, first wedding anniversary or the christening of the first child. Wrapped carefully, a good quality fruit cake may last for several years. Wedding cake is traditionally served in 2.5 cm (1 inch) square pieces and the table above gives a rough guide to servings. Square cakes are better value than round ones and are also easier to cut.

Colour and Decorations

The most popular colour for wedding cakes is white but there is absolutely no reason why the cake should not be coloured, for example to complement the colour scheme of the wedding party, or the flowers.

Generally royal icing is used for wedding cakes as it is harder and easier to pipe, but there is also the more recent fondant icing which is more versatile enabling many different embellishments. If employing a professional, they should be able to provide a choice of decorations from their portfolio. A cake may be personalised with initials or names and date of the wedding. Suggestions for decorations include: bride and groom, lovebirds, bells, rings, and flowers.

Drinks

The guests will naturally want liquid refreshments and as with the food, the drink should suit the general style and formality of the occasion. The caterer may be able to supply a glass of sherry for each guest as they arrive, wine with the meal and Champagne for the toasts. There may be a bar available at a hotel with a bar tender provided. The guests can purchase their own drinks or the bride and groom may pay the full bar bill, or they may allocate a certain sum to the barman and once this is exhausted, guests then pay for their own

drinks. If supplying drinks, quantities will naturally depend on the number and thirst of the guests and it is good advice to have a reasonable range, including a plentiful quantity of mixers, fresh fruit juices and soft drinks for children, teetotalers and drivers.

It is becoming increasingly popular to serve sparking wines throughout the reception, or a still white wine with a good Champagne for toasts. If a combination of wines is selected, the general rule for the order in which it should be served is as follows:

First	— White
Then	— Red
First	— Dry
Then	— Sweet
First	— Younger
Then	— Older

More unusual options include punch and hot mulled wine or hot port for a cold day.

Arrival at Reception

Guests like to have a drink when they arrive at the reception after passing through the receiving line and depositing their coats. Traditionally, sherry is offered at this time; medium and dry provide an acceptable choice but an alternative could be port or red and white wine. If the finances allow, Champagne may be served or Buck's Fizz (Champagne and orange juice). Each bottle will serve about six people (twelve if serving Buck's Fizz). Non-alcoholic drinks should also be made available for drivers, non-drinkers and children. Guests may, of course, order their drinks from the bar (if at hand).

Accompaniment to Meal

A white wine may be served as an aperitif, perhaps with the starter. The tradition of white wine with fish, white meat and fowl and red with red meats may no longer seem appropriate. It is usual to accompany a sit-down set menu meal with wine and an expert should be able to suggest a good quality selection to suit a particular menu but generally the white wine with the main course is med-ium to dry.

Some caterers will allow wine to be provided from another supplier but they will still charge for opening and serving the drinks. Again, a plentiful supply of non-alcoholic drinks should be available together with water, and perhaps tea and coffee.

The Toasts

Champagne is the traditional drink with which to toast the good health of the bride and groom. Many chain stores and wine merchants now stock a range of Champagnes to suit various budgets but frequently, sparkling wine is chosen as a less expensive option. A brut Champagne is very dry, while a demi-sec is sweeter. Less expensive alternatives include quality wines which may cost half the price. Sparkling wine is now very popular for the toasts. If white wine has been drunk with the meal, it is acceptable to use the same wine for the toasts, but if the meal was accompanied by red wine, it would be more appropriate to serve a different wine following the meal; perhaps Asti Spumante served well chilled or Moscato or Veuve du Vernay. A bottle will serve approximately six glasses.

After the Meal

After a very formal meal, it may be appropriate to serve a dessert wine which is usually a sweet variety, brandy, port or liqueurs. However, it is acceptable to serve tea and coffee. Unless there are unlimited funds available, an 'open' bar whereby the host and hostess pay for the drinks, should be 'closed' after a stipulated time or after a limited amount of money has been spent after which time guests pay for their own. Or there could be a cash bar whereby guests pay for all of their drinks. At a home or hall reception, the host and hostess provide all the drinks.

Teetotalers and Drivers

These days teetotalers and drivers need not confine themselves to drinking squash as there are many delicious non-alcoholic drinks available, including red and white wines, cocktails, punches, exotic fruit juices, and non-alcoholic elderflower Champagne.

Chilling and Quantities

Champagne and white wines should be adequately chilled, ideal bottle temperature is between 5.5 and 9°C (42 and 48°F) but two to three hours in cold water will suffice where no ice is available. Champagne should never be served ice-cold and a suitable method of storage should be considered prior to serving. Red wines should be served at room temperature (two hours in a typical dining room atmosphere should suffice) and uncorked one hour prior to being served to allow for 'breath-ing'.

At least half a 75cl bottle of wine (three glasses) should be allowed for each guest. Champagne is the traditional wedding drink but can be expensive. A half to three-quarters of a bottle per person should be allowed if Champagne is to be served throughout the reception. A bottle will serve six glasses.

Bottle sizes	
Quarter	187 ml
Half	375 ml
Bottle	750 ml
Magnum (two bottles)	1.51 cl
Jeroboam (four bottles)	3.0 cl
Methusalem (eight bottles)	6.0 cl
Salmanazar (twelve bottles)	9.0 cl

Preferred glasses include slender fluted and tulip-shaped.

A litre of spirits will serve approximately sixteen people. It is possible to purchase barrels of beer but it is advisable not to over-order because of possible wastage. Beer barrels can always be supplemented with cans.

Serving

If a barman is not part of the 'reception package', it is advisable to have someone who will act in this role or a number of people who will help out. It would be inappropriate to expect the best man to spend the reception behind the bar when he should be enjoying the occasion with the guests. If a barman is employed, references should be sought or he should be personally recommended. Charges for services should be agreed before the event.

When serving Champagne, bottles

must be opened carefully. The wire muzzle must be unwound and removed. The cork should be grasped in one hand and the bottle in the other, pointing away from danger! The bottle should be slowly twisted and when the cork is out, the bottle must be kept at the same angle for a few seconds to allow the escape of surplus gas.

Hotel, restaurant and club receptions invariably insist on supplying and serving the drinks themselves. The few that do allow other arrangements may charge a corkage for serving. If a firm is to supply the drink the agreement should be on a sale-or-return basis, ensuring that any over-estimate on amount is not paid for.

Seating Plan

A stand-up finger-buffet reception demands no formal seating arrangement except that the bridal party should have a formal table where they can be served and that seats should be provided for the elderly and infirm. It may also be necessary to set aside an area for young children, equipped with highchairs and maybe a room where babies can be fed and changed.

A fork-buffet will require seating; this can be formal whereby the guests have allocated seats or informal whereby they choose where to sit.

For a formally seated reception, it is traditional to reserve the top table for the wedding party with guests allocated places on the side tables which may be laid out to suit the space available. The aim is to ensure that all can see and be seen. Although the planning of seating arrangements for the guests is optional, it does make things less confusing on the day. A table plan displayed near to the entrance of the dining room will enable guests to go directly to their seats where place cards confirm their positions. However, the table plan should not be displayed in the doorway where it will cause a bottleneck into the dining room.

Seating plans should be devised as soon as all the acceptances to the wedding invitations have been received and place cards arranged on the day so that everyone can find their places quickly and with minimum fuss. If there are many guests, the display of two plans will reduce crowding and ease the flow into the dining room. Husbands and wives do not sit directly together, they are often seated opposite, and men and women should be alternated. In special circumstances, for example, when seating divorced couples, arrangements should obviously be handled tactfully.

Top Table

At most weddings there is a top table for members of the wedding party who sit along one side of a long table facing the guests, ensuring that everyone can view the top table. Bridesmaids, pages and ushers generally occupy the seats of other tables closest to the top table or on the top table itself if arrangements permit. Care must be taken not to hurt anyone's feelings by including a guest who has no connection with the wedding party, though partners of the wedding party may be included if space permits.

The bride and groom sit in the middle; the groom always sits on the right of the bride. Men and women should be alternated for integration purposes. Whoever is proposing the first toast generally sits on the bride's left. If parents are divorced and remarried they should be seated close to their new partners.

INFILL LIST							SEATING PLAN — TRADITIONAL
Chief Brides-maid	Groom's Father	Bride's Mother	Groom	Bride	Bride's Father	Groom's Mother	Best Man

INFILL LIST					SEATING PLAN — ALTERNATIVES		
Best Man	Groom's Father	Bride's Mother	Groom	Bride	Bride's Father	Groom's Mother	Chief Brides-Maid
Groom's Mother	Bride's Father	Chief Brides-Maid	Groom	Bride	Best Man	Bride's Mother	Groom's Father
Chief Brides-Maid	Bride's Father	Bride's Mother	Groom	Bride	Groom's Father	Groom's Mother	Best Man
Groom's Mother	Bride's Father	Groom	Bride	Bride's Mother	Groom's Father	Chief Brides-Maid	Best Man

Arrangement when Bride's parents are divorced and both parents have remarried

Bride's Stepfather	Chief Bridesmaid	Groom's Father	Bride's Mother	Groom	Bride	Bride's Father	Groom's Mother	Best Man	Bride's Stepmother

Arrangement when Groom's parents are divorced and both parents have remarried

Best Man	Groom's Stepmother	Groom's Father	Bride's Mother	Groom	Bride	Bride's Father	Groom's Mother	Groom's Stepfather	Chief Bridesmaid

Groom's Stepmother	Bride's Stepfather	Chief Bridesmaid	Groom's Father	Bride's Mother	Groom	Bride	Bride's Father	Groom's Mother	Best Man	Bride's Stepmother	Groom's Stepfather
Arrangement when both sets of parents are divorced and all have remarried											

Side Tables

Closest relatives are usually seated nearest to the top table. Brothers and sisters should be interspersed with their wives and husbands where applicable. A husband and wife are usually seated at the same table, or nearby, but not necessarily next to each other. Aunts and uncles follow, then friends and colleagues of the newly-weds.

Arrangements should, if at all possible, separate guests who are known to have differences and seat together people who will enjoy each other's company. Each person needs to be near to some one they know and yet have an opportunity to meet new people. Sometimes the places are allocated so that the guests from both families are intermingled, but not to the extent that nobody knows what to say to anyone!

To generalise the rules, an attempt should be made to alternate the sexes as far as possible always considering friendships or otherwise.

Seating is an important factor, especially at a formal reception as the guests will spend a long time seated and after the meal, they will need somewhere to relax more informally and mingle more freely.

Small children should be seated with their parents. Children over the age of seven can be seated; those under seven should have a crèche with a child-minder. Small children may be disruptive and hazardous at an informal stand-up buffet and for this reason, a separate room might be the answer with supervision and entertainment laid on. Children over thirteen can be seated with others of their own age. A 'singles' table for unattached guests

may be an idea and if there are several teenagers, they might prefer to have their own table too.

If the reception is informal, then the guests may be left to make their own seating arrangements. For an informal buffet, a decision needs to be made whether tables and chairs will be provided. Guests can only be expected to stand for a very short informal buffet and even then it is necessary to provide seats for any elderly or infirm guests.

If traditional arrangements seem to be inappropriate, the solution can be to opt for a room full of separate tables which can make for a much more relaxed and successful atmosphere as long as guests are grouped tactfully with a good mix of men and women so that everyone has maximum opportunity for enjoying themselves. It should be appreciated that a wedding is not always a joyous occasion for single people and for this reason it is important to seat them close to other single people with whom they are likely to share common interests.

Table Decorations

A professional caterer will arrange table decorations (usually flower arrangements) according to instructions. The arrangements may be ordered by the bride or the bride's mother to create a complementary overall colour scheme or they may be included in a hotel's wedding package. The bride may also want to add specially printed menus, place cards, napkins and coasters. For a reception held in the hall, the bride or her mother would need to check that they have access early in the morning for setting up their tables.

Configurations

Top table with two sides

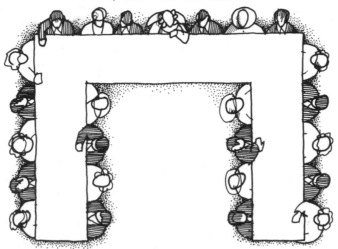

This is ideal as everybody has a clear view of everybody else.

Top table with three sides

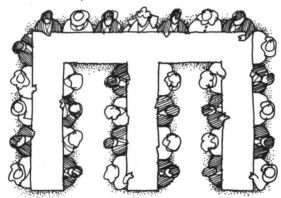

Top table with separate sides

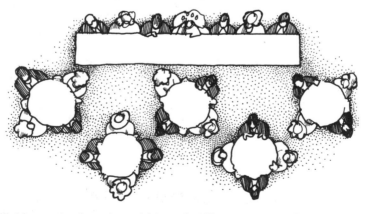

Separate tables seating four, six or eight people offer greater scope for mixing or separating certain guests. Tables can be angled so that guests do not have their backs fully turned towards the top table.

Entertainment

To start the festivities at the reception, there could be live or recorded music while drinks are served and photographs are taken. The music should be uplifting but soft and unobtrusive so that guests do not have to raise their voices in order to be heard.

The style of music for the main entertainment obviously depends on personal choice but it is wise to have a selection of music that will allow everyone to be happy and have a good time. Ages may range from five to seventy so there needs to be plenty of variety! Besides ensuring that the music is acceptable to the maj-ority of guests, it can set the tone for the style of reception. A ballroom full of two hundred or more guests will require a dance band or orchestra, whereas a smaller affair may be better with a disc jockey. If everyone is expected to dance, plenty of dance music must be provided, but if a quieter reception is planned, then sophi-sticated background music may be a better choice. Most people opt for a mixture of the two, or assume that guests will want to talk first and start dancing later. Taped music or a pianist, flautist or harpist would be ideal for a small reception at home. A string quartet or steel band makes good background music for a home outdoor reception.

Although many caterers are able to organise music, generally couples arrange their own.

Musicians

There are many kinds of musicians from which to choose including: harpists, steel bands, string quartets, singers, barbershop singers, jazz musicians and pianists. For live music, it should be possible to choose a band that can provide a variety by playing a little of everything: a waltz, rock, gentle songs, interspersed with lively dances. The band should be informed of the kind of music desired; the frequency of particular pieces; any special songs that they may need to learn before the wedding; the first dance, as the bride and groom will dance to this alone; and any preferences for the last dance.

There are many kinds of musicians playing many kinds of music. Performers can be found through recommendations from family, friends and colleagues, the caterers, the hotel or from Yellow Pages. The hotel may have a resident musician. It is wise to listen to a taped performance or to attend a function at which the musicians are entertaining and to ensure that they are willing to perform the selections and suit the atmosphere of the occasion. The cost of a band depends on their popularity, experience, the number of members, whether they have to learn new music, the time required and the distance travelled. Agreed details such as date, times, fees, deposit, cancellation/refund policy, provision of equipment, length of breaks and special requests should be confirmed in writing.

Discotheques

Live bands are expensive and for this reason many couples choose a discotheque and employ a disc jockey who is capable of varying the entertainment to suit the guests. He or she provides their own selection of records to the reception. As with bands, DJs all have their own personality and style, so it is wise to choose someone in whom there is plenty of confidence. To provide variety, the selection will need to include waltzes and foxtrots as well as the more modern popular music. Most DJs who work regularly at weddings will have a good and up-to-date selection, and understand that music at weddings should not be too loud as guests want to talk among themselves as well as join in the dancing.

Recorded Music

To economise, there is always the option of taped music. Music may be home-taped and a friend appointed to operate the equipment which may be hired or borrowed. When making the recording, the volume should be kept at a low level to avoid recording vibrations and an attempt made to ensure smooth flow from one piece of music to the next. A separate tape of background music may be used during the meal and another for the dancing later on.

Wedding Songs

Wedding theme songs include:

Get Me To The Church On Time (My Fair Lady);

Going To The Chapel (My Fair Lady);

The Wedding Song (Peter, Paul and Mary);

Love and Marriage (Sammy Cahn);

Congratulations (Cliff Richard) and

Hawaiian Wedding Song (Andy Williams, Elvis and others).

If the last dance is to be a 'waltz' the bride and groom should practise beforehand.

Entertainer

If there are many children, a clown or magician could be employed to entertain. Videos are also another entertainment idea, particularly useful for keeping the younger generation fully occupied and happy.

The Role of the Bride and Groom

When the formal part of the reception is over, the bride and groom should circulate and talk to guests informally and if possible this should be done while the couple are still in their wedding attire — it is a chance for guests to admire their outfits at close range and to convey best wishes. Before leaving for the honeymoon it is a polite gesture for the couple to thank privately those who have been particularly involved with the preparations.

··

TRADITION

It is traditional for the bride, on leaving the reception, to throw her bouquet over her shoulder into the group of unmarried female guests. Supposedly, the person who catches it will be the next one in the room to marry. In earlier days, the bride often threw one of her wedding shoes! Tossing the garter is similar except that the groom removes the bride's garter and throws it over his shoulder into the group of unmarried males.

··

INFILL LIST		Balance due date		ENTERTAINMENT
Musicians/DJ	Name			
	Address			
	Telephone			
	No. of musicians/members			
Venue	Address			
	Contact			
Booking	Date			
	Time: start	break/s	finish	
	No. of performance hours			

Music	**Choice**	**Time**
First dance		
Special requests		
Last dance		
Musicians'/DJ's attire		
Equipment facilities		

Cost	£
Deposit/cancellation policy	
Deposit due date	

8

Honeymoon

Nowadays a honeymoon is the chance to get away from it all, to wind down after the excitement of the wedding, relax and enjoy each other's company and prepare for the future. A great deal of money will probably have been spent on the wedding but it is desirable to have a holiday together that will be memorable in future years. Most people would agree that it is a good idea to spend at least the first few days of married life away from what will be, for the future, normal routine, and to escape from the worries of home, families and friends for a while. Many travel firms offer special honeymoon packages or bargain breaks for couples trying to economise.

TRADITION
In the days when a groom captured his bride, the couple hid from her parents until the search was called off. After they were married they would hide for one full cycle of the moon while drinking honey wine, hence 'honeymoon'.
Carrying the bride over the threshold may also originate from this time as a way of preventing her from running away.
The groom traditionally arranges and pays for the honeymoon.

Considerations

The honeymoon is likely to be the most expensive item next to the reception and the decision about a location which suits both largely depends on how much can be realistically afforded and how much time can be devoted to the break. If the wedding precedes the summer vacation then a long main holiday may be possible, but if a further holiday is planned for the same year it may be preferable to choose a shorter or simpler honeymoon. Availability of finances will determine the type of honeymoon of course.

Traditionally the honeymoon is held immediately after the wedding but increasingly today the bride and groom prefer a holiday some time afterwards when all the activity has subsided. Even if the groom keeps the destination a well kept secret from the bride, she will need to know the climate and the formality of the location so that she can organise her packing accordingly.

Going Abroad

Travel magazines provide much information to help decide on a suitable holiday. Travel agents are able to supply brochures and can recommend tour operators who offer special honeymoon options. Discount fares may be available as many airlines and travel agents hold back a number of lower priced seats. Generally it is necessary to book one, two or three weeks in advance and stay for at least one week (plus one Saturday night's stay over) to obtain a cheaper ticket. It is possible to order special meals to suit special diets. A telephone call to the airline a few hours before the flight will confirm any delays. However, it is important to check in at the airport at least one and a half hours before the flight time.

UK Honeymoon

If the budget is limited, perhaps a small hotel for the weekend could be considered. Low season bookings are always cheaper.

Camping or caravanning are other considerations or a combination with hotels or bed and breakfast may be an option. It may be preferable to spend one or two nights in a bridal suite rather than spending a week somewhere. It is always a good idea to pursue special rates for honeymoon couples regardless of location.

Some hotels offer a free bedroom for the bride and groom if they have a sizable catered reception held in the hotel. Hotel wedding packages may include four poster bed, jacuzzi, Champagne, chocolates, flowers, greeting card and a gift. Relatives and close friends may have a holiday home which they are prepared to rent for the honeymoon.

Documents

Some countries require a visa in addition to a passport. The travel agent or embassy or consulate of the country destination will be able to advise.

Passports and medical requirements must be arranged well in advance. If the honeymoon is abroad and the bride's passport is in her maiden name, she should have any plane tickets and travellers cheques issued in her maiden name and take the marriage certificate with her. If the bride wants a new passport in her married name, application needs to be made to the Passport Agency in London for which at least three months should be allowed for processing. The passport will not be received until the marriage has taken place but it may be sent to the appropriate minister or registrar to pass on after the wedding.

The safest way to carry money is to use travellers cheques as they can be replaced if stolen or lost. With each traveller cheque there is a serial number. These should be kept safe and separate from the cheques and produced as proof of purchase and ownership if the need arises. It is advisable to check how long it takes for the money to be refunded and what happens if a passport is lost as well. Credit card users should note the account numbers and emergency telephone numbers, keep this information safe and separate, and pay any outstanding balances before the honeymoon.

Arrangements and reservations need to be made early, especially if travelling in high season and choosing a popular holiday resort.

Insurance

It is important to choose a reputable travel agent who is a member of ABTA and to be covered by their insurance bond should anything go wrong. The travel agent or tour operator will recommend insurance covering injury, sickness, loss of property and travel delay and will also advise on baggage restrictions. When touring in a rented car, hidden costs may include insurance, petrol and late return. Some vehicle insurance policies and some credit card companies automatically provide cover for hired vehicles. Before they are driven, hired vehicles should be checked for petrol and any damage should be reported to the person in charge.

Timetable

When planning the timetable it is important to allow enough time between leaving the reception and reaching the destination.

First Night

Spending the first night in the reception hotel or in a nearby hotel before going abroad the next day provides a chance to recover from the excitement and exhaustion of the wedding day. Many airports have hotels nearby and some have bridal suites.

It is vital that documents such as passports and plane tickets are not forgotten. The best man will keep all travel documents safe on the wedding day and will hand them over prior to departure from the reception. He will also deal with the luggage.

INFILL/CHECK LIST		HONEYMOON PLANNING	
Budget		£	
Work leave from	to		
Date booked			
Departure time from reception	Transport from reception		
Honeymoon dates from	to		
Departure time			
Style Luxurious		Adventurous	
Meeting new people		Lazy	
Active		New experience	
Atmosphere/venue City		Historic interest	
Countryside		Sunshine and beaches	
Sport, for example ski resort		Night life	
Foreign customs/culture		Particular interest, for example bird watching, walking, sightseeing	
Stay One place		Tour	
Location Abroad		UK	
First night destination			
Address			
Telephone			
Honeymoon destination			
Accommodation			£
Hotel luxurious modest Bed and breakfast Special honeymoon suite Flat Villa Caravan Tent Other		Address Telephone	

INFILL/CHECK LIST	HONEYMOON PLANNING	
Travel Air Sea Train Coach Car	Travel Agent Address Telephone	
Reservation made with whom		
Airport/Station		
Flight/Train number		
Transport home		
Documents		
Passports		
Visas		
Marriage certificate		
Foreign currency/Travellers' cheques/Credit cards		
Spending money		
Insurance		
Tickets (plane, train, boat, etc.)		
Driving licences, etc.		
Maps		
Guidebooks		
Timetables		
Inoculations certificates		
Departure time for return journey		

INFILL/CHECK LIST	HONEYMOON PACKING
Documents (on previous page)	£
First aid kit including travel sickness tablets and any medication	
Luggage two medium cases	
two medium hand luggage	
(check baggage restrictions)	
Labels	
Blood group card	
Contraception	
Cosmetics	
Sunscreen	
Sunglasses	
Toiletries	
Jewellery	
Clothes informal and formal	
Sportswear, for example, swimwear	
Nightwear	
Underwear	
Jackets, coats, shoes, etc.	
Camera, films, batteries	
Recreational books	
personal cassette	
sports equipment	
TOTAL	

9

Duties

*C*hoosing *special attendants is a way of surrounding the bride on her wedding day with those people closest to her. They act as helpers in all sorts of capacities and add to the general atmosphere of enjoyment. For the bride, her attendants are her chief bridesmaid, bridesmaids, and page boys; the groom chooses a best man and ushers.*

Selection of Attendants

The number of attendants is entirely the bride's decision in accordance with the budget but generally the larger and more formal the wedding, the greater the number of attendants. Every wedding requires two witnesses, and at most weddings there is a best man and a chief bridesmaid and it is the parents, one from each side, or the best man and chief bridesmaid who usually perform this role. Anyone can be chosen to play the role of an attendant, though family are generally the first to be selected. It is thoughtful to include members from both the bride's and groom's families and to achieve an even balance if there are to be several attendants. Close friends are also often included.

The bride will probably have people in mind from the beginning and many brides find that the difficulty is not being able to ask everyone, but she should not feel obliged to ask someone to be an attendant purely because she was chosen to play a role at a previous wedding. This should not be expected. However, if there are people who cannot be included, then the problem should be explained to them and they will probably be most understanding.

Perhaps they could be asked to fulfil some other special role.

Attendants are usually honoured to fulfil wedding roles but they could be a little overawed by the responsibility, especially if the wedding is to be a large formal occasion. An informal chat with them explaining what is expected should allay any fears. If they are expecting to perform certain special duties such as providing transport, they should be asked first and then informed as to the detailed requirements. It is important that they are not expected to guess their duties! The allocation of roles is more a matter of custom and tradition than the demands of either ecclesiastical or secular practice. Those chosen for a role to play should be trustworthy people who will respond to delegated responsibility. It is very important that all attendants know both their own and everyone else's duties.

The allocation and details of the responsibilities and duties of the attendants used to be dealt with solely by the bride's family, with only symbolic consultation with the groom's family, but these days couples plan most of the details together. However, it is obviously important to consult both sets of parents and the rest of the wedding party at each stage.

INFILL LIST					THE WEDDING PARTY WHO'S WHO
	Name	Age if child	Address	Telephone	Specific duties
Best Man					
Chief Bridesmaid/ Matron of Honour					
Bridesmaid					
Bridesmaid					
Bridesmaid					
Flower Girl					
Page					
Page					
Page					
Chief Usher					Transport
Usher					Escort
Usher					Buttonholes

INFILL LIST					THE WEDDING PARTY WHO'S WHO
	Name	Age if child	Address	Telephone	Specific duties
Usher					Order of Service Sheets
Bride's Parents					
Groom's Parents					

Bride's Diary

It is impossible to be too specific about planning since this obviously depends on the type of ceremony, the style of the reception and the fact that everyone has different methods of dealing with the planning. However, most brides would agree that the earlier the planning, the better. Allowing maximum time provides an opportunity to shop around and time to arrange everything to suit.

The following diary entries are based on having six months to plan the event and suggest how time may be organised. In addition to keeping check lists of all the detailed wedding plans, the bride will need an overall timetable so that plans are made in good time and that nothing is forgotten. The entries, some of which may overlap, may be added to, deleted or adapted to suit individual needs and may be used to ensure that everything is covered.

Six Months

☐ Announce decision to bride's parents

☐ Announce decision to groom's parents

☐ Arrange for parents to meet

☐ Discuss specifics and payment with partner and parents

☐ Make a list of those to be informed

☐ Tell relatives and close friends

☐ Arrange engagement party

☐ Arrange press announcement

☐ Decide how many guests to invite to the wedding

☐ Draw up guest list with groom and bride's mother and wedding gift list with groom

☐ Consult groom's parents about guest list

☐ Draft budget

☐ Compile actual budget

☐ Decide on the type of wedding

☐ Choose and book register office and provide details

☐ Provide statements that there are no legal reasons why the marriage should not take place

□ Discuss plans with groom and attendants

□ Write thank-you letters for gifts as they arrive

□ Choose and book photographer and/or video

□ Choose and book transport

□ Choose and book entertainment

□ Check and arrange passports

□ Begin any long-term beauty treatments

□ Plan honeymoon travel arrangements and organise documents

Four months

□ Choose and acquire gown accessories, going-away and honeymoon attire

□ Choose and acquire attendants' attire, in consultation with them

□ Discuss formal wear for the groom and principal men

□ Choose and book the florist, order flowers and arrange collection/delivery dates

□ Choose and order stationery

□ Ensure that the mothers have selected their outfits

□ Acquire furnishings for new home

□ Advise best man of any specific people to mention in his speech

Two Months

□ Choose and acquire gift for groom

□ Ensure that groom has chosen gifts for the attendants

□ Address and send invitations

□ Send/circulate gift list to guests or set up a wedding list at a department store that has a bride's department

□ Acquire wedding ring(s) with groom

□ Practise making-up

□ Obtain Registrar's certificate and/or licence

□ Ensure that notice is entered in Superintendent's notice book

□ Choose and book location of and date for ceremony by applying to the minister

□ Meet minister to discuss and finalise details, with groom

□ Arrange for publication of banns or note when to apply for licence

□ Arrange publication of banns in groom's parish or obtain licence/certificate

□ Choose and book reception venue, caterers, bar and drinks supplier

□ Choose and order or make the cake

□ Visit reception venue with groom and best man to check arrangements

□ Select and appoint attendants with groom bearing in mind their duties

□ Select helpers in agreement with groom

☐ Make an appointment with hair-dresser for the day before the wedding and decide on a hairstyle

☐ Book any special beauty treatments

☐ Discuss and finalise the photography arrangements

☐ Discuss and finalise arrangements with the florist

☐ Check church/civil arrangements with groom

☐ Obtain marriage licence

☐ Arrange overnight accommodation and transport for guests if necessary

☐ Have inoculations, if necessary

☐ Write thank-you letters for gifts as they arrive

☐ See GP regarding family planning if required

☐ See GP and dentist for a check up

☐ Arrange insurance against cancellation of the wedding and loss of/damage to attire and gifts

One Month

☐ Arrange and have a final dress fitting for bride and attendants

☐ Finalise rehearsal arrangements with groom and inform wedding party

☐ Arrange pre-wedding parties

☐ Confirm guest numbers for the reception

☐ Confirm all appointments and arrangements with suppliers

☐ Ensure that groom has ordered currency and travellers' cheques for honeymoon

☐ Inform important organisations of imminent change of marital status, new name (if adopting groom's surname), and address

☐ Prepare and submit any announcements to the press

☐ Make appointment with hair-dresser, manicurist, beautician for the day before the wedding day

☐ Write thank-you letters for gifts as they arrive

Two Weeks

☐ Devise seating plan for the reception and place cards for the tables

☐ Give final numbers and seating arrangements to the caterer

☐ Begin moving into new home

☐ Write thank-you letters for gifts as they arrive

One Week

☐ Wrap gift for groom and those for attendants with groom

☐ Attend rehearsal and hold rehearsal party for attendants; pass on and receive gifts

☐ Ensure that all attendants know their duties and when and where they should be at each venue

☐ Ensure that the groom and best man know who to thank in their speeches

☐ Attend and enjoy hen party

☐ Attend shower (if organised)

☐ Arrange for a display of gifts to be viewed by friends and relatives if they are not to be on display on the wedding day

☐ Practise make-up and hair with dress and headdress

☐ Step up beauty treatments and manicure/attend beauty salon

☐ Ensure that the groom has a haircut

☐ Wear in wedding shoes

☐ Ensure groom has all his clothes organised

☐ Confirm arrangements for transport

☐ Confirm arrangements with florist

☐ Confirm arrangements for reception venue and caterers

☐ Confirm arrangements for cake collection/delivery

☐ Confirm arrangements for photographs

☐ Confirm arrangements for entertainment

☐ Collect banns certificate from groom's minister

☐ Ensure delivery of cake

☐ Pack for honeymoon

☐ Check documents

☐ Allocate as many jobs as possible to others for the wedding day

☐ Arrange for the return of any hired items

☐ Ensure that best man has or knows when to collect buttonholes, order of service sheets, for example

☐ Go through guest list with both sets of parents so that everyone's names are known

☐ Pay bills that will fall due while away

☐ Start packing

One Day

☐ Visit hairdresser, manicurist, beautician

☐ Prepare wedding outfit – iron if necessary

☐ Relax

☐ Have an early night

The Day

☐ Ensure that luggage, going-away outfit and honeymoon clothes are delivered to reception venue

☐ Ensure younger attendants are looked after

See Chapter 19 for the day's full procedure

After the Honeymoon

☐ Write outstanding letters of thanks including letters to both sets of parents expressing thanks

☐ Order photographs

☐ Deal with documentation

☐ Ensure that best man has returned hired attire

☐ Ensure that slices of cake have been sent

☐ Ensure that the best man is paid any out-of-pocket expenses incurred on the wedding day

☐ Arrange press report

☐ Entertain both sets of parents and attendants

Groom's Diary

The groom's responsibilities include: dealing with legal aspects; choosing the best man and ushers; organising the honeymoon, clothes for male members of the wedding party, wedding rings, flowers for the bride and attendants, a gift for the bride and attendants; attending the rehearsal and delivering a speech.

Six Months

☐ Announce decision to bride's parents

☐ Announce decision to groom's parents

☐ Arrange for parents to meet

☐ Discuss specifics and payment with partner and parents

☐ Make a list of those to be informed

☐ Tell relatives and close friends

☐ Arrange engagement party

☐ Draw up guest list with bride and bride's mother and wedding gift list with bride

☐ Consult own parents about guest list

☐ Draft budget

☐ Compile actual budget

☐ Decide on the type of wedding

☐ Choose and book register office and provide details

☐ Provide statements that there are no legal reasons why the marriage should not take place

☐ Obtain Registrar's certificate and/ or licence

☐ Ensure that notice is entered in Superintendent's notice book

☐ Choose and book location of and date for ceremony by applying to the minister

☐ Meet minister to discuss and finalise details with bride

☐ Arrange for publication of banns or note when to apply for licence

☐ Arrange for publication of banns or obtain licence/certificate

☐ Select and appoint best man and ushers with bride

☐ Choose and book reception venue, caterers, bar and drinks supplier

☐ Visit reception venue with bride and best man to check arrangements

☐ Select helpers, in agreement with bride

☐ Discuss plans with bride and attendants

☐ Plan attire for self and other male members of the wedding party

☐ Check all legal and practical details of the wedding

☐ Inform best man of seating arrangements for the church and reception

☐ Decide upon, arrange, book and pay for honeymoon

☐ Arrange passports, visas, vaccinations, inoculations

Four Months

☐ Acquire or book own outfit

☐ Choose and pay for going-away outfit, honeymoon attire and luggage

Two Months

☐ Choose and buy a gift each for bride, best man, bridesmaids, pages and ushers

☐ Acquire wedding ring(s) with bride

☐ Arrange and pay for transport to and from church and transport from reception, in consultation with the best man

☐ Pay for flowers for the bride and attendants, buttonholes and sprays

☐ Write speech for reception

☐ Check church/civil arrangements with bride

☐ Obtain marriage licence

☐ Have inoculations, if necessary

☐ See GP and dentist for a check up

☐ Make arrangements for out-of-town guests

One Month

☐ Order travellers cheques and foreign currency

☐ Finalise rehearsal arrangements with bride

☐ Arrange stag night

☐ Buy ribbons for the wedding cars

One Week

☐ Move belongings to new home

☐ Finalise transport arrangements

☐ Wrap gift for bride and gifts for attendants with bride

☐ Attend rehearsal and hold rehearsal party for attendants; pass on and receive gifts

☐ Ensure that attendants know their duties and when and where they should be at each venue

☐ Ensure that the best man knows who to thank in his speech

☐ Visit the barber

☐ Attend stag night

☐ Pack for honeymoon

☐ Check documents

☐ Arrange for the return of any hired items

☐ Ensure that the best man has or knows when to collect buttonholes, order of service sheets, for example

☐ Pay bills that will fall due while away

☐ Ensure that credit cards are valid for the duration of the honeymoon, check current credit limit, pay outstanding balances if necessary

☐ Ask a neighbour to keep an eye on house and car while away

One Day

☐ Relax

☐ Check any borrowed cars for petrol

☐ Have an early night.

The Day

☐ Take luggage and going-away outfit to reception

☐ Take going-away car to reception

☐ Give church fees, documentation and ring to best man

☐ Arrive at church with best man twenty minutes early

☐ Check entry in register

☐ Meet registrar to exchange papers

☐ Wait for bride at the front of the right side of the church or marriage room

☐ Place ring on third finger left hand when appropriate

☐ Sign register

☐ Lead recessional with bride

☐ Join receiving line and greet guests

☐ Respond to the bride's father's toast to the bride and groom

☐ Give speech and propose toast to the bridesmaids

☐ Present gifts if not previously done

☐ Take part in the cake-cutting ceremony

☐ Lead dancing with bride

☐ Retrieve travel documents from best man

☐ Change and leave for honeymoon

After the Honeymoon

☐ Ensure that the best man is paid any out-of-pocket expenses incurred on the wedding day

☐ Ensure that the best man has returned hired attire

☐ Entertain both sets of parents and attendants

☐ Change all necessary documentation to reflect married status

☐ Review insurance provisions, including life, property, contents, medical and car

Bridesmaid's Diary

Bridesmaids and page boys complete the beautiful picture with the bride. The bridesmaids help her whenever they are needed and if they are very young, someone should be nearby to supervise and look after them.

Bridesmaids are unmarried attendants and were, at one time, always chosen from the unmarried sisters of both families, but it is now normal practice for unmarried friends of the bride to fulfil this role. They may be of any age and although very young children may be cute as bridesmaids they can be a nuisance to the proceedings of the day!

First-time brides may have married female attendants if desired.

A bridesmaid's responsibilities include helping to choose their own outfits, attending fittings, forming part of the church procession and recession, welcoming the guests and offering wedding cake to guests.

(The bride will arrange for outfit)

☐ Attend fittings

☐ Help with bride's dress before and after ceremony

☐ Get into the car destined for the ceremony, leaving the bride alone with her mother and giver-away for a few minutes

☐ Look after wedding clothes

☐ Carry comb and pocket mirror for use by the bride

☐ Follow the chief bridesmaid up the aisle

☐ Wait at chancel steps or sit as instructed

☐ Follow chief bridesmaid and best man out of the church after the register is signed

☐ Leave for the reception with the chief bridesmaid and best man after the bride and groom and after the photographs

☐ Offer drinks to guests at the reception (older bridesmaids only)

☐ Distribute slices of cake

☐ Wear dresses and headdresses all day and evening

Flower Girls

A very young girl (between three and eight years old) may perform the role of flower girl who carries a basket of flower petals to scatter down the aisle (if allowed) in the processional and joins the recessional. She does not have to stand with the bridal party throughout the entire ceremony.

Page Boy's Diary

The bride may, of course, choose page boys as well as bridesmaids if there are relations or sons of friends who would like to attend the bride at the wedding. Page boys are usually between the ages of five and eight.

(Bride arranges for outfit)

☐ Follow chief bridesmaid up the aisle

☐ Wait at chancel steps or sit as instructed

☐ Follow chief bridesmaid and best man out of the church

☐ Leave for the reception with chief bridesmaid and best man after the bride and groom and after the photographs

☐ Hand out slices of cake

Ring Bearers

A young boy (between four and eight years old) may act as ring bearer who

leads the procession holding a satin cushion onto which the ring (or substitute) is tied. The actual ring(s) may still be held by the best man.

Chief Bridesmaid's or Maid/ Matron of Honour's Diary

Since the chief bridesmaid acts as adviser, messenger and general assistant to the bride, she is usually an unmarried sister, a cousin or best friend. A maid of honour is an unmarried lady attendant. A matron of honour is a married lady attendant. A maid or matron of honour is sometimes chosen instead of bridesmaids when she will be the sole attendant acting as chief and only bridesmaid. Her duties are those of a chief bridesmaid but she will not usually wear the finery.

The duties of the chief bridesmaid involve assisting the bride as much as possible with the wedding planning and preparation, helping to choose the bride's outfit, organising other bridesmaids, attending the pre-wedding festivities including arranging and hosting or co-hosting the hen party, and on the day ensuring that the bride looks her best, arranging her veil and train before and during the ceremony and holding the bride's bouquet during the ceremony. She may act as a witness to the ceremony and sign the register. She will help the bride into her car at the church. She will be near to the bride throughout the proceedings acting as chief helper and is the equivalent of the groom's best man. Her responsibilities include marshalling and taking charge of the young attendants – especially taking care of any younger bridesmaids, ensuring that they are looked after and that they behave themselves. There will usually be plenty of family and friends to help her, but a watching brief is never a bad idea. At the reception, she may join the receiving line to greet the guests and can be generally helpful in circulating with the guests and helping the bride to ensure that everyone enjoys themselves. She will ensure that the bride's luggage and going-away outfit are taken to the reception for the honeymoon. When it is time to leave, she will help the bride to change

and will usually look after the wedding dress, taking it home or returning it to the supplier if it is hired.

Before accepting the role, the prospective chief bridesmaid should be clear about her responsibilities and understand that the bride will depend upon her for support.

Four Months

☐ Arrange and pay for own outfit unless it is unsuitable for other future occasions

☐ Help the bride to choose bridesmaids' dresses

☐ Attend fittings

☐ Discuss plans with bride, groom and best man

☐ Attend pre-wedding parties and rehearsal

The Day

☐ Ensure that bouquets are ready for the bride and bridesmaids

☐ Help bride to dress and make-up ready for the ceremony

☐ Ensure that bridesmaids arrive promptly

☐ Carry emergency supplies: tissues, comb, make-up, hairclips, safety pins, for example

☐ Leave for the church with the other bridesmaids and bride's mother

☐ Marshal the bridesmaids and pages

☐ Assemble with bridesmaids and pages in the church porch

☐ Arrange bride's dress, veil and train to perfection for the procession up the aisle

☐ Take charge of the bride's bouquet and gloves at chancel steps

☐ Accompany best man into the vestry, following the bride and groom

☐ Sign register if called upon to do so

☐ Return bouquet and gloves to the bride in the vestry

☐ Leave church with the best man after the bride and groom

☐ Help the bride into her car

☐ Leave for the reception with the best man and other bridesmaids after the bride and groom

At Reception

☐ Form part of the receiving line and greet guests

☐ Help to display and record gifts received and offer drinks to guests

☐ Take bride's bouquet and place it in a cool place

☐ Check that bride's going away outfit is ready

☐ Check that bride's luggage is ready and help bride to change into her going-away outfit

☐ Retrieve bouquet and hand to bride when she is about to leave

☐ See bride to the car

☐ Take charge of bride's wedding dress

☐ Help bride's mother clear up

After the Wedding

☐ Return the bride's and own outfits, if hired

TRADITION
Traditionally, when the bridal couple return from honeymoon, the chief bridesmaid would wait at their home and welcome them. This tradition is now sometimes fulfilled by the bride's mother and/or the bride's mother-in-law.

Bridesmaids' Mothers

Bridesmaids' mothers traditionally pay for the bridesmaids' attire, although this is not mandatory today. The bride or bride's father generally bears the cost if the dresses are not suitable for future wear.

Best Man

The title 'best man' was previously 'groomsman' and before this he was called 'brideman'.

The 'best person' needs to be a good friend of the groom and can be a woman but as duties include helping the groom to dress, it is more usual to have a best man. The best man is the groom's assistant for the wedding, and is usually a brother, cousin or close friend. He reassures the groom when he is nervous, and is there to give support, share the organisation and help when needed.

Role

The best man is the organiser and should be relied upon to handle details such as ensuring that the ushers are in the right place at the right time and are correctly dressed. He liaises with the bride and groom on all the details concerning the church and reception and usually arranges the stag party for the groom ensuring that festivities do not get out of control. He is responsible for transport and parking arrangements and attending the rehearsal. On the morning of the wedding he helps the groom to dress and gets him to the church at least fifteen minutes before the service is due to start.

At the church he is responsible for the ushers and distribution of buttonholes, corsages and order of service sheets which he collects from the bride's mother in advance. He takes care of the ring(s), the marriage licence, the fees and may act as official witness by signing the register. He organises the procession to the vestry and the recessional. He directs and times the photographer.

The best man sees that the bridesmaids and guests have transport from the church to the reception.

At the reception he may join the receiving line and can generally be useful in ensuring that guests enjoy themselves. He introduces the speeches, makes a speech, responds to the toast to the bridesmaids, reads the congratulatory messages, introduces the cake-cutting ceremony, looks after any gifts on display, supervises the decoration of the groom's car and ensures that the groom's car is ready at the reception for when the couple leave.

Traditionally best men were bachelors

but today, married men are acceptable — and more experienced, of course! It is the job of the best man to support and bear all of the groom's worries both on the day and during the preparations.

It is a great honour to be asked to be best man, a vote of the groom's friendship and confidence but the groom should remember that the job of best man should give his friend pleasure. The groom should realise that his friend has no obligation to accept the honour, especially if he is the shy, retiring type.

At a large formal wedding it is extremely useful to have a professional toastmaster who:

- has a loud voice and an extrovert nature;
- announces guests to the receiving line in the traditional way, for example:

  ☐ Mr and Mrs John Jones (husband and wife)

  ☐ Mrs John Jones (husband is absent)

  ☐ Mrs Jane Jones (widow)

  ☐ Mr John Jones and Mrs Jane Jones (not married to each other);

- announces 'Ladies and gentlemen, pray be seated. Dinner is now being served';
- announces 'Ladies and gentlemen, pray silence for grace';
- introduces speakers;
- announces the cutting of the cake.

In the absence of a professional toastmaster, the best man performs these tasks.

Qualities

The best man is said to be the one who is level headed, confident in a crisis, a natural public speaker, a diplomat and a trouble-shooter all rolled into one. Someone who is born to be a superb best man is a rare commodity indeed, and yet people are doing a great job at it every day. He will need to be tactful, reliable, punctual, sociable, thoughtful and unflappable. With a little foresight, preparation and planning, duties can be learnt and performed perfectly on the day by almost anyone.

An element of common sense will help the best man through most problems should any arise on the day. However, if this does not happen to be a strong point, a few sensible precautions can be taken. It helps for the best man to be on good terms with the chief bridesmaid and the bride's and the groom's fathers so that they may be called upon to help out if necessary. As an all-round helper, observation and tact are essential so that problems can be spotted and everyone remains happy.

Being responsible for the groom's timekeeping makes punctuality very important. If notorious for oversleeping, an alarm call can be booked and if everything is arranged in advance there should be no problems.

To do a good job, it is important for the best man to remain reasonably sober. Taxis or lifts are essential for the stag party and it is the best man's duty to see the groom safely inside the house before going home himself if the stag night is on the eve of the wedding. On the day itself, slurred speeches are never well received!

The speech is probably the moment that the best man dreads the most. A good speech is important, but no one expects a polished, witty, professional performance. Four minutes is ample; the best speeches are always the shortest ones and with a little preparation and practice, success is guaranteed. A sense of humour will come in useful when making the speech, will put the groom at ease throughout the tense moments of the day, and will relax other members of the wedding party whose nerves may be over-stretched.

Well-informed

Preparation is the key to acquiring all the qualities and performing all the duties of the perfect best man. It is necessary for him to know the format of the day, what to expect, where to be at what time and all the duties involved. Although strictly speaking, the best man is 'employed' by the groom, in practice the kingpin of any wedding — whether during the preparations or on the day — is the bride. The groom will have plenty to contribute to the planning and decision-making but for most couples, the bride is the one whose ideas and preferences set the atmosphere for the day. Naturally, every bride has her own ideas on how the day should be planned, the atmosphere she would like, and what she would like everyone to do; so the role of any best man will be slightly different in each case. The size of the bride's family may make a difference; if she has plenty of brothers and sisters to help with the organising, the best man may find that certain jobs are taken off his hands. The best man should not be left to make vague guesses as to what is required; he should be informed of as much as possible and well in advance. The details may change as the wedding plans proceed, and a few last-minute adjustments to the best man's schedule may need to be made. However, the best man should not be put in a position where at the eleventh hour the bride expects him to chauffeur the bridesmaids, or he is expected to be in two places at once on the wedding morning. There are ways round any problems which may arise provided that the best man is well-informed and plans are made in advance. It is important for the best man to meet with the bride and groom and chief bridesmaid as soon as possible before the wedding plans are under way. The bride and groom should arrange this themselves, or the best man may meet them regularly in any case. An evening should be set aside for the purpose of working through the plans to ascertain exactly what is expected.

Best Man's Diary

The morning of the wedding will be busy for the best man as there are some things which cannot be done earlier. It is therefore important to deal with as much as possible prior to the day of the wedding. This will minimise the rush on the day and calm nerves!

Six Months

☐ Send written reply immediately on receipt of invitation. Mark the wedding date in diary and cancel any other arrangements for that date and any engagements booked for the preceding couple of days

Three Months

☐ Consult the wedding gift list

☐ Purchase special wedding gift, gift card and wrapping paper, keeping the receipt in a safe place in case of subsequent problems, for example, damaged or duplicated gift

☐ Return the wedding gift list immediately

☐ Discuss plans and responsibilities with the bride, groom and chief bridesmaid and make notes

☐ Help to choose the ushers

☐ Explain duties to ushers

☐ Help with the wedding preparations

Two Months

☐ Arrange and pay for own outfit

☐ Check that groom and ushers have organised their own outfits

☐ Help to choose groom's and ushers' clothes and accessories, if desirable

☐ Prepare and draft speech, checking with bride to see if there are specific people to be mentioned

☐ Practise and time the speech

BEST MAN'S FACT FILE		
Ceremony	Date of Wedding	
	Venue	Arrival time for Groom
	Name of Minister/Registrar	
	Telephone	Time that fees are payable
	Confetti rules	Parking arrangements
	Photographs/Video restrictions	
Attire	Groom	Best Man
	Accessories required	
	Colour scheme — Bride	
	Bridesmaid	
	Hire firm — Name	
	Address	
	Telephone	
	Fitting dates	
	Collection dates	
	Return dates	
Flowers	Buttonholes	
	Corsages	
Rehearsal	Date	Time
Stag Night	Date	Time
	Transport	Venue
Photographers	Name	
	Address	
	Telephone	
	Emergency	
	Name	
	Address	
	Telephone	

BEST MAN'S FACT FILE		
Reception	Venue	Contact Name
	Telephone	Time
	Parking facilities	Number of guests
	Guests to be announced	
	Toastmaster	Receiving line
	Seating Plan	Meal time
	Meal arrangements	Speech time
	People to thank	Bar facilities
	Entertainment	
	Changing room for bride and groom	
	Leaving time	Departure details
Transport	To Church — Groom and Best Man	
	Parking facilities	
	To Reception — Bride and Groom	
	Bridesmaids and Attendants	
	Parents	
	Guests	
	Parking facilities	
	To Honeymoon — Bride and Groom	
	Car hire firm	
	Address	
	Telephone	
	Cars to be supplied	
	Other details	
	Collection/delivery/return time	
	Taxi firm	
	Telephone	
	Emergency firm	
	Telephone	
	Address	

BEST MAN'S FACT FILE					THE WEDDING PARTY WHO'S WHO
	Name	Age if child	Address	Telephone	Specific duties
Bride					
Groom					
Chief Bridesmaid/ Matron of Honour					
Bridesmaid					
Bridesmaid					
Bridesmaid					
Flower Girl					
Page					
Page					
Page					
Chief Usher					Transport
Usher					Escort

BEST MAN'S FACT FILE				THE WEDDING PARTY WHO'S WHO		
	Name	Age if child	Address	Telephone	Specific duties
Usher					Buttonholes
Usher					Order of Service Sheets
Bride's Parents					
Groom's Parents					

☐ Compile a list of close family

☐ Pass on this list to the ushers to help them with seating arrangements in the church

☐ Liaise with ushers and instruct them on their duties and timing

☐ Organise and book stag night for a week before the wedding

☐ Visit the reception venue with the bride and groom

☐ Check parking facilities at ceremony and reception venues

☐ Offer to arrange transport for out-of-town guests and those without cars

☐ Remind the groom to acquire passports and travellers cheques, to have inoculations etc.

☐ Keep in touch with the groom and offer to help

One Month

☐ Check buttonholes have been ordered

☐ Check that honeymoon arrangements have been made

☐ Check routes to groom's home, to church and to the reception by running test runs, timing the routes on the right day and at the right time

☐ Check traffic conditions

☐ Check roadworks by finding out if there are to be any special events on the wedding day itself, for example, carnival processions

☐ Arrange transport for groom and self to church, to reception, going-away vehicle for newly-weds and own transport from reception

☐ Arrange car service, if appropriate

☐ Check that groom's car has been

serviced if it is being used to transport the groom and later the bride and groom

☐ Purchase ribbons, etc. to decorate the car(s)

Two Weeks

☐ Finalise speech and write prompt cards

☐ Check with bride any special arrangements for guests to be taken to the reception

☐ Check on parking arrangements at the church and at the reception venues

☐ Deputise ushers to assist with parking at the church and at the reception if necessary

☐ Note details of emergency taxi firms

☐ Ring up taxi firms to ascertain length of time it would take them to arrive on the scene in the event of an emergency

☐ Purchase a phonecard

☐ Ensure that ushers have made arrangements for their own transport

☐ Warn ushers of any parking and/or traffic problems

☐ Have hair cut

One Week

☐ Attend rehearsal and rehearsal party

☐ Hand over gift to the bride and groom at the rehearsal

☐ Check that ring(s) have been purchased

☐ Check that licence/banns certificate has been collected

☐ Ensure the groom's safety during and after stag party

☐ Check that the groom has all necessary documents for the wedding and honeymoon

Two Days

☐ Check and confirm car hire bookings and/or taxi arrangements

☐ Organise group of guests to decorate the going-away car

One Day

☐ Collect hired attire for groom and self, if applicable

☐ Collect order of service sheets from bride and pass on to chief usher

☐ Organise items for decorating going-away car

☐ Pack cleaning-up kit in groom's car

☐ Arrange to collect buttonholes

☐ Ensure that bride's and groom's luggage is packed

☐ Clean car, fill with petrol, check water, oil

☐ Ensure that the going-away car is filled with petrol and parked at the reception venue

☐ Tie ribbons on car(s)

☐ Arrange alarm calls

☐ Ask reliable friend to visit

☐ Set alarm

☐ Go to bed early

The Day

☐ The morning of the wedding will be busy for the best man and there are some things which cannot be done in advance but which should not be forgotten on the day.

☐ Rise early

☐ Ring the groom to check that he has ready:

   ☐ Clothes and accessories

   ☐ Certificate of banns or Marriage Licence

   ☐ Passports, visas, etc.

   ☐ Tickets

- ☐ Church fees
- ☐ Ring(s)
- ☐ Cases packed and loaded
- ☐ Car keys (if a car has already been left at the reception venue ready for the couple's getaway)
- ☐ Telemessages (which may have arrived at the groom's house)
- ☐ Remind groom of set-off time for ceremony
- ☐ Confirm arrangements with hire firm/taxi service
- ☐ Ring chief usher and ushers to check that they:
  - ☐ Are clear about the time they should be at church
  - ☐ Have clothes ready
  - ☐ Have cars ready
  - ☐ Have order of service sheets ready
  - ☐ Have arranged to collect buttonholes from the bride, florist or reception venue
  - ☐ Know of their duties
- ☐ Ring the bride or her parents:
  - ☐ Wish them well
  - ☐ Ask them about any last-minute hitches with which they may need help
  - ☐ Remind bride's father to take with him any last minute tele-messages to the reception
  - ☐ Check clothes and accessories
- ☐ Pack bag of essentials:
  - ☐ Phonecard
  - ☐ Cash for telephone, etc.
  - ☐ Taxi firm numbers
  - ☐ Emergency photographer's number

> **SUPERSTITION**
> *The best man ensures the good luck of the couple by ensuring that the groom carries a small mascot in his pocket.*

- ☐ Spare name cards
- ☐ Spare order of service sheets
- ☐ Speech cards
- ☐ Handkerchief
- ☐ Decoration for going-away car
- ☐ Cleaning kit to pack in groom's car
- ☐ Umbrellas
- ☐ Collect buttonholes from bride's mother to take to church
- ☐ Collect telemessages and order of service sheets from bride's mother, if not already done
- ☐ Deliver buttonholes to chief usher
- ☐ Ensure that the bride, groom, ushers and groom's parents all have their flowers
- ☐ Oversee and supervise the ushers
- ☐ Check that groom's luggage is ready
- ☐ Ensure that the groom's change of clothes is ready at the reception
- ☐ Check that going-away car is at the reception
- ☐ Set out for the groom's house early
- ☐ Keep the groom as calm as possible
- ☐ Take from the groom:
  - ☐ Ring(s) and place in safe pocket
  - ☐ Money for church fees
  - ☐ Documentation for safe-keeping

> **SUPERSTITION**
> *The best man should ensure the good luck of the couple by not allowing the groom to turn back for any reason after starting out for the ceremony.*

- ☐ Set off for the church to arrive half an hour before the ceremony is due to start
- ☐ Accompany the groom to the church, ensuring that he arrives on time — the most important duty of the day!

At Church

- ☐ Arrive thirty minutes early

- ☐ Hand order of service sheets to ushers (if not already handed to the chief usher)

- ☐ Check that ushers are showing guests to their seats

- ☐ Ensure that the groom, groom's father, ushers and self have button-holes and that the bride's and groom's mothers have their corsages

- ☐ Pay church fees (or later in the vestry)

- ☐ Hand over the Banns certificate from the groom's church

- ☐ Attend the groom throughout the service

- ☐ Take seats in the front pew on the right side of the church − before the bride's mother takes her seat

- ☐ Take charge of the groom's hat and gloves in church

- ☐ Wait on the right side of and a little behind the groom

- ☐ If the bride is late, find out the reason and ask ushers to talk to the congregation so that the delay passes without too much concern

- ☐ The best man and groom may turn briefly to welcome the bride as she walks down the aisle

- ☐ Move forward with the groom to stand in front of the steps

- ☐ Hand over the ring(s) at the appropriate time. Sometimes the minister offers the best man the open prayer book onto which he places the ring(s) which are then blessed and exchanged

- ☐ Return to previous position along with the bridesmaids and the bride's father

- ☐ Pick up own and the groom's hats and gloves

- ☐ Join the recessional to the vestry

- ☐ Offer the chief bridesmaid left arm and escort her into the vestry behind the bride and groom for the signing of the register

- ☐ Sign register (if called upon to do so)

- ☐ Ensure that male members of the wedding party have their hats and gloves

- ☐ Pay church fees to the minister (if not paid previously)

- ☐ Escort the chief bridesmaid out of the church following the bride and groom

- ☐ Remind the ushers to warn tactfully any confetti-throwers

- ☐ Remind the chief usher to check the church for property left behind

- ☐ Escort the newly-weds to the photographer

- ☐ Help the photographer to position guests in the right place at the right time

- ☐ Escort the bride and groom to their car on time

- ☐ Ensure that ushers have arranged transport to the reception for all guests

- ☐ Leave for the reception with bridesmaids after the bride and groom

At Reception

Join the end of the receiving line or announce the guests. At a very formal wedding, where there is a professional Master of Ceremonies to announce the guests, the best man and chief bridesmaid may join the end of the receiving line. The best man may, on the other hand, be expected to briefly announce the guests as they approach the receiving line.

- ☐ Receive, take charge and ensure

the safety of any late wedding gifts. Keep a note of them in case of theft

☐ Collect and vet the telemessages

☐ Offer drinks to the guests

☐ Supervise the reception, ensuring that guests are orderly

☐ Take and place the guests' coats

☐ Guide the guests to the seating plan

☐ Escort guests to their seats quickly and without fuss

☐ Request silence for grace

☐ If there are insufficient serving staff, draft in the ushers to help

☐ Call on speakers when the time seems right

☐ Reply on behalf of the bridesmaids in response to the toast to their health

☐ Give speech, read telemessages and cards and propose a toast to the newly-weds

☐ Announce the cake-cutting ceremony

☐ Help to keep things running smoothly by chatting to guests, making introductions and helping people to their seats

☐ If the entertainment fails to turn up, send out for a music system and tapes/records

☐ Dance with the chief bridesmaid after the bride and groom have started off the dancing

☐ Dance with the bride, the mothers and as many guests as possible

☐ Rescue the bride and groom from those guests who try to monopolise them so that they may circulate as much as possible

☐ If drinks run dry, send out for emergency supply

☐ Decorate the couple's car ensuring its safety and that no damage is caused

☐ Ensure the couple's luggage is correctly labelled and is ready for transportation

☐ Place luggage in the car ready for the honeymoon

☐ Announce that the couple are about to leave

☐ See the newly-weds to their car

☐ Hand over to the groom documentation: tickets, passports, keys, etc.

☐ Take charge of the groom's wedding attire

☐ Collect telemessages and a few mementos, for example, place cards, flowers, napkins to give to the newly-weds when they return from honeymoon

☐ Ensure that nothing is left behind at the reception

☐ Help the bride's parents to see the guests safely on their way home

☐ Ensure that all guests have transport home

☐ Help to clear up

After the Wedding

☐ Check that all gifts are carefully stored (with chief bridesmaid) and that clothes have been taken away and returned to the hire company (if appropriate)

☐ Remind the ushers to return their suits

☐ Return groom's and own wedding attire, if applicable

☐ Write thank-you note for the bride's and groom's gift

☐ Check on the security of the bride's and groom's residence whilst they are away

☐ Deliver some flowers to the house for their return

Usher's Diary

The ushers are the best man's team of helpers. They are traditionally unmarried and are usually brothers or close relatives of the bride and groom. Ushers are chosen by the groom in consultation with the best man. It makes sense to choose those who do not have to face a long journey on the day and it may also be very helpful if they can drive and better still if they have a car at their disposal. If the groom is worried about offending anyone by excluding them, he should explain the situation tactfully and they are sure to understand.

Generally there are as many ushers as there are bridesmaids and the reason for this tradition is that their duties include escorting the bridesmaids during the course of the day. However, since escorts are no longer considered essential, this particular custom is not always strictly followed but it is thoughtful if ushers can ensure that the bridesmaids are looked after during the day. The number of ushers also depends on the number of guests; generally one usher is needed for every fifty.

The responsibilities of an usher are not onerous but if the job is done well, it helps the smooth running of the wedding day and takes care of several minor worries of those principally involved in the organising. Traditionally, the best man is in charge of the ushers and he ensures that they know their duties, are properly dressed, and are in the right place at the right time. They should be armed with umbrellas and be ready to shelter members of the wedding party and guests from rain during the course of the day.

Three Months

☐ Receive from the best man a list of close family to help with seating arrangements

☐ Liaise with the best man to sort out the arrangements

☐ Arrange and pay for own suit or arrange to hire suit

☐ Acquire an umbrella

Two Weeks

☐ Have hair cut

INFILL LIST				USHERS
	Name	Address	Telephone	Specific duties
Chief Usher				Transport
Usher 2				Escort guests to seats
Usher 3				Buttonholes
Usher 4				Order of Service sheets

- [ ] Liaise with other ushers on their duties

- [ ] Confirm arrival time at church

The Day
....

- [ ] Escort the bridesmaids during the day

- [ ] Collect order of service sheets and buttonholes from the best man or bride's mother

- [ ] Carry an umbrella

- [ ] Arrive first at church about three-quarters of an hour before the ceremony is due to start

- [ ] Organise car parking facilities (duty for one usher)

- [ ] Offer buttonholes and corsages to principal guests

- [ ] Ensure that the minister has a supply of order of service sheets at the front of the church for the wedding party

- [ ] Line up on left side of entrance

- [ ] Greet guests and hand out hymn books, prayer books and/or order of service sheets

- [ ] Warn any guests carrying cameras not to take photographs inside the church if the minister does not allow this

- [ ] Conduct guests to pews, escorting any unescorted lady to her seat in church, bride's family and friends on the left, groom's on the right. Offer left arm to females; simply escort (without the arm) single men to their seats. If two single ladies arrive together, the usher should escort the elder first while the other lady waits for him to return or for another escort. At less formal weddings, it is simply a matter of directing the guests to their seats. The first one or two pews at the front should be reserved for close family. The next one or two are for more distant relatives. The groom's parents sit in the second pew from the front. If there are any divorced parents in the family, the ushers should be informed of such special circumstances by the best man who should explain the relevant seating arrangements. Normally, if the bride's or the groom's parents are divorced but not remarried they would be seated together as usual. If they are divorced and remarried, the mother would sit in the first pew with her new husband and the father in the second pew with his new wife.

- [ ] If the number of guests on each side of the church will clearly be unbalanced due to one of the partners having few guests, the ushers may use their tact and discretion in filling the seats and positioning guests evenly.

- [ ] The last guest to arrive is the bride's mother, who should be escorted to her seat by the chief usher to the front pew on the left where she will leave a spare seat on her right for the giver-away (usually her husband) when he has given away the bride. Late-comers should be quietly directed to pews at the back of the church with minimum fuss and attention so that the service is not disrupted in any way.

☐ Families with young children and babies should be positioned near the exit so that they are able to make a swift retreat in case of loud disruptive crying or misbehaviour.

☐ Take own seat ready for the service

☐ Deal with disturbances discreetly

After the Ceremony

☐ Join the recessional

☐ Request that anyone carrying confetti keeps it for the reception if the minister does not allow it to be thrown in the church grounds

☐ Direct guests to the venue for photographs

☐ Help the photographer

☐ Ensure that all guests have transport to the reception

☐ Direct guests to the reception venue

☐ Ensure that the church is left tidy, for example, collection of order of service sheets

☐ Check that nothing is left behind, particularly hats and gloves

☐ Clean up confetti

At Reception

☐ Try to make a positive contribution to the smooth running and friendly atmosphere at the reception

☐ Offer drinks to guests as they arrive

☐ Introduce people to one another

☐ Assist with seating the guests

☐ Look after elderly or infirm guests

☐ Be sociable and polite

☐ Dance with as many guests as possible

After the Wedding

☐ Return outfit, if hired

☐ Send thank-you note for gift to the bride and groom

Bride's Father's Diary

The giver-away is usually the bride's father but if this is not possible for any reason, the bride's eldest brother, male guardian or uncle are generally called upon to perform this role but any or all of the tasks may be undertaken by other members of the bride's family or friends.

Traditionally, the bride's father is responsible for paying for the reception, his own wedding suit, escorting and giving away the bride and delivering a speech. If he is funding the entire wedding, he should set the budget and advise his daughter of its limit.

It is acceptable for the father to pass on his responsibility to make the speech to another senior member of the family who need not take the bride's father's position at the top table.

Six Months

☐ Decide the budget

☐ If sharing the costs, meet the groom's parents to decide on financial responsibilities

One Month

☐ Ask the minister to say grace at the reception.

If a minister of religion is to be present at the reception, he must be invited to say grace and should be approached in advance. If the minister will not be present, grace may be said by the toastmaster or the bride's father. Grace is not obligatory these days but if it is to be said, the best man should request silence

☐ Buy or hire wedding suit

☐ Write speech

The Day

☐ Escort the bride from home to the church

At Church

- ☐ Arrive last with bride

- ☐ Lead procession to chancel steps with the bride on right arm

- ☐ Take bride's right hand to give to the minister at the appropriate time

- ☐ Give away the bride

- ☐ Step back to join the bride's mother

- ☐ Escort the groom's mother to the vestry after the service (followed by the best man and chief bridesmaid)

- ☐ Leave the church with the groom's mother in the recessional

- ☐ Leave for the reception with other parents after the best man and bridesmaids

At Reception

- ☐ As host of the wedding reception make the occasion enjoyable for all

- ☐ Arrive early at the reception with the bride's mother to host the reception

- ☐ Form part of the receiving line and greet the guests with the bride's mother

- ☐ Ask the minister (if present) to say grace, after the best man has requested silence

- ☐ Indicate to the waitresses that they may start serving

- ☐ Make the first speech and propose the first toast to the health and happiness of the newly-weds

- ☐ Pay for the reception

Bride's Mother's Diary

It may appear that the bride's mother has very little to do with the ceremony and reception on the day. This is because all her hard work will have been put in beforehand and behind the scenes. She will have done most of the work arranging the reception, devising a seating plan, placing the announcement, helping to choose the bride's and bridesmaids' dresses, organising the flowers, wedding cars, photography, her own outfit, accommodation for guests, sending the invitations, not forgetting the help and advice she will have given the bride concerning wedding attire and trousseau.

On the day she ensures that the best man has the order of service sheets, buttonholes, helps to dress the bride, receives her guests and may need to clear up.

The bride's mother acts as hostess of the wedding and helps in all aspects of the planning arrangements. Her responsibilities overlap with those of her daughter and may be undertaken jointly or separately.

Three Months

- ☐ Arrange own outfit and accessories well in advance

- ☐ Inform the groom's mother of chosen outfit so that colour clashes can be avoided

- ☐ Arrange reception and catering with the bride

- ☐ Draw up the guest list in consultation with the bride and the groom's parents

- ☐ Arrange press announcements

- ☐ Order stationery: invitations; order of service sheets; printed napkins, place cards, cake boxes, etc.

- ☐ Send out the invitations

- ☐ List the responses

- ☐ Devise seating plan in consultation with groom's parents

- ☐ Help to choose bride's dress and those for the bridesmaids

- ☐ Display gifts at home

- ☐ Organise flowers with bride

- ☐ Hire transport with bride (transport for the groom and the best man is not the responsibility of the bride's mother)

- ☐ Order and arrange delivery/ collection of the wedding cake to the reception venue

- ☐ Select and book a photographer with the bride

- ☐ Finalise the number of guests and inform caterers two weeks before

- ☐ Arrange changing room facilities for the bride

- ☐ Arrange overnight accommodation for guests in consultation with groom's parents

- ☐ Arrange entertainment with bride

The Day

- ☐ Take delivery of flowers

- ☐ Check that deliveries and arrangements are progressing

- ☐ Help bride to dress and fix the veil (the fixing of the veil by the mother is traditional)

- ☐ Travel to the church with the bridesmaids

- ☐ Arrive at church before the bride

- ☐ Enter the church escorted to seat by the chief usher just before the bride

- ☐ Sit in the front pew on the left of the aisle

- ☐ Ensure that there is a vacant seat alongside and to the right for the giver-away who will take his seat after giving away the bride

- ☐ Enter the vestry to sign the register, led by the groom's father and followed by the bride's father who escorts the groom's mother

- ☐ Leave the church on the left arm of the groom's father following the bridesmaids and page boys in procession with the groom's mother and bride's father behind them

- ☐ Leave for the reception

- ☐ Pose for photographs

At Reception

- ☐ Act as hostess

- ☐ Form the receiving line and greet guests with the bride's father

- ☐ Arrange display of gifts

- ☐ Take charge of the wedding gifts

- ☐ Take charge of the cake

- ☐ Ensure that all guests leave safely and that the clearing up is attended to

- ☐ Leave last

After the Wedding

- ☐ Send slices of cake to those who were unable to attend the wedding

- ☐ Organise the distribution of photograph proofs and collect orders

- ☐ Give orders to the photographer

- ☐ Collect and distribute photographs

Other roles

Parents

It makes for the best atmosphere if the two sets of parents have met before the wedding. Usually, they co-operate in the arrangements and the finances.

Bride's Parents

The bride's parents usually host the wedding (as they are generally responsible for the majority of the expenses involved) and help in all aspects of the planning and arrangements. They are responsible for sending out the invitations and receiving the replies. Wedding gifts are usually sent to their home prior to the wedding date where they are displayed for callers to view.

As host and hostess, the bride's parents are first in the receiving line at the reception. They are usually responsible for ensuring that all guests leave safely and that the clearing up is attended to.

Groom's Parents

By comparison, the groom's family have little to do, though they should be consulted about the venue of the ceremony and the reception. If they already know the bride's parents well, this usually presents no problems but if they do not, then a small supper party should be arranged by the bride and groom, when both sets of parents of the engaged couple can get acquainted.

If the bride's parents are overseas or not living, the wedding arrangements should be made by her closest relatives available. If there are no close relatives, then the arrangements are normally taken over by the groom's family.

The groom's parents sit at the front of the church on the groom's side (the right), and join the wedding party when they go to sign the register. They usually join the receiving line at the reception to greet the guests as they arrive.

Special Circumstances

If there are cases of death or divorce in the family, the situation should be handled tactfully and with the understanding to suit the particular circumstances involved.

If either set of parents is divorced and remarried, the mother sits in the first pew with her new partner, and the father and his new partner take the second pew on the relevant side of the church.

The receiving line at the reception is headed by the host and hostess of the reception — usually the bride's parents — and the groom's mother and father. New partners are not normally included in the receiving line.

Seating at the top table should accommodate all those involved if possible.

Speeches

Speeches at engagement parties are usually very short. If the bride's parents are paying for the wedding, the bride's father starts by toasting his daughter and her fiancé. The groom-to-be replies with a toast thanking his fiancée's parents and toasting the health of everyone present. The groom's father may then make a short speech before the best man's speech if he wishes.

At a wedding the speeches and toasts take place after guests have finished their meal and usually before the cutting of the cake.

Although the bride is seldom expected to give a speech, she will want to know about protocol (the order of speeches and toasts) to be able to advise the principal men of the number and order of speakers, and be in a position to pass on useful hints to those giving speeches, namely her father, her fiancé and the best man.

For those brides who choose to make a speech, the guidance will help her to plan and perform. In the past women were considered too modest to attract such attention but today it is perfectly acceptable.

Expectations

The purpose of the speeches are to congratulate the couple, wish them well in their future life together and thank appropriate people. They include the toasts and usually occur after the last course of the meal.

Delivery of speeches and toasts is the part of the day that many bride's fathers, grooms and best men dread the most, but with a little planning and preparation it really need not be a terrifying experience. Very few people are practised public speakers and unless speakers are experienced in this activity, the prospect of standing up and addressing a crowd that probably includes many strangers is probably daunting, but there is no need to worry as every speech maker is nervous. In any case, it is not difficult to make a wedding speech as the audience is already warmed by the happiness of the occasion and they do not expect or want a long and important oration. They simply expect a few sincere and perhaps amusing words from speakers and the toasts so that they can get on with really enjoying themselves. It should be remembered that the speeches are not the most important part of the wedding and if the speaker loses his or her nerve, he or she need only say a few words of thanks, congratulations and good wishes.

Although traditional, it is not compulsory for any of the leading men to deliver a speech, especially if they feel that doing so will ruin the day. If the bride's father feels this way, he may ask a brother to step in. Similarly, the bride may speak instead of the groom. Those expected to step in must be given sufficient prior notice so that they have plenty of time for preparation.

Order of Toasts

Each speaker should be announced briefly by the toastmaster or the best man.

When the guests have finished the dessert course of their meal, the toastmaster or best man introduces the speeches and calls each speaker in turn. Traditionally everyone stands for the toast except the people being toasted.

First Toast

The first toast is made by the giver-away (usually the bride's father) who stands and says a few words about the bride and groom before proposing the toast to the health of the bride and groom.

Reply to First Toast

The groom responds on behalf of the bride and himself.

Second Toast

Following on, the groom proposes the toast to the bridesmaids.

Reply to Second Toast

The best man replies on behalf of the bridesmaids, gives a speech and reads out the telemessages and cards.

End of the Speeches

The toastmaster or best man announces the cutting of the cake and the programme for the rest of the reception.

Planning a Speech

Unless extremely accomplished in delivering speeches on the spur of the moment, plans should be made in advance. A speech taken from a book and recited word for word will sound false and stilted; personal sentiments are always far better. There are various ways of presenting a speech: read the speech from notes; recite the speech from memory; refer to brief 'headline' notes which serve as memory joggers for previously memorised text.

The first method may be disastrous in that the speech may sound like a public announcement. It may be unnatural and lacking in liveliness and spontaneity. It also leaves little or no opportunity for mentioning unexpected events of the day.

Similarly, if the speech is recited from memory, it may be too inflexible as it prohibits comment on some little incident of the day such as the black cat that crossed the bride's path that morning. The speech may also sound like an audition before the local amateur dramatic society. There is also the problem of what to do with idle hands.

The third method is a compromise used by many public speakers and seems to produce the best results in that the speech will have shape and will include all the main points which should not be forgotten. It is perhaps the best option for a wedding speech. It will have been carefully planned and yet will possess flexibility for improvisation when delivered. It is these last minute additions which can really bring a speech to life.

The headers (written on cards) allow the addition of amusing comments or development of the material as best suits the occasion.

When the wording of the speech is finalised and sounds natural, key (memory) words should be highlighted and transferred to plain post cards — a separate word or phrase written boldly on each card followed by a few memory joggers. Each card should then be numbered so that they remain in the correct order. The cards need to state the things that must be included, for example: thank groom for the toast to the bridesmaids; congratulations to the happy couple. The things that should be said may then be added, perhaps the recollection of an incident about the couple which would make an amusing story.

Cards do have the advantage of giving the speaker something to do with his hands. They can be held in front and can be flipped from the front to the back of the pile during natural pauses ready for the next prompt. Cards are more manageable and do not flap and crumple like paper. They look professional and can be hidden in a pocket until needed. It is probable that several drafts will be needed until the wording and order take the shape of a reasonable and structured speech lasting no longer than five minutes. The first draft should be put to one side for a few days — a fresh reassessment will work wonders.

Practice

The fact that the speaker has not spoken in public before is no cause for worry. Timed practice runs in front of a mirror or video, and perhaps the comments of a close but critical friend, will enable the speaker to hear how well the items run together, measure pace, and will aid confidence. Sometimes a seemingly good and logical flow of composition appears to flow on paper but does not work when spoken. A tape recorder can be useful here. Some people use certain phrases repeatedly without realising, for example 'you know', 'like', 'sort of', 'um'.

Presentation

The secret of good delivery is to take control of the audience from the very first moment by being confident with an easy relaxed manner. The audience will then feel reassured enough to relax comfortably, sit back and enjoy the speech.

There will always be a babble of comments between speeches as well as the scraping of chairs and fidgeting as people get comfortable. This time can be used to take a few relaxing deep breaths, and cast a glance through the speech notes.

Speech Manner

The way a speech is spoken is very important. It is easy to sound pompous or patronising when speaking on your feet but on the other hand, too much informality should also be avoided. Even a highly informal reception is an important occasion and the manner of speeches should reflect this fact. The speaker must judge for himself an appropriate manner. The audience will almost certainly be made up of well-known family or friends and some strangers. These strangers should be borne in mind and will not expect an address that is too familiar. It should be remembered that guests at a wedding are there to enjoy themselves and they will be tolerant of inexperienced speakers — but not rude or over-familiar ones.

Formal words, phrases and clichès should be avoided as they will sound either boring or pompous, or both. The use of slang should be avoided as it detracts from the sense of occasion and also because some listeners will be left in the dark, particularly those who are too young or too old to understand modern slang usage. The speaker must not be tempted to swear. Even a 'damn' or 'blast' can offend some people.

A natural accent should be used. It is foolish to assume a 'stage' voice or put on a refined, posh accent if this does not come naturally. On the other hand sloppy pronunciation should be avoided. It is worth noting the fact that consonants at the ends of words can get lost when spoken, especially when the next word starts with another consonant. For example when saying 'that time' or 'and did', there should be a tiny pause between the words. The best way to avoid this particular pitfall, which is good advice to many inexperienced speakers, is to speak just a little more slowly than normal.

The one thing that a novice speaker forgets is to breathe. In normal conversation there is hardly any need for extra breathing effort to make oneself heard and conversation is normally a dialogue where rests occur between exchanges. Yet for the speech maker there are no such pauses, unless these are deliberately made. The best advice is not to hurry, taking a leisurely pace and pause between sentences or even between phrases.

The speaker should position his feet slightly apart and should stand upright but relaxed in a natural posture. This aids comfort and gives an air or confidence. There are certain things which nervous first-time speakers do unconsciously and which should be avoided at all costs: clinking loose change or keys in pockets; mopping face with handkerchief; shuffling from one foot to the other; and rocking backwards and forwards.

A lively manner improves speech delivery but the inexperienced speaker should avoid making gestures to illustrate speech unless they come absolutely naturally, otherwise they will look posed and peculiar. There is nothing worse than watching a speaker flinging his arms around like an orchestra conductor. It detracts from the speech and there can be few people who can concentrate on the words when the speaker appears to be trying to swat a mosquito!

Some speakers grip their coat lapels, but this tends to give them the appearance of a racecourse bookmaker, shouting the odds. Others lay their hands palm down on the table and rest their weight on them, giving the stance of a shopkeeper waiting for a customer. The best advice is to do whatever comes naturally. Note cards can be something to hold on to even if they are not referred to. An accomplished speaker stands with his hands loosely at his side and gestures naturally as appropriate but this is very difficult for the beginner to achieve. Practising in front of a mirror is a good way of assessing gestures and performance.

From the point of view of good manners, it would perhaps be unforgivable to stand with hands in pockets, but if this is the only way that a speaker can feel happy and by feeling comfortable can deliver a good speech, then perhaps it is forgivable. A drink of water will satisfy a dry throat during the speech. Alcohol has a disastrous effect on speech-making ability, so it is vital that the speaker restricts himself to just one or two drinks beforehand. A little alcohol stimulates and relaxes, whereas several drinks will slow the thought processes.

The speaker should not look at floors, walls or ceilings, he should look just above the heads of the audience and towards the subject of the toast when proposing, without staring fixedly, thus causing embarrassment.

Being Heard

Everyone knows the old advice to speakers: 'Stand up, speak up, shut up'. The most important of these without a doubt is 'speak up'. A speaker's voice simply must be heard, or there is no point in making a speech at all. Nervousness often makes a speaker inaudible; so does a large room and it can be foolish to assume that a microphone will improve matters. The technique of using a microphone must be practised if it is to be of benefit and if this is impossible, the advice of an experienced user should be sought. It is also important to ensure that there is someone on hand who will know what to do if the system misbehaves. Prompt action can avoid a most embarrassing pause in the proceedings. Microphones tend to create a distance between speaker and audience and are perhaps best forgotten for a wedding speech.

Another point the speaker should remember is never try to compete with extraneous noise. When a speaker first stands up there is usually a continuing babble of conversation, perhaps the clinking of glasses being put down, or the clattering of chairs being re-arranged to face the speaker. The speaker must wait until all noise has died down and the listeners' full attention is attracted before starting. When all is quiet, the speaker should jump straight into the speech, perhaps with a witty remark so that the audience responds and is eager for more. The voice needs to be projected so that it is heard by those at the back of the room. Deep breaths and natural pauses will help.

Duration

Speeches must be brief and should be times to take no more than five minutes. Breathing time must be allowed. This may sound obvious but when a speaker is nervous, there is a tendency to hold the breath unintentionally. A few practice runs will facilitate relaxation and help to give a good presentation.

A nervous speaker wishing to do the bare minimum but at the same time satisfying the need for courtesy, should concentrate on the purpose of the speech, i.e. respond to or propose a toast and thank people.

General Speech Content

Like every properly constructed speech, a wedding speech must have a beginning, a middle and an end. Speakers should begin by addressing the guests. The wording depends on the formality of the occasion. Examples include 'Ladies and gentlemen', 'Relatives and friends' and if someone with a title is present, it is courteous to acknowledge this. A speaker might follow this by saying that he has never made a speech before, or with the carefully chosen joke or short amusing story. This will immediately set a pleasantly relaxed tone and ensure that the audience is really attentive.

When it comes to the serious content of the speech, it is important to remember that this is the proposal or the response to a toast, or both. So if proposing the toast, the speaker simply says, at the end of his speech, 'I ask you to rise and drink the health of ...' or simi-

lar words. If responding to the toast, the words need not be quite so formal, but it must be made clear in the opening sentence that the speaker is thanking the company for drinking the speaker's health. A simple 'thank you very much' is often surprisingly effective, or 'I (or we) thank you most sincerely for your kind wishes ... It was most kind of you to drink to my/our health ...' and so on. It is advisable to use plain conversational English and to make it grammatically correct. Archaic expressions such as 'Please be upstanding' are no longer necessary.

To finish off a speech, it is quite acceptable to repeat the thanks for the toast that has been drunk, thus avoiding any need to devise a clever ending.

After the toast has been drunk, the speaker and guests may sit down.

At an informal reception where most guests are standing, the speeches should be short as guests will find it difficult to see, hear and balance food and drink while standing still for any length of time.

Specific Speech Content

The Bride's Father

The first speech is normally made by the bride's father. If the bride's mother is a widow, the speech should be made by a relative of mature years (an uncle for example, or an old family friend) and should last for three to five minutes.

Specific content obviously depends on the relationship of the speaker to the bride but it will normally be of a semi-serious nature and include four or five important elements:

- The speech should praise the bride and indicate the happiness that the speaker has had in seeing the bride grow up from a delightful child to a fine young woman. A brief anecdote or short story relating to the bride's

NOTES

early life or events leading up to the wedding may be included, providing that it is in no way embarrassing.

- The speaker should congratulate the groom, exclaim his (and his wife's) happiness in getting to know him and his family and express a welcome to their family to the new son-in-law and the groom's parents.
- The speaker should express his confidence in the couple's future together and wish them a long and happy marriage. He is entitled to offer some advice from an 'old hand' perhaps by way of a quotation to convey his message.
- He should say how happy he is to see his daughter marrying the man of her choice and ask the guests to join him in wishing the couple well.
- The toast to the bride and groom is made at the end of the speech. This can be 'to the bride and groom' or 'to the happy couple' or he may use their first names. As this is not the moment for the speaker to suddenly find himself lost for words, it is advisable to reiterate planned lines or refer to notes in order to make a clear speech.

The Groom's Reply (and Toast to the Bridesmaids)

The groom replies to the toast on behalf of his wife and himself and will need to make seven or eight specific points in his speech, although again it should certainly not last for more than five minutes. The groom's response is usually the one that gives least scope for wit as his primary task is to thank the people concerned.

- The groom should thank the bride's father for the toast just proposed.
- The groom should express his happiness and how fortunate he is to have such a lovely wife and how happy he is to be joining his wife's family. He

may want to add a few words about how he met her and express his future intentions to secure happiness.

- The groom must express his and his wife's thanks to the bride's father for his daughter's hand in marriage.
- He must thank the bride's parents (or whoever is hosting the occasion) for a wonderful wedding and for their generosity.
- He may wish to thank his own parents for all their care and attention to his upbringing and sacrifices that they must have made and acknowledge all that they have done for him both over the years and during the preparations for the wedding.
- He may want to respond to any advice offered by the bride's father if something appropriate comes to mind at the time.
- It is important to say what a pleasure it is to see so many guests and friends gathered together, and to thank all for their good wishes and for their generous gifts.
- He should thank anyone who has been particularly helpful, such as a relation who made the cake, for example. If a close family member or an old friend is unavoidably absent, regret can be added here.
- The groom must declare his admiration, with a few complimentary remarks, for the beauty and efficiency of the bridesmaids and thank all helpers who have made the reception a success, particularly the best man and ushers. He may then present the bridesmaids, pages and ushers with gifts if he has not already done so either at the rehearsal get-together or earlier in the day.
- He then proposes the toast to the bridesmaids. The toast may be 'to the bridesmaids' or he may use their first names. If there are no bridesmaids, he may make a toast to his bride.

NOTES
The bride and her mother may want the groom to relate particular thanks to certain people. The bride can make a note here and pass on details to the groom.

Best Man's Reply (on Behalf of the Bridesmaids)

Traditionally, the best man's speech is the highlight of the reception. He replies to the toast on behalf of the bridesmaids. His speech needs to be lighter in tone than those of the bride's father and the groom.

- He thanks the groom on behalf of the bridesmaids and generally adds a few complimentary remarks of his own. He may thank anyone who has helped him to do the job properly, or the bride may ask him to thank someone on her behalf.
- He then offers his congratulations to the bride and groom and offers some thoughts on their future. These can be amusing but never of a *risqué* nature. He may add a story about how the couple first met or some suitable amusing anecdote or a quotation.
- The best man may propose a toast to absent friends if important guests have been unable to attend the wedding. Jewish wedding receptions end with a final toast: 'Ladies and gentlemen, Her Majesty the Queen!' He may then propose a toast to the bride and groom's future happiness.
- The best man introduces and reads any telemessages and cards from absent friends. These should be vetted beforehand and any hint of vulgarity excluded from the public recital. It is acceptable to group together several messages of simple good wishes, merely announcing the names of the senders.

NOTES
The bride and her mother may want the best man to relate particular thanks to certain people. The bride can make a note here and pass on details to the best man.

The Bride's Speech

There is really no need for the bride to make a speech and she is seldom expected to do so. However, the custom is growing for the bride to say just a very few words if she wishes — a few sentences to thank her parents and husband are sufficient.

Sometimes the bride speaks immediately after her husband has responded to the toast to the two of them, but as he is proposing the toast to the bridesmaids, this is difficult because he has to rise again after the bride to propose the toast. For this reason, it may be better that someone else proposes the toast to the bridesmaids. The best man sometimes introduces the bride and again the order of speakers will need consideration in advance.

In any event, the best man's response usually concludes the speeches when he announces the cutting of the cake and the programme for the rest of the reception.

NOTES

Comic Stories and Jokes

The art of witty public speaking cannot be acquired in a few weeks, however intense the practice, nor will success be achieved in sounding witty by either learning or reading someone else's script written specially for the occasion. A natural or professional comedian's success lies in the ability to act, in facial expression, in the confidence that comes with assured popularity and perfect timing. Few people possess these talents and if the speaker is not one of these lucky people, he is best advised not to attempt a witty speech as the result will, almost certainly, be painful and boring.

However, there is no reason why a suitable joke should not be included as this does help to relax both speaker and audience. The best man's speech traditionally includes humorous references and it is vital that these are pitched correctly. Jokes that are witty, innocent or affectionate may all be suitable for wedding speeches but those that are malicious, blue, sick or insulting must not be used at such an important public occasion. Making jokes at the expense of the bride or her mother is unforgivable but making jokes at one's own expense is a good way of interesting and maintaining the attention of the audience. Jokes at the expense of the groom are acceptable as long as they are in good taste. One-liners are often safer and more effective than long jokes and funny stories.

Twenty years ago a wedding reception was considered no place for comic stories but times change and even at the grandest weddings these days the amusing story or quotation is quite acceptable provided that it is of the kind that could be told to the vicar, or an elderly maiden aunt! What is important is that vulgar and even *risqué* stories are avoided as these embarrass people and spoil a very public and important occasion. References to the newly-weds' honeymoon, any previous marriage or liaisons, the family they may or may not have in the future, or to sex in any form must be avoided. What a speaker can do to raise a laugh is to make fun of himself, his shyness, and his inadequacy as a public speaker.

Funny stories or anecdotes tend to be the easiest 'lighteners' to fit into a speech. They should flow naturally into the speech and not be slotted in for their own sake. Mild jokes about nagging wives and lazy husbands are permissable provided that they are followed by a disclaimer making it clear that the jokes relate in no way to the bride and groom. Some people are good at telling jokes and some are not. If the speaker falls into the latter group, taking a joke from a book could be a disaster, because the chances are that the punchline will be forgotten or it will be badly recited and people will not laugh. It is wise to remember that nothing falls flatter than a joke which no one understands or thinks is funny.

Poems

Orators and actors might like to include a poem but generally verses over five lines should be avoided. A Limerick can add humour but it needs to be in good taste.

Quotations

Quotations, like jokes, can be adapted to suit the circumstances and can add purpose and shape to a speech. However they should only be dropped in as the source of an idea, i.e. used as an introduction to a story, and not to show off the speaker's literary knowledge. More than two quotations can sound awfully pompous, but a few can be useful to start a train of thought which makes the thread of a speech particularly if there is one that is especially apt to the circumstances of the wedding.

Marriage

For in what stupid age or nation,
Was marriage ever out of fashion?
SAMUEL BUTLER

The concept of two people living together for twenty-five years without having a cross word suggests a lack of spirit only to be admired in sheep.
A.P. HERBERT

Any man who says he can see through women is missing a lot.
Marriage is a wonderful institution, but who wants to live in an institution?
GROUCHO MARX

When I said I would die a bachelor, I did not think I should live till I were married.
Love and marriage, love and marriage, go together like a horse and carriage.
Marriage has many pains, but celibacy has no pleasures.
Marriage is popular because it combines the maximum of temptation with the maximum of opportunity.
GEORGE BERNARD SHAW

Hanging and marriage, you know, go by destiny.
GEORGE FARQUHAR

It won't be a stylish marriage.
I can't afford a carriage.
HARRY DACRE

Marriage is like life in this: that it is a field of battle not a bed of roses.

It is a woman's business to get married as soon as possible, and a man's to keep unmarried as long as possible.

Times are changed with him who married; there are no more by-path meadows, where you may innocently linger, but the road lies long and straight and dusty to the grave.
ROBERT LOUIS STEVENSON

Marriage the happiest bond of love might be, if hands were only joined when hearts agree.
GEORGE GRANVILLE

Though marriage makes man and wife one flesh, it leaves 'em two fools.
WILLIAM CONGREVE

I wish you health — a little wealth
And a happy home with freedom.
And may you always have true friends
But never have cause to need them.
ANON

If men knew how women pass the time when they are alone, they'd never marry.
O. HENRY (W.S. PORTER)

Wives are young men's mistresses; companions for middle age; and old men's nurses.
FRANCIS BACON

Chumps always make the best husbands. When you marry, Sally, grab a chump. Tap his forehead first, and if it rings solid, don't hesitate. All the unhappy marriages come from husbands having brains. What good are brains to a man? They only unsettle him.
P.G. WODEHOUSE

Marriage is an attempt to turn a night owl into a homing pigeon.
ANON

I have always thought that every woman should marry and no man.
BENJAMIN DISRAELI

I chose my wife, as she did her wedding gown, not for the glossy surface, but such qualities as would wear well.
OLIVER GOLDSMITH

If it were not for the presents, an elopement would be preferable.
GEORGE ADE

Bigamy is having one wife too many. Monogamy is the same thing.
ANON

Love

Love is best.
ROBERT BROWNING

Love is more than gold or great riches.
JOHN LYDGATE

Love makes the world go round.
She who has never lov'd, has never liv'd.
JOHN GAY

Two souls with but a single thought,
Two hearts that beat as one.
MARIA LOVELL

Women are meant to be loved, not understood.
OSCAR WILDE

And all for love, and nothing for reward.
EDMUND SPENCER

The course of true love never did run smooth.
WILLIAM SHAKESPEARE

Oh! She was good as she was fair.
None — none on earth above her!
As pure in thought as angels are,
To know her was to love her.
SAMUEL ROGERS

Alas! The love of women! It is known to be a lovely and a fearful thing.
LORD BYRON

Did you ever heard of Captain Wattle? He was all for love and a little for the bottle.
CHARLES DIBDIN

Women

All women become like their mothers. That is their tragedy. No man does. That's his.
OSCAR WILDE

A mother's pride, a father's joy!

Oh Woman, in our hours of ease,
Uncertain, coy and hard to please.
SIR WALTER SCOTT

Women have their faults,
Men have only two;
Everything they say,
Everything they do
ANON

Apologise to a man if you're wrong, but to a woman even if you're right.

Blest is the bride on whom the sun doth shine.
ROBERT HERRICK

A woman is only a woman, but a cigar is a good smoke.
RUDYARD KIPLING

Women will be the last thing civilised by man.
GEORGE MEREDITH

She was a lovely girl.
Our courtship was fast and furious —
I was fast and she was furious.
MAX KAUFFMANN

Bridesmaids

Why am I always the bridesmaid,
Never the blushing bride?

A happy bridesmaid makes a happy bride.
LORD TENNYSON

Various

I am no orator as Brutus is;
but you know me all a plain, blunt man.
WILLIAM SHAKESPEARE

Be sure to leave other men their turns to speak.
FRANCIS BACON

An honest man's the noblest work of God.
ALEXANDER POPE

A wise man makes more opportunities than he finds.
FRANCIS BACON

An after-dinner speaker is a man who rises to the occasion and then stands too long.

In public speaking, if you don't strike oil in five minutes, stop boring.

Often when we ask for advice we want approval.

Men are like fish;
neither would get into trouble if they kept their mouths shut.
ANON

Blessed is the man who having nothing to say, abstains from giving us wordy evidence of the fact.
GEORGE ELIOT

An old man gives good advice in order to console himself for no longer being in a condition to set a bad example.
LA ROCHEFOUCAULD

Never to go bed mad.
Stay up and fight.
PHYLLIS DILLER

Telemessages

Guests who are unable to attend a wedding should write to the bride's parents expressing regret and perhaps send a gift. If the guest is a close friend of either the bride and groom, they should also send another note (informally written) to the couple.

A greetings telemessage timed to arrive on the wedding day is a good way of conveying best wishes and can be informal. The reading out of wittily composed telemessages can add gaiety to a wedding reception.

Telemessages should be vetted prior to their reading and anything unsuitable discarded. If there are many, it is wise to select a few, otherwise the guests will be quickly bored. All those with the same or similar messages such as 'best wishes' can be grouped together and the greeting mentioned only once. The best man should check with the bride beforehand to find out if there are any which she would specifically like included.

Messages should be read clearly with deep breaths taken between each one. This allows everyone the time and opportunity to mutter and exchange comments amongst themselves.

10

Guest List

The guest list for the wedding and the reception afterwards may require careful thought and a lot of tact and common sense, especially where both families have many relations and friends.

Having decided the ceremony and reception venues and the type of reception, it is time to compile the guest list. The engagement party list and address books provide a useful starting point.

Considerations

Preparing a guest list may not be an easy task since it can be the most contentious part of the preparations and as it is often restricted by the confines of the agreed budget, it may not be possible to invite all family members and friends. Both sets of parents will often want to invite all relations, when the bride and groom may be more interested in inviting many friends, so great tact, consultation and consideration for others are vital if resentments are to be avoided. If young children are not invited, this may mean that their parents are automatically excluded if they are unable to arrange baby-sitters. Letters of explanation must be extremely tactful — even the nearest and dearest are sensitive about their children.

Traditionally the bride's mother compiles the guest list in consultation with the groom's parents but today the decisions largely depend on whoever is paying for the reception and he or she must be decisive by setting a maximum number. As a general guide, approximately eighty per cent of those invited will attend. It may be possible to send out late invitations if a significant number of guests are unable to attend but it is impolite to send these less than three weeks before the wedding.

Draft List

A draft guest list will help to calculate numbers for the ordering of invitations and when finalised may also be used for recording gifts from guests and those not attending the wedding. It will probably be necessary to make adjustments to suit the allocated budget, so a pencil will come in handy.

Some time needs to be devoted to making a draft list divided into three categories: definite, probably and possible. It is easier to list members of the wedding party, relations and close friends first and then consider other friends, colleagues and neighbours, double checking to ensure that no one is forgotten. Relatives in the couple's immediate families are always included. Those relatives who are one step removed, aunts, uncles and cousins, are usually included. The temptation to invite acquaintances should be avoided, otherwise the length of the list will soar. When the draft list is complete, the groom and his parents should be consulted. However many guests on the list, there is usually an attempt to achieve a fifty/fifty division — half from the bride's family and half from the groom's side but if the groom's family is three times larger than the bride's and the bride's parents are paying the reception in full, then a tactful compromise will have to be arranged. However, an even split may not be the fairest solution if, say, many of the groom's close friends have had to be excluded while the bride has had to include more acquaintances to make up the numbers.

If the list is too long, it can be reduced to include close family and friends only or the groom and his parents can contribute towards the cost if they have many family members. On the other hand, the bride's mother should not insist that she has the lion's share of the guest list because she and her husband are financing the event.

If the guest list needs to be very limited, the solution may be to invite friends to the evening celebration only. If the ceremony venue is very limiting, guests may be invited to the reception only. The minister should be invited together with his or her spouse.

When drafting the list some decisions need to be made about the following situations to avoid possible embarrassment. In the case of small informal weddings, most people understand that the guest list will be limited, but it can be more difficult for a large formal wedding.

- An invited guest may ask to bring a friend.
- If there are twenty cousins, but the couple are close only to a few of them, should they all be invited to avoid hurt feelings?

- Will children be invited? This should be made clear on the invitations. The fairest solution may be to have either an 'adults only' wedding or invite all children. However, it may be necessary to exclude children because of cost and late night celebrations.

Final List

When the draft list has been devised with the groom's parents and checked for duplication and last-minute additions, it can then be finalised and provision made for any special needs, for example, vegetarian diets, highchairs for children, facilities for disabled guests. The list may also include anyone who cannot be invited but to whom a personal letter will be sent to inform them of the good news.

The idea of combining the guest and the gift list, is that all the addresses and telephone numbers will be readily available when the time comes to write the thank-you letters.

Acceptances and refusals should be logged as they are received and anyone who sends a gift should be included on the list so that thank-you notes are not forgotten. It may be an idea to invite gift donors to dinner sometime after the wedding.

Out-of-town Guests

It is important to make distant relatives and old friends feel special and that their presence is appreciated by preparing for their arrival and departure and making their stay as comfortable as possible. They have made a special effort to be at the wedding so the very least that should be done is to ensure that they have somewhere to stay. The bride's mother may feel that she would like some guests to stay with her or with relatives or even close friends. Some guests may prefer to stay in a hotel or bed and breakfast in which case it is polite to provide them with details of local places. It will make life easier if guests are staying nearby. Information for out-of-town guests might include maps, telephone numbers, invitations to pre-wedding parties and literature detailing local sights of interest.

INFILL/CHECK LIST					
Total numbers adults: children: to suit church/marriage room and reception					
Name (incl. children)	Address	Telephone	Definite ✓	Probable ✓	Possible ✓

					GUEST AND GIFT LIST
Invitation					
Sent ✓	Accepted ✓	Refused ✓	Special needs	Gift received	Thank-you note sent (date)

11

Announcements and Printing

In much the same way as for engagements, most couples like to announce their wedding in the local papers so that any casual friends may, if they wish, join in wishing them well at the church or register office, or send a card, for example. Details about engagement announcements are contained in Chapter 2.

Press Announcement

When arranging press announcements, it is wise to check the submission date for entry in the appropriate edition and to ensure that the details are sent well in advance. Entries may be acceptable in handwritten letter format or the press office may provide a form specially designed for this purpose. If the proposed entry contains too much information, the editor may find it necessary to cut it to suit the limited space available, so it is obviously better to keep the announcement relatively short. Something along these lines may be suitable:

> *Mr and Mrs Nigel North*
> *are pleased to announce*
> *the marriage of their daughter*
> *Nel*
> *to*
> *Mr Samuel South*
> *at . . . am/pm*
> *on Saturday 2 May 19 . . .*
> *at . . .*
> *All friends welcome at the church.*

Letters of Announcement

If there are people whom the couple would particularly like informed about their marriage, but because of the limitations of the guest list they have not been able to invite to the wedding, a personal letter is probably the best way to let them know the news in a friendly way.

Personal Letters of Invitation

Before the formal invitations are despatched, relatives and close friends should be informed by personal letter, the wording for which could be as follows:

> *'You will be glad to hear that Nel and Sam's wedding has been arranged for 2 May. We shall, of course, be sending you a formal invitation later, but we felt sure you would be delighted to have the news as soon as possible.'*

Formal Invitations

The wedding arrangements should now be falling into place and about four months before the wedding, invitations should be ordered and despatched to the guests named on the guest list, having been finalised in consultation with the groom's parents.

Invitations serve both a practical and a decorative purpose and should be pleasurable to send and to receive. They are traditionally from and sent out by the bride's parents as they generally host the occasion (indicating their responsibility for payment of the reception) but if the wedding is being hosted by anyone else, such as the bride and groom themselves, the couple should deal with this task. Ideally invitations should be despatched simultaneously as prospective guests do not like to assume that they are second choice! It is obviously important to ensure that nobody feels overlooked.

Although the best man and attendants will already know the details, they must also receive invitations to which they should reply both formally and immediately. Similarly, the groom's parents should also receive an official invitation. It is courteous to invite the minister and his or her spouse to the reception, although, unless he is a personal friend, he or she will probably acknowledge the generosity and decline. The name and full address of the place of the marriage must be double checked for accuracy as in some towns there may be more than one church dedicated to the same saint!

Style

The style of invitations can give the guests clues about the style of wedding. For example, very formal invitations may indicate to the recipients that the wedding will be a very formal occasion. The style chosen for the invitations should reflect the style for the entire wedding and set the tone for all other stationery.

For a very small informal wedding with perhaps fewer than twenty guests, hand-written invitations on attractive stationery are acceptable but for a larger wedding, they will probably be standard printed (obtainable in packs from stationers) or custom printed (from a printer) according to individual requirements. For an ultra-formal wedding they will be engraved in Roman or Script typefaces of black or silver ink on heavy white or ecru folded paper with minimum decoration. A separate reception card and reply card are included. There may be two envelopes; the outer will have the full name and address and the inner will have the guest's name. A cheaper alternative is thermography which simulates engraving.

The many styles of invitations about which the local stationers and printers can advise include formal, informal, traditional, modern, hand-written with fancy envelope seals. The stationer will be able to supply plain card for hand-written invitations — this is obviously the most economical option.

To be really original, invitations may be self-designed with an original monogram or even a small illustration. Local printers may be willing to give guidance and help to create a really professional unique job.

If the ceremony venue is too small to accommodate all guests, it may be appropriate to send a reception card or an evening invitation.

A printer will allow freedom of choice concerning the colour of the card and ink, choice of motifs, monograms, pictures, borders, typefaces and embossed print. Black is the traditional colour for the lettering on wedding invitations. Invitations can also include a photograph, a drawing of the couple or other relevant symbols.

To economise, invitations may be delivered by hand to family and friends.

Ordering

The printer will need accurate details of the date, times and venues and these must be double checked again prior to bulk printing. When calculating the number of invitations to order, each couple or each family needs only one invitation, although teenagers over the age of eighteen should receive their own invitation even if they live with their parents. A few extras for last-minute additions, lost invitations and souvenirs should be ordered.

The printer should be given instructions at least two weeks before the date the invitations are to be sent out and he should be asked to provide written confirmation of the agreed deadline. It is also important to check a proof before bulk printing goes ahead.

Wording

All invitations need to make clear the following vital information:
Host(s)
Couple
The relationship between the bride and host(s)

Ceremony and/or reception venue
Exact time and date
Invitee
'RSVP'
Address for reply

As a wedding is a formal event, invitations should reflect this.

Traditionally, the invitation is addressed to the wife of a couple or family. The wording of the invite(s) should be specific in that people should be named so that numbers will be exact. If a guest would like to be accompanied by another person, 'and Guest', should be included in the wording. The invitation can be formal (Mr and Mrs Alan Smith) or less formal (Alan and Rita Smith) or informal (Alan and Rita) depending on the formality of the wedding and the sender's relationship to the invitees. Their names are normally handwritten in the top left-hand corner if not included as part of the main wording. The wording should make clear whether children are invited as this can avoid embarrassment later.

If there is to be a discotheque or dance after the meal, this should be stated, together with an indication of suitable dress ('Black Tie' or 'Formal Attire') in the bottom right-hand corner of the invitation. For ultra-formal events it is more correct to inform guests of the dress code by word of mouth than print it on the invitation.

The rules for the wording of the main part of invitations can be varied if the wedding is anything other than the most formal affair. By tradition, invitations are composed in the third person. Very formal wording requests the 'honour' of a guest's presence rather than 'pleasure' as in the examples below. The bride's surname is not normally included, but it can be appropriate if it differs from that of the host and hostess. The wording must be perfectly clear and free from ambiguity.

It may be necessary to order two differently worded sets of invitations if some guests are to be invited only to a particular part of the day's celebrations.

The abbreviation 'RSVP' represents 'Repondez s'il vous plait' and means 'Reply, if you please'. A telephone number beneath the reply address and postcode may encourage recipients to relate their acceptance or refusal in advance of the post and may help in the case of any queries.

Before sending out invitations, a check on their individual weight at the post office will ensure that guests do not have to pay any shortfall in postage.

Wedding Given by Bride's Parents

> *Mr and Mrs Nigel North*
> *request the pleasure of your company/*
> *request the company of*
> *. . .*
> *at the marriage of their daughter*
> *Nel*
> *to/with*
> *Mr Samuel South*
> *at St. Mark's Church, Northton*
> *on Saturday 2 May 19 . . . at 2.30*
> *pm*
> *and at the reception afterwards*
> *at Stone Manor, Northton*
> *(Reply address)*   RSVP

Wedding Given by Bride and Groom

> *Nel North and Samuel South*
> *request the pleasure of your company/*
> *request the company of*
> *. . .*
> *at their marriage*
> *at . . .*

Wedding Given Jointly by Parents of Bride and Groom

> *Mr and Mrs Nigel North*
> *and*
> *Mr and Mrs Sidney South*
> *request the pleasure of your company/*
> *request the company of*
> *. . .*
> *at the marriage of*
> *Nel*
> *to*
> *Samuel South*
> *at . . .*

Wedding Given by Divorced Parents of Bride

Mr Nigel North and Mrs Nancy North
request the pleasure of your company/
request the company of
. . .
at the marriage of their daughter
. . .

Wedding Given by Bride's Divorced Mother (now re-married) and Bride's Father

Mr Nigel North and Mrs Nancy Black/
Mrs Nancy Black and Mr Nigel North
request the pleasure of your company/
request the company of
. . .
at the marriage of their daughter
. . .

Wedding Given by Bride's Divorced/Widowed Mother

Mrs Nancy North
requests the pleasure of your company/
requests the company of
. . .
at the marriage of her daughter
. . .

Wedding Given by Bride's Widowed Mother (now re-married)

Mr and Mrs Benjamin Black/
Mrs Benjamin Black
requests the pleasure of your company/
requests the company of
. . .
at the marriage of her daughter
Nel North

Wedding Given by Bride's Divorced Mother (now re-married) and her Husband

Mr and Mrs Benjamin Black
request the pleasure of your company/
request the company of
. . .
at the marriage of her daughter
Nel North . . .

Wedding Given by Bride's Divorced/Widowed Father

Mr Nigel North
requests the pleasure of your company/
requests the company of
. . .
at the marriage of his daughter
Nel

Wedding Given by Bride's Divorced/Widowed Father (now re-married) and his Wife

Mr and Mrs Nigel North
request the pleasure of your company/
request the company of
. . .
at the marriage of his daughter
Nel North

Wedding Given by Bride's Stepfather

Mr Edwin East
requests the pleasure of your company/
requests the company of
. . .
at the marriage of his stepdaughter
Nel North

Wedding Given by Bride's Foster Parents

Mr and Mrs William West
request the pleasure of your company/
request the company of
. . .
at the marriage of their foster-daugh-
ter
Nel North

Wedding Given by Bride's Godmother

Mrs Susan Southwest
requests the pleasure of your company/
requests the company of
. . .
at the marriage of her goddaughter
Nel North

Wedding Given by Bride's Godmother and her Husband

> Mr and Mrs Daniel Southwest
> request the pleasure of your company/
> request the company of
> . . .
> at the marriage of her goddaughter
> Nel North

Wedding Given by Bride's Uncle and Aunt

> Mr and Mrs Walter Westward
> request the pleasure of your company/
> request the company of
> . . .
> at the marriage of their niece
> Nel North

Wedding Given by Others (for example if bride's parents are deceased)

> Mr and Mrs Guy Grey
> request the pleasure of your company
> at the
> marriage of
> Nel North
> daughter of the late
> Mr and Mrs Nigel North
> to
> Mr Samuel South

Service of Blessing

> Mr and Mrs Nigel North
> request the pleasure of your company
> at a Service of Blessing
> following the marriage of their
> daughter
> Nel North
> to
> Mr Samuel South
> at . . .
> on . . .
> and afterwards at . . .

Ceremony and Reception

An invitation to a wedding is normally considered to include the reception afterwards, but this need not necessarily be so. It is important to clarify matters on any invitation. Wedding ceremonies cannot really be private in that no one can be prevented from attending. Thus, well-wishers and friends do not strictly need an invitation to attend the ceremony but they do need to be invited to the reception.

Civil Ceremony – Reception-only Invitations

Register offices are often unable to accommodate many people and consequently it may be impossible for everyone to attend the ceremony, in which case reception-only invitations may be sent, including an explanatory note if desired.

> *Mr and Mrs Nigel North request the pleasure of/request the company of . . .*
> *at the Reception to celebrate the marriage of their daughter Nel North to/with Samuel South to be held at Stone Manor, Northton on Saturday 2 May 19 . . . at 4.30 pm*

Explanatory note:

> *Owing to the small size of the church/ register office, only immediate family can be invited to the ceremony. We do hope you will join us for the reception afterwards.*

Evening-only Invitations

> *Mr and Mrs Nigel North request the pleasure of/ request the company of*
> *. . .*
> *on the evening of the wedding of their daughter*
> *Nel*
> *to/with*
> *Mr Samuel South*
> *at Stone Manor, Northton*
> *on Saturday 2 May 19 . . .*
> *at 8.00 pm*

OR

> *Mr and Mrs Nigel North request the pleasure of/ request the company of*
> *. . .*
> *at an evening reception*
> *at . . .*
> *to celebrate the marriage of their daughter*
> *Nel*
> *to/with*
> *Mr Samuel South*
> *on . . .*

Ceremony-only Invitations

It used to be considered improper to invite people to the service only but this is no longer the case. Work colleagues, associates and other acquaintances may appreciate an invitation to witness the service. If there are only a few they could be invited informally by telephone but for more than this, invitations may be printed detailing only the service information.

> *Mr and Mrs Nigel North request the pleasure of your company/ request the company of*
> *. . .*
> *at the ceremony of marriage for their daughter*
> *Nel North*
> *to*
> *Samuel South*
> *at . . .*
> *on . . .*

Double Weddings

When two sisters are to be married in a double wedding ceremony, the elder sister and her fiancé are mentioned first.

In the case of a daughter and a niece or goddaughter, the daughter takes precedence as she is closest in relationship to the host and hostess.

If the two couples to be married are acting as hosts and hostesses for a double wedding, the older couple is mentioned first.

There are, of course, numerous variations to the wording of invitations even on the possibilities listed above.

Checking the Invitations

The printer will supply a proof for checking before printing the bulk supply. The following points must be checked for accuracy:

Paper/card — colour
— quality
Lettering style
Borders/designs
Text — date
— times
— spelling
— punctuation
Print bulk deadline
Quantity

Enclosures

Unless everyone is local, it is useful to photocopy a map or sketch of the area and highlight appropriate places, describing the most favourable routes to the designated locations, for example to the ceremony venue, reception venue, railway station, taxi ranks, bus stops, car parks. If cars are to be provided, this should be clearly stated.

Although there are no rules of responsibility for the provision of lodging, or transport for that matter, it would be helpful to provide some information about accommodation and rates in the area, for those guests who are having to travel some distance. It might be possible for all guests to stay in one place so that a group discount can be arranged.

It is, of course, possible to send a wedding-gift list with the invitations, but it is obviously more tactful if this is done at a later stage and only on request.

Replies to Invitations

Formal invitations require formal replies and should be composed in the third person and sent within three days of receipt, so that the bride's mother will have a more definite idea of numbers. It may be possible to send out a few more invitations if a number of people are unable to attend.

Acceptances and refusals should be entered on the guest and gift record as they are received.

In order to make replying quick and easy, a reply card (printed in the same style and on the same paper as the invitation) may be enclosed with the invitation for which it is courteous to stamp the envelope so that the sender bears the cost of reply.

Reply Card

> . . .
> *are pleased*
> *to accept your kind invitation*
> *for Saturday 2 May 19 . . .*
> *Number of guests . . .*

Acceptance

> *(Date)* *(Address)*
> *Mr and Mrs Don Day and their son*
> *thank Mr and Mrs North for their kind*
> *invitation to the wedding of their daughter, Nel, to Mr Samuel South at St Mark's*
> *Church, Northton on . . . and have great*
> *pleasure in accepting.*
> *(No signature required)*

OR

> *Mr and Mrs Don Day thank Mr and*
> *Mrs North for their kind invitation and*
> *will be delighted to accept . . .*
> *(No signature required)*

OR

> *Don and Debbie Day will be delighted . . .*
> *(No signature required)*

Early Refusal

It is courteous to acknowledge the invitation within three days of receipt (so that the organisers can finalise numbers) and to state apologies clearly. The refusal should be formal and fairly brief. No one wants to know the reasons for refusal in great detail. It is sufficient to state, for example, that owing to illness, it would be impossible to attend, or something like the following:

> *(Date)* *(Address)*
> *Mr and Mrs Don Day and their son*
> *thank Mr and Mrs North for their kind*
> *invitation to the wedding of their daughter on . . . but regret they are unable to*
> *accept because of a previous engagement.* *(No signature required)*

Late Refusal

Unforeseen circumstances may necessitate a refusal following acceptance. A note should be sent immediately, for example:

(Date)   *(Address)*
Mr and Mrs Don Day and their son sincerely regret the necessity, because of a bereavement in the family, to have to inform you that they will now be unable to attend your daughter's wedding on . . .
(No signature required)

Order of Service Sheets

The benefit of printed order of service sheets is that the congregation can follow the service and the hymns without referring back and forth from prayer book to hymn book. They also eliminate the need to share church books and can be printed in enlarged and emboldened print to aid reading. Although the sheets do provide use useful benefits, they can be unnecessary where a sufficient number of hymn and prayer books are provided. The printer will probably have a sample design on which individual requirements can be based, however, he or she will require a separately typed copy of the wording.

Details may include:

- Names of the bridal party
- Church
- Minister's name
- Date
- Time of the ceremony
- Music selections
- The processional
- Prayers and their responses
- Marriage service
- Readings
- Hymns
- Signing of the register
- The recessional

A sample layout concludes Chapter 5.

The minister must be consulted before bulk printing is authorised to ensure that all elements are complete and correct. For example if prayers and responses are to be included, they need to appear in the correct order. Printing the music to which the wedding party will enter and leave the church may ensure that the congregation stands at the right time.

Quantity

It is sensible to have a few extra order of service sheets printed for unexpected friends. The minister and choir members need to be included in the calculation, as well as all the attendants.

On the wedding day, the groom holds two copies and passes one to the bride inside the church. Bridesmaids and page boys acquire their copies from pew ends when they reach the chancel steps.

Stationery for the Reception

Menus

If there is a choice of fare at the reception, menu cards may be printed for the guests.

Place Name Cards

These are useful so that the guests know where to sit at the reception. They can be printed, but it is possible, of course, to do these by hand using white card.

The full names of the guests should be used. In the case of a divorced or widowed lady, her own initials or her first name should be used. The best man should hold a supply of additional blank cards to cater for the arrival of any unexpected guests.

Seating Plan

In addition to place name cards, an overall seating plan is usually prepared so that guests know the general location of their seats as they enter the dining-room.

Compliments Cards

Compliments cards are dispatched with cake slices to those who were unable to attend on the day.

Mr and Mrs Samuel South
(address)
With compliments on the occasion of their wedding
2 May 19 . . .

Cake Boxes

It is possible to purchase attractively designed cake boxes with grease-proof inner linings to protect the cards from the cake.

Guest Book

It is possible to purchase guest books into which guests sign their names at the reception. This may be retained as a keepsake.

Other Stationery and Souvenirs

Additional Items for the Reception

A multitude of items including napkins, napkin rings, drink mats, matchboxes and match books for use on the wedding day may be monogrammed (personalised with the couple's names and date of the wedding) and kept as souvenirs. There is also a vast choice of stationery and souvenirs which can be personally printed. These items may be very attractive but can be a rather extravagant luxury which is certainly not essential. It is therefore prudent to consult the budget carefully before being tempted to order too many additional items.

Thank-you Cards and Letters

Thank-you cards or letters can be preprinted with standard text so that a signature is all that is required together with an addressed envelope. These do make life easier but they will give far less pleasure than a personally hand-written letter of thanks. For this more personal, and more acceptable, option it is possible to purchase pre-printed letterheaded note paper detailing the new address and telephone number. Preprinted thank-you cards or letterheaded paper for letter of thanks are usually in a style which complements the wedding invitations, but can also be used for future correspondence.

Desk Diary and Records

A desk diary with plenty of space for daily entries is a good investment to aid the planning of the wedding. Records become souvenirs and in years to come it can be informative to be reminded of just how much or little the whole event cost!

Keepsake Books

Books with pre-printed layouts or large scrap books can be used to display the various souvenirs such as: guest list; copy announcements; pressed flowers; sample stationery; replies to invitations; order of service sheets and fabric samples.

Post-wedding News

Many couples like a press report of the wedding to appear in the local newspaper. This is the responsibility of the bride's parents and the newspaper office will usually supply a wedding form which requests certain details such as in the Post-Wedding News Infill List at the end of this chapter.

The service is sometimes free, though some newspapers will not print a report unless a small advertisement in the marriages column is taken. Some local newspapers arrange to take a wedding photograph and in this case they frequently print this with the report.

Mr Samuel South and Miss Nel North The marriage took place on ... at the Church of ... of Mr Samuel South, only son of Mr and Mrs Sidney South of Southton and Miss Nel North, younger daughter of Mr and Mrs Nigel North of Northton.

Where one party has been divorced:

A service of blessing was held on ... at the Church of ... after the marriage of Mr Samuel South, only son of Mr and Mrs Sidney South and Miss Nel North, younger daughter of Mr and Mrs Nigel North of Northton.

Postponement or Cancellation

Ideally, there will be no hitches with the wedding plans, but having said this, they can and do happen. If it is necessary to delay the wedding, for example, through illness or the loss of a job, there is no need to give a reason to anyone except close family and friends. If it seems appropriate to disclose the reason, a simple statement of fact is sufficient.

Whatever the situation, if the invitations have not been posted, the bride need only notify immediate family members, close friends and members of the wedding party. If the invitations have been sent, guests should be notified by printed card in the same style as the invitations; if these were formal then the cancellation notes should be formal too, but if there is little time, a personal note or telephone call will have to suffice. It is unwise to send the information by post if the guests will not receive it at least one week before the wedding date for they may not have adequate time to change their arrangements.

---

*Mr and Mrs Nigel North announce
that the marriage of their daughter
Nel
to
Mr Samuel South
will be postponed until . . ./
will not take place*

OR

---

*Mr and Mrs Nigel North
announce that
owing to the illness of
. . .
they are obliged to
postpone the marriage of
their daughter
Nel
to
Mr Samuel South
which was to have taken place
on Saturday . . .
and will now be held
on . . .
The time and place
remain the same*

OR

---

*Owing to the recent
illness/sudden death
of Mrs North's father,
the wedding
of her daughter
Nel to Samuel South
at . . .
at . . .
on . . .
has been postponed/
will not now take place
until . . .am/pm
on . . ./
The marriage will be held privately in
the presence of the immediate family
at a date to be arranged.*

OR

---

*Mr and Mrs Nigel North
regret that they are
obliged to cancel/recall
the invitations to the
marriage of their daughter
Nel
to
Mr Samuel South
owing to the death of
Mr South's father,
Mr Stephen South.
The ceremony will be held privately in
the presence of the immediate family*

As well as informing the guests, all suppliers of goods or services need to be informed regardless of whether or not a deposit has been paid. If the wedding is postponed, it may be possible for the suppliers to re-schedule but if not, a request should be made for the refund of any deposit paid.

Postponement does not require the return of wedding gifts. In the event of cancellation, which results in the holding of a private ceremony, gifts may be returned. With total cancellation however, gifts should definitely be returned.

INFILL/CHECK LIST

	Invitations	Envelopes and seals	Maps	Order of service sheets	Thank-yous Letterheads/ Cards
Supplier/ printer					
Address					
Telephone					
No. required					
Style					
Size					
Paper or card					
Paper colour					
Print style					
Print colour					
Monogram					
Photo or illustration					
Other personal touches					
Wording					
Cost £					
Date ordered					
Proofs ready for checking					
Collection date					
Deposit due date					
Balance due date					

						PRINTING
Place Cards	Seating Plan	Cake Boxes	Napkins	Napkin Rings	Match-boxes	Postage

INFILL LIST				POST-WEDDING NEWS	
Publications	Press Office address	Telephone	Editor	Deadline	Entry date

Submitter's	Name	
	Address	
	Telephone	
Wedding:	Date	
	Time	
Ceremony venue		
Parents' names: Bride's		
	Groom's	
Minister/registrar		
Dress description		
Bouquet description		
Attendants' names		
Bridesmaids' dresses and bouquet description		
Reception venue		
Couple's professional background		
Grandparents' names		
Honeymoon plans		

12

Photography and Videography

The special day would not be complete without a permanent record on film to be looked back on with pleasure as the years pass, and consequently photographs and videos are a very important reminder of the wedding day not only for the couple but for parents, family and attendants. The skills of the photographer and/or videographer create the most important memento of all.

Photography

The Photographer

Most brides and their mothers would recommend that a professional, reputable and trustworthy photographer is employed for the occasion. Well-meaning friends may offer their services for the day but this is generally not ideal since there is no guarantee of good results and if the volunteer is a guest, the bride will naturally want them to enjoy the cele-bration and not spend most of the day behind the camera. Most relations and friends will take their own photographs anyway so if some informal snapshots are needed to add to the album, this should be easy enough to achieve.

The most difficult choice of all the service suppliers is perhaps the photographer and for this reason a decision should not be rushed. The Yellow Pages, the local press and the local high street will reveal a good choice and it is the bride's and her mother's choice as to who will take those photographs that will be treasured for years to come.

Taking good photographs takes years of experience and the professional photographer will know how best to tackle the inclement weather conditions so common in the United Kingdom and can make even the most posed picture look quite natural. An assessment of a photographer's experience can be checked by the examination of previous work. The shots should be clear, sharp and varied and not catch anyone in awkward positions or include backgrounds which detract from the subject of the picture.

The photographer should be a full-time operator and a member of a professional association such as the Master Photographers' Association or the British Institute of Professional Photographers which insist on conformation to a code of practice and if it is felt that performance is in any way unprofessional, reference can be made to the appropriate association. There should be no doubt as to who will be taking the pictures on the day. In the case of illness of the appointed photographer, there should be provision for a back-up. It is advisable to compile a list of alternative locally based photographers and to ensure that the best man has this with him on the day for if the appointed photographer fails to show, it may be necessary to recruit someone else at short notice. It would also be worth checking the length of time that the chosen business has been established and whether wedding photography is their speciality.

When a professional is employed, guests should be instructed tactfully not to take their own photographs when the expert is working and informed of the reasons why, one of which is that if two or more flashes occur simultaneously, it is probable that the employed photographer's pictures will be ruined.

Most photographers have brochures detailing their services and costs and those who specialise in weddings generally offer 'wedding packages' but these do vary. Some photographers charge a standard fee which includes the photographer's attendance at the wedding to take a certain number of photographs, plus one album of about twenty photographs, some charge an hourly rate with a lower price per print, and some incorporate their attendance fee in the cost of the prints. There may also be a charge for the proofs and in most cases VAT will need to be added to the bill. Packages offered may or may not include the cost of an album. Additional albums and individual photographs will be charged as extra. The couple must decide on the number of photographs they want taken on the wedding day as this will determine their choice of package. The photographer may offer to handle the photograph and/or the announcement for the press but this may incur an additional charge. Deposit requirements and refund policy should be checked and discussed. The deposit will be demanded when booking a photographer and at this stage he or she will probably need a decision on the choice of package and the album required. Both sets of parents will often decide to have an album of their own, or the couple could buy these for them as thank-you gifts. The photographer should be asked to confirm a date for the availability of proofs and state the length of time that they can be retained by the family.

When choosing a photographer, it is folly to accept the cheapest, or indeed the most expensive, quotation; neither the cheapest nor the most expensive is necessarily the best and considering that after the wedding, photographs are all that remain of the great day, it is wise to opt for the best value/quality combination and the photographer whose style best suits the type of wedding planned. For a relatively small wedding, it may be more economical to choose a firm that simply charges per print, whereas for a large wedding, it may be prudent to opt for the photographer who charges a flat fee for the day plus a smaller fee per print. It is not economical to order black and white photographs as these are rarely used nowadays and are generally more expensive than colour.

Many photographers have busy diaries with many advance commitments, so the couple should make the booking at least three months before the date of the wedding. They will need to meet the photographer in person several weeks before the wedding to discuss the type and subject of pictures to be taken if this is not done at the time of booking. The details should then be confirmed in writing.

Most couples find that a mixture of candid and more formal shots are best at capturing every aspect of the day but the photographer must be informed of any specific requirements: there may be certain times when photographs may not be appropriate; there may be a request for a particular double-exposure shot; or the couple may not like very formal poses. If the photographer is unaware of any such requirements, he cannot be expected to take the right pictures. Having said this, it needs to be remembered that an experienced wedding photographer knows his or her job and can give invaluable advice on how to create the best album possible.

The photographer will probably take a set number of photographs both before and after the ceremony and may arrange a list of groups with the bride, but obviously choice depends on particular requirements and personal preferences.

The photographer will then print proofs of all the shots so that the bride and groom may choose the pictures they would like to buy. These are generally sent to the couple about a week after the wedding. Generally, the proofs may be retained for a short time so that they may be shown to family and friends so that they may order prints if desired, in which case they should indicate the proof number, the size required and the quantity. The chart provided towards the end of this chapter may be used for this purpose.

It is possible to take out insurance against the photographer not turning up or against loss of or damage to or non-development of wedding photographs. The insurance should cover the cost of hiring replacement services.

The Photographs

The Photographs Infill List may be used to agree with the photographer the shots particularly wanted. The ones marked 'P' (popular) are those favoured by couples who opt for a small number of photographs. Some photographers' packages do not include attendance at the reception but this can be arranged specially or perhaps a friend can oblige. The photographer should be allowed some discretion to add to the list anything which he thinks would be especially effective. It is important to check whether photographs are allowed inside the church, register office or approved premises marriage room. The decision of the minister or registrar is final and must be respected. Some ministers allow photographs as long as no flashes are used whilst others may allow photographs as long as these are not taken during the actual marriage itself. Others will not allow any photographs inside the church.

Once the photographs have been ordered, it will usually take a few weeks before they are ready when the final balance will be payable and the photographs are collected.

SUPERSTITION

It is considered good luck for the fully attired bride to glance in her mirror just once before leaving for the wedding, but bad luck to return to look in her mirror after she has left the bedroom to commence her journey to the wedding.

INFILL/CHECK LIST	THE PHOTOGRAPHER
Photographer	
Address	
Telephone Opening Hours	
When was the firm established?	
Do you specialise in weddings?	
See brochure	
See price list, check proof charges and VAT	
Who will take the photographs?	
Is he/she experienced?	
Is he/she qualified?	
See sample work	
Is there a back-up photographer?	
Is there back-up equipment?	
Package details	
Attendance fee	
Set number of prints	
Is the cost of the album included?	
Who keeps the proofs?	
Are the proofs over-stamped (rendering them worthless)?	
Who owns copyright and negatives?	
When will the proofs be ready?	
How long may the proofs be retained?	
When will the photographs be ready?	
Do you handle the photograph announcements in the press?	
Check with minister/registrar about restrictions	
Appointment to discuss order of shots	
Quotation – Cost of proofs	£
Cost of each finished photograph	£
Cost of additional albums (Couple and both sets of parents)	£
Cost of additional individual photographs	£
VAT	£
When do prices increase?	

INFILL/CHECK LIST	THE PHOTOGRAPHER
Deposit/cancellation arrangements Is it refundable?	
Confirmation in writing	
Insurance against photographer not attending, loss of/damage to or non-development of photos	
Deposit due date	
Balance due date	

INFILL LIST					PHOTOGRAPHS
Date of Wedding		Meeting dates			
	Time	Shots			
		Popular	Formal	Informal	Both
Before the ceremony at home Address					
Close up		P			
With mother					
With father		P			
With mother and father					
With family					
With attendants					
At gift table					
Full length					
Adjusting veil					
With flowers					
At dressing table, for example, looking through mirror					
Putting on veil or hat					
Bridesmaids getting bride ready					
In the garden					
Mother and attendants leaving					
Leaving with father					

INFILL LIST					PHOTOGRAPHS
Date of Wedding		Meeting dates			
	Time	Shots			
		Popular	Formal	Informal	Both
At the ceremony Address					
Arrival of guests					
Arrival of groom and best man					
Groom					
Groom with best man		P			
Groom with ushers					
Groom with best man and ushers					
Arrival of bridesmaids, pages and bride's mother					
Arrival of bride and giver-away					
Bride, bridesmaids and pages		P			
Bridesmaids					
Pages					
Ushers					
Bride outside church					
Wedding party assembled					
Bride and father entering church		P			

INFILL LIST					PHOTOGRAPHS
Date of Wedding		Meeting dates			
	Time	Shots			
		Popular	Formal	Informal	Both
During the ceremony (if allowed)					
In the church					
Bride going down the aisle (processional)					
The marriage itself (if allowed)					
In the vestry for signing the register		P			
Leaving the church (recessional)					
At the church door, bride and groom together		P			

INFILL LIST					PHOTOGRAPHS
Date of Wedding		Meeting dates			
	Time	Shots			
		Popular	Formal	Informal	Both
After the ceremony					
Leaving the church — weather permitting					
Bride and groom at the church door		P			
Outside the church/ register office/approved premises					
Bride and groom together		P			
Couple with best man, bridesmaids and other attendants		P			
All attendants					
Couple with bride's parents		P			
Couple with groom's parents		P			
Couple with both sets of parents					
Couple getting into car					

INFILL LIST				PHOTOGRAPHS	
Date of Wedding		Meeting dates			
	Time	Shots			
		Popular	Formal	Informal	Both
Formal after-ceremony photographs					
Exact location					
Bride alone					
With bridesmaids					
With bride's parents					
Couple together		P			
With best man, bridesmaids and pages					
With bride's parents					
With groom's parents					
With both sets of parents		P			
Entire wedding party		P			
With best man, bridesmaids and bride's parents		P			
With best man, bridesmaids and groom's parents		P			
With best man, bridesmaids and both sets of parents		P			
With bride's family					
With groom's family					
With all attendants, both sets of parents and respective wider families		P			
With friends					
With guests throwing confetti					
Leaving for reception		P			
In car					

INFILL LIST				PHOTOGRAPHS	
Date of Wedding		Meeting dates			
	Time	Shots			
		Popular	Formal	Informal	Both
At the Reception Location					
Bride and groom arriving		P			
Receiving guests					
With bride's parents					
With groom's parents					
With both sets of parents					
With special friends					
With godparents					
Top table		P			
Side tables					
Proposing toasts					
During toasts and speeches					
Cutting the cake		P			
Bride and groom eating cake					
During first dance (bride and groom)					
Bride and father dancing					
Groom and his mother dancing					
Musicians/DJ					

INFILL LIST					PHOTOGRAPHS
Date of Wedding		Meeting dates			
	Time	Shots			
		Popular	Formal	Informal	Both
Leaving the Reception					
Bride throwing bouquet					
Good-byes					
Getting into the car		P			
Car leaving					
Special requests					

INFILL LIST			GUESTS' PHOTOGRAPH ORDERS		
Name	Address	Telephone	Proof no.	Size	Qty

Ordering Photographs for Guests

Once the proof prints are available, the families and close friends may wish to order copies. They could do this direct with the photographer, or it may be easier to collect all the requests into one order and for the bride to send in a form.

Videography

Many brides now decide to have their wedding recorded on video either in addition to or instead of photographs. The minister may decide not to allow the service itself to be recorded on video but may permit some recording, in which case it is advisable to visit the church with the technician to decide on positioning for lights and microphones – they will need to be unobtrusive. A video will need editing, otherwise the tape could be five to six hours long!

The Videographer

Videos can be dealt with by a professional firm or by an experienced and trusted amateur. It is tempting to allow a well-meaning but inexperienced friend or relative to oblige but, unless there is evidence that their results are impressive, the services of a professional should be employed for a high-class production of a commercial standard and, as with photographers, they are keen to protect their reputations as well as being insured. It is usually possible to have the original video reproduced.

As with photography the abilities and fees of professional firms should be checked and compared with particular attention paid to the quality of sound, naturalness and continuity.

Keepsake Album

It is surprising how quickly many details of the wedding day are forgotten so it is a good idea to combine the photograph album with a collection of souvenirs of the day. It is possible to buy books with pre-printed layouts or large scrapbooks for this purpose. Insertions could include: guest list; copy announcements; pressed flowers; sample stationery; replies to invitations; order or service sheet; fabric samples; guest book.

INFILL/CHECK LIST	THE VIDEOGRAPHER
Videographer	
Address	
Telephone Hours of work	
When was the firm established?	
Do you specialise in weddings?	
Back-up operator	
Back-up equipment	
Package details	
Attendance fee	
Length of video	
Can we select music dub-ins?	
When will the video be ready?	
When will the video copies be ready?	
Quotations	
Attendance	£
Cost of video	£
Cost of editing	£
Cost of additional video copies	£
VAT	£
TOTAL	£
When do prices increase?	
Deposit/cancellation arrangements	
Is it refundable?	
Please confirm all points in writing	
Double check date and times nearer the date	
Deposit due date	
Balance due date	

13

Attire

A couple's wedding day is probably the most spectacular celebration of their lives, for which most participants like to dress up in new clothes purchased specially for the occasion. As far as the wedding party members are concerned, the most important consideration is the overall co-ordination, and the style of the bride's wedding dress which will set the scene for the remaining members of the party.

Bride

. . . .
: **SUPERSTITION AND TRADITION** :
: *Something old, something new,* :
: *Something borrowed, something blue,* :
: *And a silver sixpence in your shoe.* :
: *The custom of wearing 'something blue'* :
: *originates from ancient Israel where a* :
: *bride wore a blue ribbon as a symbol of* :
: *her fidelity. The placing of a coin in her* :
: *shoe is said to bring wealth. Something* :
: *'old' was frequently an old garter. Other* :
: *ideas for this tradition include family* :
: *jewellery, accessories from past family* :
: *weddings and blue flowers.* :
: *When brides were no longer 'captured', the* :
: *role of the wedding party was to ward off* :
: *evil spirits. The women in the wedding* :
: *party (including the bride) all dressed in* :
: *the same way and similarly the men* :
: *attired themselves in the same way as the* :
: *groom in order to confuse the evil spirits* :
: *as to the identity of the real bridal couple.* :
: *Oriental brides frequently wear elaborate* :
: *outfits and jewellery.* :
. . . .

Some brides have a clear image of what they would most like to wear for their wedding, or they may have a dozen ideas! Sorting out the wedding attire will probably take some considerable time and this chapter may help the bride to make her choice.

The hunt for the perfect wedding attire should start as soon as possible and at least four months before the day. Every bride wants to take her time when making such an important decision and she will be choosing a complete outfit which can be very expensive whether it is bought or hired. The style of her dress will set the tone for other members of the wedding party.

Dress

The bride should enjoy choosing her wedding dress, probably assisted by her mother and her chief bridesmaid. For a church wedding, the bride may decide to have a long dress or something less formal.

First time brides generally wear white for church and register office/room weddings but it is acceptable to wear any other colour. They may feel that a full-length dress and train with a veil might look out-of-place in a register office but many do wear this full regalia without looking overdressed.

Most wedding dresses are white, ivory or cream and the choice of colour should complement skin tones. Dress style will depend on formality and the time of day of the ceremony. Here are a few ideas for the formality of the bride's dress.

SUPERSTITION AND TRADITION

The bride should not try on her complete outfit before the wedding day.
It is considered bad luck for the groom to see the bride on the wedding day or see her in her wedding dress before she appears in church.
The bride should not finish dressing until the last minute.
It is difficult to define tradition regarding attire. In Roman times the traditional wedding dress colour was yellow. Brides were not expected to wear white until the sixteenth century when it became popular after Anne of Brittany married Louis XII in white and even then brides continued to wear their best dresses, whatever the colour, and sometimes one which had been handed down through the generations, or sometimes her national costume. Furthermore, Queen Victoria broke with the royal tradition of wearing a silver dress when she chose white for her wedding to Prince Albert in 1840. The colour white became popular as a symbol of purity reserved for maidenhood and was thought to ward off evil spirits.

		Colour	Fabric	Dress Length	Train	Veil Length	Jewellery
ULTRA-FORMAL/ FORMAL	**Daytime**	White Champagne Ivory Cream		Floor	Brush Court	Long	Pearls
	Evening	White Champagne Ivory Cream	More orna- mental than for daytime	Floor	Cathedral Chapel	Long	Simple
SEMI-FORMAL	**Daytime/ Evening**	White Champagne Ivory Cream or pastel	Evening: More ornamental than for daytime	Optional	Optional	Elbow or shorter	Simple
INFORMAL	**Daytime/ Evening**	Pastel	Optional	Optional		Short or hat with or without veil	Simple

Dress Suppliers

There are a number of ways of acquiring a wedding dress and it can prove to be very expensive so it is good advice to start shopping early and adhere to the budget. Every bride wants to look wonderful but it should be remembered that very formal dresses are worn for the one day only so it may be prudent to spend a little less money on the wedding dress, thereby allowing extra outlay for some new clothes for the honeymoon. Brides who buy expensive wedding dresses sometimes regret it later when they see it hanging in the spare bedroom wardrobe. Hand finishing, special fabrics and trim-mings all add to the cost. Polyester dresses may be less expensive than silk or satin but they look equally wonderful. Some stores reduce the cost of wedding dresses when styles have been discontinued or at the end of the season. This latter incentive is obviously tempting but any bargain should of course be suitable for the time of year of the wedding.

If the budget is restricted, it may be desirable to hire or borrow a dress. A moderate budget will allow for purchase from a cheaper range, dress hire or a second-hand gown. High prices can be paid for originality, individuality, quality fabric and finish, but a mass-produced dress accompanied by a personal variation of accessories will not be instantly recognisable as such and can look marvellous.

Purchase

It can be reassuring to have the dress made by a professional dressmaker or an experienced and confident relation or friend. To have a dress made by a professional dressmaker takes many weeks and several fittings and is obviously the most expensive choice which is out of the question for most brides. However, if this is the choice, it is advisable to set-

tle the price before the work starts and obtain a written guarantee date in advance of the wedding date.

It will be cheaper to buy a dress ready-made from a specialist bridal-wear shop where there is a range of beautiful gowns from which to choose.

A much cheaper way of buying a dress is to procure it ready-made off-the-peg from a department store or catalogue. Many large stores have their own bridal sections with extensive ranges of beautiful gowns and most offer a fitting and alteration service at a small extra cost. An inexpensive way of personalising a bought dress is to decorate the dress neck, waist and/or hemline with fabric flowers, silver decorations and/or imitation pearls.

An early 'window-shopping trip', with no intention to purchase, will avoid any feelings of being bulldozed, pushed or rushed into a hasty decision. It is a good tip to avoid peak shopping times. When choosing the dress, the shop assistant should be made aware of the amount of money set aside in the budget so that only the dresses in that price range are considered, otherwise temptation will lead to extravagance and possible regrets later. Early shopping may reveal unexpected bargains as dresses go on sale at the end of the season.

Second-hand dresses from agencies or through advertisements can be beautiful bargains. They can be modified by changing the lace panels or buttons or by adding a train and decorations. The bride needs to start looking early and should not be embarrassed into buying a dress of which she is unsure. An in-depth conversation over the telephone regarding the style, prior to visiting someone with a dress for sale, will give the bride a good visual image of the dress before it is actually seen.

The Internet has a wealth of information. Search for dress hire, bridal wear and wedding dresses, under which there are hundreds of web pages to visit.

Hire

It is possible to hire a really special dress without paying a great deal of money. An extensive range to suit all budgets can be found in the many hire shops, both specialist and within fashion stores. The procedure for hiring a dress is the same as for purchase in that shopping should start as early as possible and then a booking made for the wedding day.

It is wise to obtain a written agreement that the dress will be available on the date needed and that the previous wearer will have returned it in time for it to be cleaned and prepared ready for collection. It is also worth checking whether the dress will be available at some point prior to the wedding date so that the suitability of accessories may be assessed. The bride should have some alternative arrangement if the dress is damaged or otherwise unavailable, know who is responsible for cleaning and whether the dress can be insured against damage. Compliance with collection and return dates is essential. It is probable that a deposit will be necessary and the bride should find out when the balance of the hire charge is payable. Normally the hire firm is responsible for the cleaning of the dress.

The chief bridesmaid should be asked to return the dress after the wedding if the bride will be away on honeymoon.

Loan

It may be worth borrowing a dress if it is suitable in every respect. There may be a family heirloom which mothers or perhaps grandmothers, relatives or friends are willing to provide for the occasion.

Self-made

Bridal dressmaking should be left to an experienced hand, and unless the bride happens to be an experienced and confident dressmaker, it would be inappropriate to attempt the job as the making of a wedding gown is far more difficult than an ordinary day dress and demands skills of the very highest standards for a perfect finished result. If there are any doubts about ability, then one of the other options should be chosen, but for those who do feel qualified then this is a great opportunity to create a unique style from an original design or modified patterns. The bride can feel really proud of her achievement as she walks up the aisle. Here are a few tips which are worth remembering even if the dressmaker is very experienced.

- Paper wedding dress patterns are available or suitable dress patterns may be adapted. Alternatively it is possible to design the pattern from scratch. However, it is important to choose a design which is within the capabilities of the dressmaker.
- The chosen fabric should be enjoyable to work with; some are more difficult than others.
- It is advisable to make up the dress in a cheap fabric first so that it may be adjusted in size, fit and length before the expensive fabric is cut.
- The correct equipment for dealing with the fabric is vital, for instance long fine pins, special needles and threads.
- A friend or relation who is an experienced dressmaker should be asked to help with final fittings as it is impossible to achieve the perfect fit alone or on a tailor's dummy.
- The weight of the garment demands that it is stored flat and carefully in a plastic cover or inside a duvet cover. It may be pressed using a very cool iron on the day before the wedding.
- Plenty of time for dressmaking is essential.

Style

For the perfect figure and complexion the choice of style is the bride's, but for most people different styles can be more or less flattering. It is folly to opt for a style simply because it is the most fashionable if it does not suit.

Magazines provide many ideas for style and should be perused before visiting the stores, otherwise the wealth of choice may be bewildering. On the other hand, it is perhaps a good idea to retain an open mind, trying on various styles, colours and lengths. The most important considerations, after cost, are whether the style suits so that the bride looks her best, and whether it is comfortable and reflects her personality. The bride does not want to be worrying about a tight bodice at the chancel steps or a split seam when dancing at the reception.

Trains are extensions of the fabric at the back of the skirt and are generally worn at formal weddings. If the dress has a long train, some thought needs to be given as to how it will be carried and kept out of the way to avoid spoiling at the reception and also when getting in and out of vehicles such as small cars and carriages.

The key to successful outfitting seems to be the selection of a style that suits the bride's shape, colouring and personality. Weddings can follow a specific theme. For a Valentine's day wedding the groom might wear a red waistcoat, the bridesmaids red dresses, groomsmen red bow ties, the cake might be heart shaped and there could be pink champagne for the toasts. For a Christmas wedding, the colour scheme might be red, green and white and the music and decorations 'Christmassy'.

Fashion Terms Explained

Style

A-line skirt	Close-fitting waist, flared hemline
Ballerina skirt	Full skirt which falls to ankles
Bell sleeve	Long sleeve which flares from top arm to wrist
Bolero	Jacket to waist, without collar, mostly worn open
Bouffant	Puffed, baggy
Bustle	Pad or frame puffing out top of skirt behind
Dropped waist	Long waist which falls below actual waistline
Fitted bodice	Tight-fitting top
Juliet cap	Fitted cap worn at back of head

Fabric

Batiste	Thin and fine, e.g. cotton or rayon
Brocade	Woven with raised design
Chintz	Cotton, generally glazed
Crêpe	Thin, crinkled cotton, rayon, etc.
Organza	Sheer silk or synthetic fabric
Raw silk	Natural silk
Satin	Smooth glossy, e.g. silk, rayon or nylon
Tulle	Fine netting

The Bride's Figure

Stout and Roundish

For brides with a fuller figure, a simple well-fitted, but not tight dress is important. Particular problem areas can often be hidden by choosing the right style; for example, for a thick waist, a high waisted or A-line dress could be appropriate. For large hips, an A-line skirt is still appropriate with extra detail added elsewhere, for instance at the neck or shoulders. Frills, flounces, puffed sleeves or trimmings, should be avoided. Elegant shoulders may be emphasised.

Thin

To appear more curvaceous, a full but softly gathered skirt and full long sleeves in a gently draping fabric should do the trick. A slender waist may be accentuated by wearing a pretty sash or fitted bodice. Trimmings, crinoline or layers of pretty lace and intricate detail can be effective.

Big-busted

A neckline that draws attention away from the bust should be selected. High necklines and high waistlines that gather under the bust should be avoided. The bride may have to spend some considerable time on her knees in front of the minister who will disapprove of a revealing neckline.

Broad Shouldered

A simple neckline or a wide draping collar creates a diversion.

CHECK LIST	DRESS FITTING
Does the style suit?	
What is the back view like?	
Does the neckline flatter?	
Is there free-movement of arms?	
Is there free-movement of wrists?	
Is it possible to breathe, walk, kneel and eat?	
Will the dress fit if a few pounds are gained or lost before the wedding?	
Are the sleeves the right length?	
Is the hem length correct with shoes?	
Are the seams neat?	
Are the threads fastened neatly?	
Are buttons firmly attached?	
Is the zip straight and unobtrusive?	
Is the dress anti-static?	
Do creases fall out instantly?	
Will it be easy to iron?	
Does it have to be dry-cleaned?	
Is the dress the same in both artificial and daylight?	
Do the accessories, including make-up and jewellery, suit?	
What is the cost?	

Short

It is possible to add to apparent height by choosing a neat style perhaps with a bell skirt and a design with vertical lines of appliqué. A dress with some delicate detail around the neck and shoulders raises the eyes of others to the wearer's upper half. Horizontal lines and horizontal rows of frills should be avoided.

Tall

Trimmings, crinoline or layers can be effective. A dress with a flounced skirt and a simple low neckline lowers the eyes of others. Tall brides should avoid vertical stripes and elaborate headdresses which add further height.

The general principle is to create a diversion — a counter-attraction. Whatever shape or size, a beautiful bride is possible if the choice of dress makes the most of her good features and disguises those of which she is less proud.

The advice of the bride's mother and/or her chief bridesmaid can be of invaluable assistance for a second opinion. Dresses must be tried on and ample time taken to study their effect, their co-ordination with the headdress and shoes (or footwear with a similar heel) to assess their hemline and suitable underwear.

Fit

It is very important to achieve a proper fit, otherwise the dress will not look good.

Fitted styles should be well tailored and fit snugly, but should not be too tight. If the dress pulls out of shape anywhere, this is a sure sign that it needs alteration. The waistline needs to be correct in that it will feel awkward if too high, and will crease round the middle if it is too low. The shoulders should not be too wide, and the armholes should allow room for comfortable movement. A high neck should fit neatly and not push up under the chin; a rounded neckline should not be loose. The key to correctly fitting sleeves is comfort and ease of movement. Long, tightly fitting sleeves are probably not the best choice because they will inevitably restrict arm movements. A long sleeve should fall to the wrist, with any lace or trim extending over the upper part of the hand. A full-length dress should not trail on the floor when worn with shoes, or the skirt will drag on the ground; it should hang beautifully and move with the wearer when she walks.

For a custom-made dress, enough time needs to be allowed for several fittings and for alterations if necessary. An allowance should be made for any gain or loss of weight — usually the latter — before the wedding day.

Trimmings

There are many finishing touches which can transform a simple dress into a stunning one, as well as help to accentuate and disguise features.

Sashes made from any material can be used around the waistline. Fabric, silk or lace flowers can be dotted over the dress, or larger flowers can be used to emphasise a scooped hemline, decorate a sash or add interest to a plain bodice.

Lace can be used in all sorts of ways for inset panels, necklines, sleeves and underskirts or as a fine layer over a different fabric. Net may be layered over the main fabric and embroidery can be used to decorate any part or all of the dress.

Ribbons can be used to highlight embroidery, emphasise the clever shaping of a dress, tie in sashes or bows to decorate a simple hem, neckline or sleeve.

Pin-tucks can give an elegant, Victorian look to a fitted bodice and may also be used in the fabric of the skirt or sleeve.

Frills, flounces and ruffles are very popular in wedding dresses because they make the dress look different from even the most sophisticated evening dress and give a really old-fashioned feminine effect.

Care of the Dress

The dress should be unpacked and hung on a hanger. Any creases should fall out but if it is necessary to iron the fabric, the manufacturer's or the supplier's instructions should be followed.

Preserving the Wedding Dress and Veil

A less formal style of dress may be dyed or altered so that it can be worn again, or it may be sold, loaned to others, or kept for another family wedding. All fabrics suffer deterioration, including discolouration, rust damage, rot and attacks from insects after a period of time. The following ideas are suggestions for keeping the dress at its most beautiful, although it must be stated that results cannot be guaranteed.

The dress may be dry cleaned making sure that no starch or sizing is applied as this will attract damaging bugs. Once cleaned, it should be removed from the plastic bag, detached from the metal hanger and freed of any pins or tape which may have been attached by the cleaner. It should be hung on a padded, unscented hanger which has been wrapped in clean muslin and then left to air thoroughly until there is no longer any smell of cleaning fluid. Any bouffant parts of the dress should be stuffed with acid-free tissue paper so that their shape is maintained. A bag to protect the dress should be made from unbleached cotton muslin, washed several times in hot water. The bagged dress needs to be stored in a clean, dry place. The bag should never be sealed with pins or sticky tape as such fixers may damage the dress fabric.

The best way to clean a veil is to wash it in the bath. It should be removed from the headdress and any tears mended. Again using unbleached cotton muslin which has been washed and well rinsed, the veil should be tacked to a piece of muslin. The bath should be filled to about ten centimetres deep with lukewarm water and a soapless detergent. The veil should be gently rubbed clean using a gentle action of the fingers. It should not be twisted but left in the bath while the soapy water is drained and the bath refilled with lukewarm rinsing water. After about three rinses, the veil should then be allowed to drain. Excess water may be pressed out using a white (or colour matching) towel then lifted out of the bath on to a dry matching towel, covered with another matching towel and as much water pressed out as possible, keeping the towels flat. The veil should then be laid on a dry towel in front of a breezy window out of direct sunlight. When completely dry, it should be rolled with the muslin still attached and covered with acid-free tissue paper and then stored in a bag similar to the one made for the dress. It is possible to have the dress professionally preserved by a specialist firm whereby the gown is treated and then sealed in an airtight container.

Train

Trains are extensions of the fabric at the back of the skirt and are mostly suited to formal dress at formal events.

Traditional trains trail yards behind the bride and are often heavy and bulky. Shorter trains can look equally beautiful and are much more manageable.

Headdress

Choice of headdress ranges from traditional sweeping veils which are longer than the longest train to neat stylish pillbox hats with a hint of netting. A headdress with a detachable veil may be convenient at the reception.

Headdresses can be worn with or without a veil. Purchased headdresses can look superb; materials can include: pearls; diamanté; silk or fresh flowers (to match bride's and bridesmaids' flowers).

The headdress is a very important part of the costume and should be tried on with the dress as well as the chosen hairstyle for the day to create an overall effect. The headdress should complement the style, fabric and colour of the dress, any decorative features that it may have, hairstyle and facial features. When shopping for the headdress, it is helpful to take along a photograph of the dress, to wear the hairstyle planned for the day and a similar top.

Veils

The veil is still the most symbolic part of the bride's wedding attire because of its significance as a face cover until the ceremony. It needs to match the dress style generally; the more formal the dress, the longer the veil but, more importantly, it has to look good, suit the bride and be manageable.

Old lace veils are heavy to wear and are best held in place by a heavy tiara. Today's veils can be of many types and lengths: frothy, lacy and fringing the face, piled high over a head piece. Lengths include to the eye, ear, shoulder, hand, floor and even longer held in place with a traditional tiara. They can be made of many fabrics but generally they are of transparent or semi-transparent material such as lace or tulle. Silk net is expensive but light to wear and easy to hold in place. Nylon net is the least expensive but is slippery and difficult to keep in place.

Tiaras

Tiaras generally complement a formal dress with a full veil. Tiaras, comb clips, Alice bands or circlets can be used to secure certain types of veil. Tiaras with real or paste gems were very popular with the traditional white dress for many years and some brides still make this choice.

Alternatives

Optional headdress includes hats and caps

especially with less traditional wedding attire, in which case a veil is not necessary but some hats and caps do have short veils as part of their design. However large brimmed hats can shade the bride's face in the photographs and can be a nuisance throughout the day. Strictly speaking, if a bride and her attendants wear hats, they should not carry bouquets as well. Prayer books are often carried instead.

Other options include a circlet of flowers or ribbons or ribbons trimmed with flowers which, although perhaps more appropriate for informal weddings, look very effective with a fall of lace. Fresh or silk flowers make attractive headdresses and can be used in many different ways. They usually echo the flowers of the bride's bouquet.

A real flower headdress could be delivered along with other flowers on the morning of the wedding. Fabric flowers are available from bridal shops and department stores.

To economise, a headdress could be borrowed and adapted to suit or specially made. A simple wreath or cap with the veiling attached or a white hat with flowers, bows, lace and pearls attached would be relatively easy to create. It is possible to purchase headdresses second-hand. The bride and attendants could, of course, choose to wear just a few flowers in their hair.

Footwear

Shoes should be bought, dyed or covered to match the dress in colour and fabric. Raw silk or synthetic materials are popular. The bride should remember that shoes will be worn for most of the day when she will be standing and dancing so footwear that is comfortable and of a sensible and practical heel height is obviously essential.

Non-slip soles are a good idea but if the chosen shoes happen to be smooth soled, they can be scratched to obtain a satisfactory rough, scored surface. It is important to try on the shoes when shopping for the dress and to practise walking about to ensure comfort and to make sure the shoes do not slip. The price sticker may be a source of interest if not removed from the base!

To economise, it would be wise to purchase a pair of shoes that can be worn later as dress shoes, or perhaps dyed to match other garments. Off-season sales can save money.

Underwear

As with other accessories, lingerie should be purchased after the dress has been chosen. The colour of underwear must be chosen with great care to avoid any shadows showing through the dress. It is for this reason that white or soft pastel colours are good choices. It is wise to experiment with the style of bra and slip so that there is no danger of riding up or coming undone and to ensure that the dress is set off to the best advantage from the front, back, sides and shoulders angles. The bra should not be seen through the dress and the straps should also remain invisible. If special underwear such as a crinoline petticoat is necessary, this can be hired or borrowed.

Hosiery

The best advice concerning the choice between tights and stockings is to wear what is most comfortable. They should be sheer and either completely transparent or the same colour as the dress. If the dress is white, ultra-pale hosiery is complementary. Buying two pairs will make life more convenient if there is an accident. It is traditional, though optional for the bride to wear a garter.

. . . .
: **SUPERSTITION** :
: *Wearing a garter is believed to bring good* :
: *luck.* :
. . . .

Accessories

Accessories should complement the mood and style of dress and of the wedding in general. It is important to keep the dress in mind and if possible try on all accessories with the dress to obtain the overall effect.

...*Jewellery*...

Jewellery should be simple so that onlookers' attention is not distracted

INFILL LIST			BRIDE'S ATTIRE
Wedding			
Dress supplier			
Address			
Telephone			
Dates for fittings		Dates for alterations	
Date last hired			
Date for collection		Date for return if hired	
Will it be cleaned?			
Responsibility for cleaning			
Dress	Colour		£
	Style and measurements		
	Neckline	Bodice	
	Sleeves	Skirt	
	Hemline	Train	
	Fabric	Trimmings	
Headdress			
Footwear			
Underwear			
Accessories	Gloves	Handbag	
Jewellery			
Something	Old	New	
	Borrowed	Blue	
Garter and extra garter for tossing			
Payment details	Deposit due date Balance due date		
Cancellation policy			
Insurance for damage during hire period			
Make-up		Perfume	
Going-away	Outfit	Accessories	
Payment details			

from the dress. A simple locket, gold chain or a strand of pearls are the most popular neckline jewellery. Generally the bride does not wear a watch on her wedding day; the time being the last thing on her mind. Earrings should be tried on with the dress, the chosen hairstyle and head-dress, and need to be of a flattering size in proportion to suit the face and other accessories and should be in keeping with the style of the dress. If the engagement ring is transferred to the right hand early in the day, there is less to remember at the ceremony. However, if the engagement ring locks into the wedding band, the groom will need this in advance to pass on to the best man.

Gloves

There is no need to wear gloves unless the wedding is very formal and they are never worn with long sleeved dresses. Fingerless gloves or those with the ring finger split will remove the necessity to take off the whole glove at the ceremony.

Handbag

Handbags are used for carrying essential personal items such as make-up, comb, tissues, safety pins and perfume and should match the dress, but as it will probably be concealed on the day, it may be preferable to choose a bag to match the going-away outfit. The chief bridesmaid is usually placed in charge of the bride's handbag on the day.

As an alternative or in addition to carrying flowers, some brides carry white prayer books, bibles, parasols, fans, pomanders, Dorothy bags with draw strings or other things, but the bouquet is usually enough to handle on its own.

It may be an idea to have a pretty umbrella to hand and hope to leave it in the car! Chauffeurs and photographers will sometimes carry large white umbrellas.

Perfume

Wearing a new perfume on the day of the wedding will ensure that when it is worn again, memories come flooding back. It would however, be advisable to try it out first to check for the smell it produces on the skin and for allergy.

Shawl

For winter weddings it may be an idea to wear a warm but lacy shawl which will not spoil the visual effect of the dress.

Going-Away Outfit and Trousseau

The going-away outfit is worn when the bride changes out of her wedding dress in order to leave the reception. It can be anything the bride desires but a wise choice would be something special that is suitable for her honeymoon and can be worn again afterwards, for example suits, casual outfits and dresses are popular. Fabric which is easily crushed will be unsuitable when travelling long distances.

> **TRADITION**
> *The trousseau dates from the days when a bride took with her enough clothing and household linen to last at least a year.*

Nowadays, the trousseau is not necessary, however many brides like to start a 'bottom drawer' for which they buy and accumulate items for their new home.

It is desirable to invest in some new clothes, especially if going away on honeymoon but it is prudent not to be too extravagant with those items that will not get much wear at some future date. Subsequent lifestyle should be a consideration and how the new clothes will be useful in addition to the existing wardrobe.

Mothers

Traditionally the bride's mother dresses for the season; a formal suit or dress-and-coat with a hat for the cooler seasons; a lightweight suit or dress and light hat for a summer wedding. Gloves normally form part of her accessories.

Many mothers buy or make a special outfit which should be comfortable, practical and smart. Popular choices for less formal weddings include the classic combination of a smart suit and hat but a beautiful dress or skirt with an attractive blouse without a hat is perfectly acceptable. A formal evening wedding may favour a floor-length or cocktail-style dress. For semi-formal day-time, ankle-length might be preferable.

The two mothers should consult closely with the couple concerning style and colour choices so that the wedding party's attire tones into an overall scheme that is visually pleasing and complementary. While their outfits should never be the same, they could dress similarly and complement the overall style of the wedding party. The formality of the wedding and personal preference will determine dress length. The mothers will obviously want to look their best, though they must ensure that they do not try to upstage the bride.

Adult Male Members of the Wedding Party

Once the formality of the wedding is set and the bride has decided on the type of dress she will wear, the groom should choose something complementary. The adult male members of the wedding party, i.e. the groom, best man, ushers and fathers of the bride and groom should all dress alike. The wedding party may all wear exactly the same but the groom may elect to be slightly different in some way.

The groom should consult with the principal men and advise them to choose something which looks compatible with his choice and does not in any way outshine him. If the best man wears brown or maroon when everyone else is in grey, he will be the one who stands out rather than the groom which would be very impolite and the photographs will look extremely odd. When choosing a lounge suit, even though there will be a range of styles and colours, the best man should take his cue from the groom. It can be wise for the groom and best man to shop together; they can each provide a useful second opinion. If a member of the wedding party rushes out to buy a suit without consulting, there could be a big disappointment if he is asked to wear something else. The best man generally buys his own attire if it is not hired so it is wise to choose something that can be worn again after the wedding.

The groom should select his suit first, so that others can take their cue from him. The colour of the suits and accessories should match the rest of the wedding party. If the bridesmaids are wearing peach, for example, the men's attire should be complementary. The men in the wedding party will be aware of the style of wedding from discussions initiated by the bride and groom.

For most weddings there are two main options, either morning dress or lounge suits. If the wedding is very formal, and if morning suits are not already owned, they are usually hired. They are very expensive to buy and this is only economical if the men attend formal occasions on a regular basis. The internet has a wealth of information. Search for bridal suits under which there are hundreds of websites to visit.

For a less formal wedding, the principal men may choose two- or three-piece lounge suits. It is important to feel comfortable and to look and feel good in a suit that fits. Trousers must be the right length, and time must be allowed for alterations to be carried out if necessary.

Morning Suit, Top Hat and Gloves

For most very formal weddings, the men in the wedding party wear formal attire which complements a bride in white. This is usually morning dress together with silk top hat, gloves and waistcoat. A traditional morning suit is a black or grey three-piece with a tail coat, or a black tail coat with pinstripe trousers, white collar and grey tie. As a general rule, dark colours are worn for winter and afternoon weddings, lighter colours for summer and morning weddings. However, morning suits are available in a range of colours and if the bride decides to allow a free choice, she will probably expect the colour to be grey, so it would be wise to consult her and the groom. Accessories such as the waistcoat, cummerbund (waist sash), tie, handkerchief and buttonhole can be co-ordinated with the bride's and bridesmaid's colours.

The hat is removed when entering the church and is carried by the brim together with the gloves in the left hand, leaving the right one free for shaking hands. When the groom approaches the chancel steps, he leaves his hat and gloves in the pew. Although the hat and gloves will be carried for most of the

		Jacket	Trousers	Waistcoat	Shirt	Tie	Top Hat	Gloves	Shoes	Socks
Formal	Day	Traditional	Morning coat or tails. Black or grey	Morning-striped	Grey	Wing-collar Double-cuffs. White	Cravat-silk-grey	Grey	Yes	Black	Black
		Modern			Patterned	Turn-down collar. White	Tie-silk-grey/navy				
	Evening	Traditional	Tails		Matching bow tie	Wing collar Double-cuffs. White	Bow tie matching waistcoat	Black	Yes		
		Modern	Dinner black	Black		Wing collar	Bow tie				
Semi-formal	Day		Lounge black or grey	Morning-striped	Grey	Soft collar. White	Patterned				
	Evening		Dinner with silk facing	Black	Cummerbund	Dress	Bow tie				
Informal	Day/Evening		Suit								

INFILL LIST	ATTIRE	GROOM, BEST MAN, FATHERS, USHERS					
	Groom	Best Man	Bride's Father	Groom's Father	Ushers 1	2	3	£
Supplier								
Address								
Telephone								
Dress rehearsal date								
Dates for fittings								
Dates for alterations								
Date for collection								
Date for return								
To be returned by whom								
Colours								
Style								
Jacket size								
Trouser size								
Waistcoat size								
Cummerbunds								
Shirt size								
Shirt studs								
Cuff links								
Tie/Cravat								
Gloves size								
Top hat size								
Shoes colour								
Shoes size								
Socks								
Underwear								
Handkerchief								

time and will only be worn for the photographs, they are an essential part of the morning dress. They should be with the men at all times and not left idle, misplaced or lost!

The shirt is usually white and can be plain collared with a normal tie, dress tie, or one with a high winged collar worn with a cravat. Shoes and socks are generally black. A tie or cravat can be chosen to match the outfits, but should never be black. The bride may want a colour to complement the bridesmaids' dresses and the flowers for which she will make available a fabric sample or a colour match. It is very difficult to

INFILL LIST	ATTIRE		GROOM, BEST MAN, FATHERS, USHERS					
	Groom	Best Man	Bride's Father	Groom's Father	Ushers			£
					1	2	3	
Jewellery								
Tie pin								
Watch chain								
Cufflinks								
Suit alteration costs								
Deposit								
Date due								
Balance								
Date due								
Refund policy								
Going-away outfit								

remember a colour sufficiently well to match it, especially under the artificial lights of a shop.

Some people will buy morning suits but unless it is common practice to attend formal occasions on a regular basis, this can be a waste of money since quality formal wear is very expensive. It is for this reason that most people hire morning suits. A reputable firm should be chosen and visited well in advance and a firm booking made as soon as possible. It is wise for the wedding party men to visit together so that they may all be fitted and can select suitable ties or cravats, at the same time.

If hiring a morning suit, it is as well to remember that the proper fit is more important than the price. A deposit will be necessary and dates and times need to be arranged for collection, final payment and return. The best man may be expected to collect both his and the groom's suits and will almost certainly be responsible for returning them both as the groom will be on his honeymoon.

Lounge Suit

Although less formal, lounge suits are a very popular choice and may be worn again after the wedding. The shirt should be white and the tie, in the case of the groom, should be pale blue or grey with little or no pattern. Loud ties, while fun, are mostly thought inappropriate.

Many brides prefer a less formal approach to their wedding, where the men in the wedding party wear lounge suits. If the men are not accustomed to wearing formal dress, then this is probably the preferred option. Shoes and socks should match the suit. No hat is worn with a lounge suit.

As for formal attire, it is important to check on the bride's choice of colour scheme for the bridesmaids and flowers, since if she is wearing a cream dress with bridesmaids in cream and rust, the groom and best man may look better in brown suits rather than blue. It should be remembered too that the occasion will be one of celebration so there is no need to be over-traditional. A bright tie (but never black) and handkerchief may add a welcome splash of colour.

Smart lounge suits are also very suitable for the register office wedding as morning attire may look out of place. A lounge suit would be appropriate for the marriage of a widower or for those marrying for a second time.

Dress Rehearsal

A quick dress rehearsal for the groom and best man a week or so before the wedding (or as far in advance as possible if hired) will provide a final check that nothing is forgotten. New shirts should be unpacked and ironed, price tags removed from shoe soles, and everything should feel and look good together.

Maid/Matron of Honour

As the sole attendant to the bride, the maid or matron of honour wears something extra special.

Bridesmaids

Dress

As with the bride's dress, the same options for acquiring attire apply to bridesmaids' dresses in that they may be made, bought or hired. The bride need not restrict herself to the specialist bridal shops; if she is looking for something different, there are many boutiques and department stores. If the bridesmaids' costumes are chosen at roughly the same time as the bride's wedding dress, there should be enough time to allow for their design, ordering, fitting and alterations.

If the dresses are very expensive or cannot be worn again, the bride or her mother should offer to pay for them. Ideally, the chief bridesmaid's dress should distinguish her from other bridesmaids, for example, a difference in colour or style or, if this is not possible, a different bouquet.

Although bridesmaids should dress in accordance with the wishes of the bride, they should be allowed an element of choice so that they feel happy and comfortable. After all, they will be expected to wear their dresses and headdresses all day and perhaps all evening.

The bridesmaids' dresses need to complement the bride's attire both in style and colour and should suit the girls themselves. They may wear similar dresses differing slightly in style but all in the same colour, or they may have dresses of different colours. The basic colour scheme should complement the bride's dress, accessories and flowers. Pastels are the traditional colours and most people prefer these or subtle shades; anything too strident will not set off the bride's dress and will look odd in the photographs.

- -
SUPERSTITION
Green is considered to be unlucky.
- -

Styles need to suit ages, colourings, shapes and the personal preferences of the bridesmaids themselves. Many off-the-peg bridal gowns have co-ordinating dresses available to complement them. Dresses need not be plain, they can be print for example, check, striped, spotted, floral or a mixture of fabrics. If the bridesmaids are very different in colouring or age, it may be necessary to be more flexible in approach. A six-year-old will not look her best in the same dress worn by a twenty-year-old, similarly a blonde may not look as good in the same colour as a redhead or a brun-ette. Even if the older bridesmaids have floor-length dresses, it is inadvisable for the younger bridesmaids to wear hems of this length since they will find them awkward and uncomfortable to wear and have an uncanny habit of tripping up!

It is important to maintain the general style and to use similar features in perhaps quite individual dresses to make them complement one another. For example, the older bridesmaids might be wearing satin dresses with fitted bodices, full elbow-length sleeves and full long skirts trimmed with lace. The child's dress in the same fabric can still be trimmed with lace and have a full sleeve, but the sleeves can be slightly shorter and the skirt length shortened to mid-calf.

There is no shortage of styles from which to choose, ranging from elegant formal satin and lace and extravagant frills and lace to peasant-style with broderie anglaise.

The girls may be brought together at one time to select or try on the dresses. If the dresses have to be chosen for them, it is thoughtful to send them a picture so that they feel more involved in the wedding plans.

INFILL LIST	Chief Bridesmaid	Bridesmaids			Page Boys			£
		1	2	3	1	2	3	
Name								
Dress supplier								
Address								
Telephone								
Dates for fitting								
Dates for alterations								
Date for collection								
Date for return (hired)								
To be returned by								
Dress – colour								
Style/measurements								
Neckline								
Bodice								
Sleeves								
Skirt								
Hemline								
Fabric								
Trimmings								
Headdress								
Footwear								
Underwear								
Accessories								
Gloves								
Handbag								
Jewellery								
Make-up								
Perfume								
Deposit								
Date due								
Balance								
Date due								

ATTENDANTS' ATTIRE

Headdress

As with the bride's attire, headdresses should complement dresses.

Accessories

Again these need to complement the style of the bride and the bridesmaids. The bride should find out their preferences and how they like to wear their hair for example.

Bridesmaids' shoes could be sandals, court shoes or satin slippers and footwear for younger bridesmaids could be pale party shoes or ballet slippers. Again, shoes should complement or match the dresses in fabric and colour and need to have non-slip soles. Allowing the bridesmaids to choose their own shoes, given the colour and style, ensures a comfortable fit.

Neutral or cream shades for hosiery are popular. Jewellery should be minimal and simple.

It is usual for the bridesmaids to be allowed to keep their dresses and accessories after the wedding regardless of the purchaser.

Flower Girl

A flower girl is a very young girl whose role could be purely decorative in that she will add some visual advantage to the attendants or she could precede the bride down the aisle scattering flower petals or confetti (if the minister allows). The flower girl's outfit should be distinct from those of the bridesmaids. Her dress could be of the same fabric but a different style or she could wear a completely different dress or a miniature version of the bride's if the style is appropriate for a three to eight year old.

Page Boys

Ideas for page boy's attire include: velvet jackets and grey trousers with bow tie; morning suit with top hat; velvet knickerbocker suit; formal suit with waistcoat and striped trousers; Scottish outfit including kilt and sporran; and sailor suit.

14

Transport

*A*t one time couples walked to the church together and then on to the
reception. Earlier this century when few people owned vehicles, the
ushers were responsible for organising transport for all guests. Today,
it is only members of the wedding party who arrive at the church in
grand hired transport.

Responsibility

It is a tradition for the bride's parents to pay for transport and consequently they are responsible for its organisation but if both the bride's and groom's parents are sharing the costs of the wedding, very often the groom's parents will pay for the cars and the bride's mother will make the arrangements. In either case, the groom should pay for himself and his best man's transport to the church and his and the bride's transport to and from the reception.

There are no strict rules concerning responsibility for transport except to emphasise that everyone must be transported safely and that no one should be left stranded.

Bride and her Family

The bride and her family usually organise the following transport:

To church	Bride and giver-away
	Bride's mother, bridesmaids, flower girl and pages
To reception	Bride and groom
	Bride's parents Bridesmaids, flower girl and pages
From reception	Bride's parents

A church wedding will require transport for the bridal party from home to the ceremony. One car may be adequate but two would make life easier. Traditionally the bridesmaids occupy the second car and the bride's mother and immediate family ride in the third but very often today the bridesmaids travel with the bride's mother in the second car. To economise further, the best man could drive the groom to the ceremony and the hired car used by the bride and her father to the ceremony could be used to take the bride and groom to the reception. A relative could drive the bride's mother and bridesmaids or the bridesmaids could travel with the bride and her father.

When booking venues for the ceremony and reception, it is worth considering how far guests will have to travel and the distance that the bride and groom have to travel after the reception.

To Church

The bride's mother, bridesmaids and pages are first to depart from the house, leaving the bride and her father to follow later. The bride's mother needs to get to the church in good time, whereas the bride should arrive unhurriedly, just as the ceremony is due to start.

To Reception

After the ceremony the bride and groom should leave first in the wedding car, followed by the best man (if he is to greet guests at the reception and if ushers have been delegated the responsibility of seeing that everyone has transport from the church), the bridesmaids, flower girl and pages and then the rest of the wedding party, i.e. the parents of the bride and groom.

Best Man

The best man is usually responsible for organising the following transport:

To Church	Groom and best man
To Reception	Best man, guests (and ushers if necessary)
From Reception	Bride and groom Best man

To Church

The groom's request to the best man is to 'Get me to the church on time!' and is one of the most important duties that he will perform on the wedding day. The ideal arrival time at the church is half an hour before the ceremony is due to start. If the groom's hire car fails to show at the appointed time or his chosen transport refuses the trip, the best man must be prepared to provide or organise transport immediately.

If the best man is responsible for hiring any cars, he should do this well in advance and double check the arrangements a day or so before the wedding. He will also need to know when the car is being delivered or whether it should be collected, the deadlines imposed and the charges to be paid.

If the best man is to use his own car, he should ensure beforehand that it has been serviced and is in good working order by checking levels of oil, water and petrol the day before the wedding. In order to be suitably prepared and as sure as possible about the timetable, he should do a couple of test runs before the day, at the right time and on the relevant day of the week to check timing. Traffic con-

ditions and anything unusual, for instance roadworks and special events such as a carnival, will need checking. He will also need to check parking arrangements at the church and reception venues. If this proves to be insufficient, he should explore nearby facilities and inform the bride's mother so that she may alert guests in advance.

Although not an essential duty of the best man, it is helpful if he checks with the bride or her mother to establish whether anyone will need a lift to the church, the reception and home so that he may arrange this by approaching members of both sides who have transport. Most guests will make their own arrangements but if the best man is sure of their intentions beforehand, then last-minute hassles may be avoided. Out-of-town guests should not be left stranded. Transport should be arranged so that they can get to the church, the reception and back to their accommodation.

To Reception

The best man is sometimes responsible for transporting the couple, the bridesmaids and pages to the reception but it is more useful for the bride's mother to arrange additional wedding cars for the wedding party as it is probably easier for her to make these arrangements.

The best man and ushers are usually expected to play a major role in ensuring that all guests have transport from the church to the reception but it is quite acceptable to ask friends to help out here. If the best man is expected to take any of the wedding party to the reception, the bride should inform him in advance so that he may make the necessary arrangements beforehand. He may arrange for the ushers to act as chauffeurs or ask guests with room in their cars to give lifts to other guests.

From Reception

The best man should ensure that the going-away transport is safely parked and available after the reception. If the bride and groom leave for their honeymoon in a hired car or taxi, the best man should ensure that it is booked a

INFILL/CHECK LIST					
Venues	Ceremony				
	Supplier		Address		
Booked					
Emergency					
		Organiser		Car booked	Chauffeur booked
		Bride	Best man		
To church Bride and giver-away Bride's mother, bridesmaids, flower girl, page boys Groom's parents Ushers Groom and best man Guests					

To reception
 	
Bride and groom
Bridesmaids, flower girl,
  page boys
Parents:
  Bride's
  Groom's
Ushers
Best Man
Guests					

From reception
 	
Bride and groom
Bridesmaids, flower girl, page boys
Parents:
  Bride's
  Groom's
Ushers
Best man
Guests					

Cost £					
Date deposit due					
Date balance due					
Refund policy					

		TRANSPORT
Reception		
Telephone	Notes	
Pick-up times	Pick-up location	Insurance

couple of weeks before the wedding and that this is confirmed nearer the time. If the groom will be using his own car, it is the best man's responsibility to ensure that it is safely parked at the reception venue and filled with petrol. Luggage can be left in the boot the day before or taken to the reception venue and loaded at the last minute. The bride and groom should inform the best man of the time they intend to leave the reception so that he may have the car ready at the main entrance at the right moment.

The best man will probably organise the decoration of the going-away car and it is his responsibility to ensure that no damage results. Traditional decorations are 'Just Married' notices, confetti, balloons, old tin cans, old boots/shoes. More recent wording for notices includes, 'It's Legal', 'Off to get a Little Sun and Air'.

```
········································
:  TRADITION AND SUPERSTITION  :
· At one time, boots and shoes were thrown ·
·  at the newly-weds! A pair of the bride's ·
·   shoes, given to the groom by the bride's ·
·  father, was said to represent the transfer ·
:  of responsibility from father to son-in-law. :
········································
```

Hire Firms

Most brides like a special vehicle for their wedding day and some may choose anything from a horse-drawn carriage to a hot-air balloon. Usually people hire one special car to take the bride and her father to the ceremony, and later the bride and groom to the reception. In most cases, these cars are chauffeur-driven. Popular choices for hired transport include: Rolls Royce, Daimler; Limousine; Jaguar; Mercedes; Bentley; Rover; vintage; horse-drawn carriage with coachman; pony and trap. White is the most popular car colour but the bride's white dress looks more outstanding against a dark colour. More unusual transport choices include helicopter, London taxi or bus, hot-air balloon; or other smart prestigious modes of transport all of which are likely to be more expensive than the more traditional alternatives. Some choices are obviously expensive but to

have something a little unusual does add a little flair to the day. A hired car will have the traditional white ribbons but it may be necessary to decorate the cars for the bridesmaids and others in the wedding party.

Transport needs to be booked as early as possible. It is important that quotations are obtained from reputable firms (preferably local ones) and that details of the chosen supplier are confirmed in writing: date; times; venues; full cost; deposit required; the type of car(s) that the hire company will provide; the substitute car(s) should anything go wrong; whether a chauffeur is provided and if so whether he will be in uniform; insurance cover; and whether there are any extra charges. Reputable firms usually offer packages which make everything quite clear.

If hire cars are beyond the budget limitations, it may be possible to economise by borrowing a smart car from a relation or friend. It does not have to be white or black, as silver, scarlet, maroon or something to complement the overall colour scheme can look classy and unusual, particularly if decorated with wedding ribbons and a few flowers (either fresh, dried or silk) in the back window. To economise on the number of cars hired, the ushers should be responsible for chauffeuring the bridesmaids and pages with friends (and perhaps relatives) providing transport for others who do not have their own. If people are recruited to help out, it is important that everyone is clear as to whom they are to transport or who is to transport them and that transport providers and drivers are at least reimbursed any costs incurred. Regardless of arrangements, it is sensible to have a few reserve cars on stand-by in case of emergencies.

```
·····································
:           OLD SONG            :
·          Daisy, Daisy,           ·
·     Give me your answer, do!      ·
·          I'm half crazy,          ·
·       All for the love of you.     ·
·  It won't be a stylish marriage   ·
·      I can't afford a carriage    ·
·       But you'll look sweet       ·
·          Upon the seat           ·
·    Of a bicycle made for two.     ·
·····································
```

15

Flowers

*F*lowers have formed a part of marriage ceremonies since at least Roman times and even today a wedding would be incomplete without the presence of flowers of some kind. Wedding flowers complete and complement the bride's outfit and provide attractive displays both at the church and the reception. Flowers should reflect the tone and mood, suit the surroundings and may be elaborate or simple according to preference and suitability. For instance, very large formal elaborate arrangements may be inappropriate for a small reception room or country church. When the wedding attire and accessories have been chosen, decisions need to be made about the floral arrangements.

Flower Types

The type of wedding, the number of wedding party members and guests and the colour scheme will determine the style and number of flowers needed. Decisions need to be made about the type of arrangements, for example, bouquets, buttonholes, corsages and flowers for the church and reception venues. Ideas of the type of arrangements available may be sought from bridal magazines, florists' catalogues and books from which preferences should be noted, for example, large-headed flowers, small simple flowers or elaborate arrangements. The florist should be informed of particular requests and be able to give expert advice on final choice, the availability of particular flowers, their cost, how long they last and how well they mix with other flowers and greenery. Fresh flowers are popular but do not last long and wild ones tend to wilt very quickly. Alternatives include dried and silk imitation flowers.

TRADITION AND SUPERSTITION
Carrying flowers is obviously decorative but the tradition may be connected to the belief that a bouquet of strong smelling herbs from the onion family, such as garlic or chives, would ward off and drive away evil spirits. At Anglo-Saxon ceremonies, the bride and groom wore garlands and in the Middle Ages, these were entwined with ears of wheat, symbolising fertility.

Seasonal Flowers and Shrubs

Some seasonal flowers may be obtained at other times but they will be expensive. Some flowers are available all year round. Listings to follow marked with an asterisk have a symbolism which is explained in 'Language of Flowers'.

Style and Colour

The flowers can be limited in colour range or may be a bright, colourful pot pourri. However, they do need to suit attire and surroundings, blending

Seasonal Flowers and Shrubs

Spring	Summer	Autumn	Winter
Apple Blossom*	Aster	Chrysanthemum*	Carnation*
Azalea	Azalea	Dahlia	Chrysanthemum*
Bluebell	Carnation*	Daisy*	Forsythia
Broom	Chrysanthemum*	Freesia	Freesia
Camellia*	Cornflower	Gladioli	Gentian
Carnation*	Daisy*	Gypsophila	Gypsophila
Cherry Blossom	Delphinium	Hydrangea*	Iris*
Chrysanthemum*	Freesia	Iris*	Lily*
Clematis	Fuchsia	Lily*	Orchid
Daffodil*	Gladioli	Morning Glory	Rose*
Daisy*	Heather	Orchid	Snowdrop*
Forsythia	Hollyhock	Rose*	Stephanotis
Freesia	Iris*		Winter Jasmine
Gladioli	Jasmine*		
Honeysuckle*	Lilac*		
Iris*	Lily*		
Jasmine*	Lily-of-the-Valley*		
Lilac*	Lupin		
Lily*	Marigold*		
Mimosa*	Orchid		
Orchid	Peony		
Polyanthus	Rhododendron	**Foliage**	
Rhododendron	Rose*	Popular choices include:	
Stephanotis	Stock	Asparagus Fern*	
Tulip*	Sweet Pea*	Bracken	
	Sweet William	Ivy*	
	Tiger Lily	Lily-of-the-Valley leaves*	

together tastefully with the complexions and hair colours of the bride and bridesmaids. They should reflect the mood of the occasion and, most important of all, the bride's personality.

Red, orange and yellow are warm, vibrant colours which attract attention. In contrast, blues and purples are cool colours and create the feeling of a more restrained atmosphere. The colours in any arrangement, whether carried or displayed, should harmonise and look attractive together. Colours which are too similar to each other will be lacking in effect, whereas opposites may be too stringent. The strength of colour is also important. A strong, dark colour will overpower a pastel, for example. Various colour combinations should be tried out until harmony is achieved.

Bouquets

Bouquets are traditionally carried by the bride who wears a veil.

The bride's bouquet can be white, or colours which blend with the colours of the dresses of the bride and bridesmaids. Until relatively recent times, it was customary to have only white flowers – carnations, orchids, lilies and roses – for weddings. When considering colour, a point to remember is that a white bouquet may not match a white wedding gown as not all whites are the same shade.

If the bride is wearing a colour other than white, a sample of dress fabric or colour match will help the florist with the colour scheme.

Sizes and shapes range from small round designs to long trailing ones. Styles include cascading posy, hand-tied and single blooms. A fairly large bouquet would suit a long formal dress with a sweeping train whereas a neat posy, simple bunch or even a single bloom would complement a shorter and more informal dress.

LANGUAGE OF FLOWERS		
Flowers generally	Purple	The blood of Christ
	White	Innocence
Almond Blossom		Hope
Apple Blossom		Good Fortune
Asphodel		My regrets follow you to the grave
Barberry		Ill temper
Burdock		Touch me not
Camellia		Gratitude/Perfect loveliness
Carnation		Fascination, love
Chrysanthemum	Red	I love you/Sharing
	White	Truth
Columbine	Red	Anxious and trembling
Cyclamen		Excessive modesty, shyness
Daffodil		Regard
Daisy		Innocence
Fern		Fascination, sincerity
Forget-me-not		True love, remembrance
Gardenia		Joy
Heather		Luck
Heliotrope		Devotion, faithfulness
Hellebore		Scandal
Honeysuckle		Generosity/Devotion
Hyacinth	White	Loveliness
Hydrangea		Boastfulness
Iris		Flame/Burning love
Ivy		Good luck, eternal fidelity, marriage
Ivy Geranium		Bridal flower
Japonica	White	Loveliness
Jasmin		Amiability/Grace
King Cup		I wish I were rich

A fresh flower bouquet should be freshly made but if dampened, covered with moist tissue and kept cool (not in the refrigerator), it will remain good for many hours. Silk or dried flowers are ideal for the bride who wants her flowers to last indefinitely and for those who suffer with hay fever. They come in a wide variety of colours.

Some brides like to include flowers which are symbolic of hidden messages as in the 'Language of Flowers'. Orange blossom has the closest and longest association with weddings.

Language of Flowers		
Larkspur		Fickleness
Lemon Blossom		Fidelity in love
Lilac	White	Youthful innocence
Lily		Majesty/purity
	Pink	Talent
	White	Purity, modesty
Lily-of-the-valley		Happiness, return of happiness
Magnolia		Perseverance
Maidenhair		Discretion
Marigold		Grief, chagrin
Meadow Saffron		My best days are past
Mimosa		Sensitivity
Myrtle		Love
Narcissus		Egotism
Orange Blossom		Chastity, fertility, virginity, happiness. The bride's purity equals her loveliness, everlasting love for each other
Orchid		Beauty
Peach Blossom		Captive
Pink		Boldness
Rose		Love, beauty, happiness
	Red	I love you
	White	I am worthy of you
Snowdrop		Hope
Sweetpea		Pleasure, delicate pleasures
Tulip	Variegated	Beautiful eyes
	Red	Love
	Yellow	Hopeless love
Veronica		Fidelity
Violet		Faithfulness

To economise, the bride should carry a single bloom and the attendants could do the same. Other alternatives include carrying a nosegay, small bouquet or a basket of flowers rather than a large cascading bouquet. A single flower attached to a prayer book is simple, yet effective and inexpensive. Choosing popular flowers in season can also save money. If there is sufficient time, flowers can be home grown and arranged by the bride.

The bride may want to wear a corsage as part of her going-away attire and the groom may like a matching buttonhole in which case these can be included in the bride's bouquet and removed just before it is tossed.

Throwing the Bouquet

Preserving the Bouquet

The bride will need to remember to keep a few flowers from the bouquet before it is thrown if she wants to press them as a keepsake. On the other hand, if the bride decides that she would rather keep her bouquet, it is possible to have a collage made from the flowers which represents the arrangements of the wedding bouquet. Fresh flowers soon lose their bloom and perfume but it is possible to preserve them by making a collage from dried blooms. To dry flowers, they should be placed in a box full of silica gel crystals and left until all the moisture has been absorbed by the crystals or they may be tied in bunches and hung upside down in a cool dry place for about a month. To make a flat picture, the flowers are laid flat and apart on a sheet of absorbent paper, covered with more absorbent paper, a heavy object placed on top and left to press in a cool dry room. After two months the flowers may be rearranged on backing and placed in a frame with glass.

Another option is to have a replica made from silk flowers. The local florist will be able to clarify and expand upon the procedures involved.

Alternatives to Bouquets

Alternatives to bouquets include: white prayer books; bibles; parasols; fans; pomanders; Dorothy bags with draw strings.

Posies

The bridesmaids traditionally carry posies which often complement the colours in their dresses or the colour and style of the bride's bouquet. They may also wear a floral wreath or hair comb. Again colour matching is important. If the bridesmaids are very young, they will be bored holding a bouquet; a basket is less of a burden and will look charming.

Headdresses

The florist should be able to create a design to complement bouquets. However, fresh flowers suffer as a result of hairstyling and also run the risk of wilting in the heat of the day.

Flower Arrangements

Flower arrangements for the church or register office/room and the reception can be the crowning glory of the occasion; they often complement the bridesmaids' dresses. For a pleasing show, floral arrangements need to reflect the scale and formality of the event. A formal wedding in a large church followed by a grand reception in a hall or marquee with over a hundred guests requires a number of elaborate displays. An informal event in a register office/room with a small reception requires fewer and much simpler displays.

Infill List								
Florist								
Address								
Telephone								
Period of notice required by florist								
Ceremony venue								
Permission obtained for personal flowers								
Restrictions								
General style of flowers								
Particular favourites								
Seasonal/All year								
	Colour	Style/ shape	Flowers	No.	Delivery/ collection	Delivery/ collection. Date & time	£	Payer
Bouquets Bride Extra for tossing								
Posies Chief Bridesmaid Bridesmaid Bridesmaid Bridesmaid								
Basket Flower Girl								
Flowers (Headdress) Bride Chief Bridesmaid Bridesmaid Bridesmaid Bridesmaid Flower Girl								

THE FLORIST								

	Colour	Style/ shape	Flowers	No.	Delivery/ collection	Delivery/ collection. Date & time	£	Payer
Buttonholes Principal men: Groom Best Man Usher Usher Usher Father Father								
Corsages Mother Mother								
Flower arrangements Church: Altar Aisles — pew ends Windows Register Office Marriage Room								
Reception: Receiving line Top table Side tables Cake table Cake Beverage table Changing room								
Gifts Bride's mother Groom's mother Package details								

The bride may want several arrangements of flowers for the church but some ministers have restrictions especially if there are several weddings on the same day. In addition to the main church decorations (behind the altar, on window sills and on the pulpit), it may also be possible to decorate pew-ends with posies. There may be volunteer flower arrangers who will decorate the church for which a small donation may be appropriate. If those who normally decorate the church are buying and arranging the flowers, the bride or her mother should offer to pay for this service. If the couple are given permission to arrange their own flowers, they should agree with the minister an appropriate time for delivery and flower arranging. Many register offices and marriage rooms are decorated with fresh flowers at all times.

For the reception, decorations, table settings and flowers create a mood so they should tone in with the wedding style and be appropriate for the scale of event. They can range from elaborate to simple depending on taste and budget. Generally, establishments which specifically cater for weddings may offer flower decorations as part of the wedding package but will usually permit the bride's own arrangements if this is her preference. It is usual to have a floral centrepiece for the top table but this should not block the view of the guests. The cake table and the dinner or buffet table usually have arrangements but if the budget is restricted, attractive pots of flowering plants or candles decorated with flowers and greenery, look effective. The cake may need to be topped or surrounded by fresh flowers of some kind.

To economise, it could be an idea to decorate the ceremony and reception venues with potted plants and flowers that can be used later to adorn the new home. Artificial flowers such as silk could be cheaper. A single flower bud in a vase as centrepieces for reception tables is effective. Although flowers add atmosphere they need not overpower the setting; a few well chosen arrangements can create the perfect effect.

Fresh or artificial flowers may be used to add the finishing touches to the cake.

The choice of fresh flowers should include those which do not wilt quickly.

Buttonholes

> **TRADITION**
> *The tradition of buttonholes has evolved from the custom of ribbons or bows worn by the male guests.*

Buttonholes are usually for the principal men of the wedding party. The groom normally wears a single white carnation to match the bride's dress. The best man and fathers sometimes have double red carnations but may wear white, pink or yellow, or roses of any colour. Ushers usually have single red or white buttonholes.

The couple may provide buttonholes for all of their guests if the budget allows.

Corsages

A corsage is an ornate buttonhole containing two to three flowers, for example orchids or roses which are popular and are usually worn by the bride's and groom's mothers and should match or complement the colour of the outfits.

The Florist

If the wedding is informal, the bride or her mother may like to arrange the flowers herself but for a formal event the work should be left to the professional, especially since most of the work needs to be done on the morning of the wedding when there is little time to spare.

A florist should be selected as soon as possible. Other brides, photographers, dressmakers and friends can be good sources of information concerning the abilities and capabilities of florists and may be able to make a recommendation. If unsure, it is wise to visit more than one to inspect their work, an assessment can then be made as to the care they take in preparing flowers, the quality of the blooms and whether each flower head is carefully arranged and wired. Membership of a professional organisation is a useful check on standards. It is important to note that prices vary and the total cost of flowers should not be underestimated.

When a florist has been chosen, a reservation should be made ideally four months before the wedding, but if the date is near Christmas, Valentine's Day or another special day, extra time may need to be allowed. An appointment can be made six to eight weeks before the wedding for a planning session. This could be especially important if the florist has to prepare the arrangements for the church or reception as well as for members of the wedding party.

The cost of arrangements is determined mainly by the number and types of flowers used. The florist needs to be made aware of the allocation set aside in the budget and should be expected to work within these guidelines. It is easy to get carried away and spend more than originally planned. The florist should be asked to provide an itemised price list. There is no need to choose out-of-season flowers if the money could be better spent in other ways. Flowers which are readily available at the time of year will be just as beautiful and cost a great deal less. A deposit will be required and this will probably be payable when the flowers are ordered. The balance may be payable either when the flowers are delivered or beforehand.

The florist should be able to give expert advice on all kinds of flowers, the season that they are readily available, how

their shapes and colours blend, their cost and how well they will last in a bouquet or arrangement in a hot room. If confronted with an unsuitable suggestion, the experienced florist will be able to suggest acceptable substitutes.

From the catalogue of arrangements, a choice should be made to suit style, taste and budget. Requirements, preferences, wedding style and colour should be discussed. It is wise to provide the florist with a photograph or brochure print of the wedding dress and samples of the fabric and colour swatches to help with selection. If there are ribbons and bows in the arrangements, they should be in matching colours. The colour of the flowers should complement the colours being worn by the wedding party.

The florist will usually arrange for bouquets and buttonholes to be delivered to the bride's parents' home on the morning of the wedding, or they may need to be collected. The florist needs to know exactly where and when to set up the arrangements and any details for delivery. The best man should ensure that the bride and groom, the ushers and the groom's parents all have their flowers on the day.

A telephone call to the florist a few days before the wedding will ensure that everything is ready and confirm the detailed arrangements. It is important to leave a contact telephone number with the florist in case of emergencies.

Rings and Gifts from the Bride and Groom

*E*ngagement rings, wedding rings, gifts between the bride and groom, gifts for the attendants and mothers of the couple are the presents given by the bride and groom.

Rings

Traditionally the prospective groom offers an engagement ring to his 'intended' as a token of the promise of marriage. It is worn on the third finger of the left hand where the wedding ring will be placed during the marriage ceremony. Although it is not general practice for the prospective bride to give her fiancé an engagement ring, she may decide to give him a signet or similar ring.

Some women choose not to have an engagement ring, preferring to spend the money on something more practical. This is acceptable so long as it is the bride's choice.

Although the wedding ring is blessed by the minister and placed on the bride's finger as a token of the promises made, the law does not in fact compel the giving of a ring at the marriage ceremony. Despite this, the act of giving a ring or the exchange of rings is considered to be the heart of the church marriage service and is a part of its ritual and tradition. A prospective second-time bride would not expect her first wedding ring to be re-used at her second wedding!

It is not regarded as necessary for the bride to give the groom a wedding gift but a ring or some other item of jewellery often forms part of the ceremony.

Supplier

Although it is legal to be married without a ring, it is more usual to have a new ring for the wedding. A parent or another close relative might offer a ring, in which case the bride might feel obliged to accept but if it is not exactly right, a tactful rejection should be made, perhaps with the explanation that a specially selected ring has always been the intention.

There is an extensive choice of both engagement and wedding rings from which to choose and it is worth shopping around prior to purchase. Unless the groom-to-be is giving his betrothed a family heirloom, it is useful for the couple to choose the ring together. The more known about availability, the better the chance of making a good selection and shopping together will ensure a satisfactory choice. A ring will be worn constantly for years so it is important to make the right decision. Rings may be of a traditional type, antique, or contain a birthstone.

Most people choose from the range offered by the jeweller, but it may be possible to buy an individual design such as an antique ring from a reputable and expert dealer which may be less expensive but equally beautiful and durable. Antique rings can be more decorative than modern designs. Edwardian rings with their stones flat within the settings are popular with those who want durability. The late Victorian rings with their protruding settings are popular with those who have large hands. Another option is to have the ring designed specially but this will cost more.

SUPERSTITION

Buying the engagement and wedding rings at the same time is thought to bring back bad luck.
Wearing the wedding ring before the ceremony is also considered bad luck.

It is important to choose a reputable jeweller. Friends and relatives may be able to make a recommendation or alternatively the high street jeweller should be able to assist. It is very difficult for anyone other than an expert to value jewellery and unless the couple are professionals themselves, the jeweller's skill needs to be relied upon. However, an independent valuation is advisable if at all possible. If purchasing from an antique shop, the ring should be examined by a qualified appraiser prior to purchase. The jeweller should explain and clarify the store's policy with regard to exchange, refund, repair or replacement and guarantee. In addition to a statement of payment, the store's receipt should include details of the ring; the materials from which it is composed; gem quality; and carat weight as all this information will be required as an insurance valuation document for subsequent insurance purposes. If a credit agreement is entered into, it is important to ascertain exactly how much interest is payable; when the payments and balance are due; the procedure in the event of late payments; details of warranties; and insurance cover.

It is the groom's responsibility to collect, pay for and safeguard the ring or rings. He should ensure that it is properly insured as soon as possible after purchase. A photograph of the ring should be kept with the receipt.

The best man should ensure that the ring(s) is insured against loss before the ceremony and obtain a similar ring (of nominal value) in case of an emergency.

It is prudent to have the ring re-valued and re-insured every three to five years.

Cost

Most jewellers stock a good choice of rings to suit every pocket so it is prudent to ensure that the jeweller is aware of the budget limitations. Naturally, the rings are important but there are many practical items to consider when setting up home for the first time and a less expensive ring symbolises no less of a commitment!

If rings are to be engraved, perhaps with the couple's initials or their names and the wedding date, at least four to six weeks must be allowed. Such extras and any alterations to rings will obviously take time and incur additional cost.

Style

Many styles are available and it is possible to buy matching wedding and engagement rings and men's and women's versions of the same wedding ring style.

Traditionally engagement rings are dress rings, i.e. they have a gemstone. When choosing the engagement ring, the couple should consider the type of wedding ring they might choose. The same carat value will ensure that the metals are less likely to erode each other.

Wedding rings are usually plain bands of yellow or white gold — they may be flat, rounded, carved or plain and should complement any engagement ring as most people wear them together. When deciding on the size, it is advisable to choose a ring which is slightly too loose rather than too tight to allow for growth of the fingers.

An eternity ring is traditionally given to a woman on the birth of her first child or at another significant event, such as their fifth or tenth wedding anniversary.

Stones

The only true precious stones are diamonds, rubies, emeralds and sapphires. All others are known as semi-precious or ornamental stones. Precious stones and some hard semi-precious stones are cut to maximise their sparkle.

TRADITION AND SUPERSTITION

Symbols have been used throughout history to mark important events in people's lives such as weddings and christenings.

The giving of rings has been part of the marriage ceremony for centuries. Early man tied plaited grass circlets around the bride's wrists and ankles to prevent her spirit from escaping. In some ancient cultures, married couples wore a rope of twine around their wrists. Later, it became customary for the groom to give his future bride a gift when they became betrothed and also a gift at the wedding itself and this practice has developed into the custom of giving rings which is still retained today. Gold became popular because of its high value and the ease with which it could be valued. The ring is a sign of possession, a token of the couple's pledge to each other and an announcement to other would-be suitors that the bride is otherwise engaged. The popularity of diamonds stems from their hard wearing qualities and the belief prevalent in Italy during the Middle Ages that they represented reconciliation and were capable of restoring harmony. Engagement rings first appeared in the Medieval period. Traditionally, the man buys the ring and then makes the proposal, but today most women help to choose the ring.

The ring has always been a symbol of harmony and unity, and very early in history was adopted as a suitable symbol for a married couple. Jewish law deems that the exchange of the ring legalises the marriage. The earliest examples of wedding rings are Roman and were made of iron, representing the durability of marriage and a sign that a down-payment or contract had been made. As women's role in society has changed, brides have begun to give a ring to the groom in return. In fact this now happens in many wedding ceremonies.

The completeness of the circle shows love flowing in a continuous stream. Two matching rings, one for the bride and one for the groom suggest togetherness. Exactness of fit signifies harmony and perfection and never taking the rings off determines permanence. Placing the ring on the third finger of the left hand recalls the ancient belief that the 'vein of love' ran directly from the heart to the tip of the left hand's third finger, although this practice is not held in all cultures.

Diamonds

TRADITION

The first diamond engagement ring was given in the fifteenth century; the diamond has become the most popular stone for an engagement ring in the world.

The traditional Solitaire (single) diamond for an engagement ring is still very popular despite the expense (due to scarcity, value and durability). The choice of settings is practically infinite and includes everything from a single gem to elaborate arrangements of many diamonds combined with other stones.

The quality of a diamond is assessed by four characteristics; cut, clarity, colour and carat.

The number of facets cut into the stone is known as the cut, and it is the cutter who uses his skills to create a stone with maximum sparkle. A stone with fifty-eight facets has great sparkle. Not all rough diamonds can be cut into any shape, hence the fact that some stones of the same carat weight are more expensive than others.

The most perfect diamonds are clear and colourless, and a diamond under a concentrated light should sparkle with as white a colour as possible when held at all angles. Magnified ten times, a perfect diamond shows no flaws, and this is known as 'perfect clarity'. A minutely flawed stone can still be exceptionally beautiful of course.

Before buying a diamond, the jeweller should be asked to review the International Colour Grading System.

The carat of a diamond is the measure of its size and weight whereas for gold, a carat is a measure of purity. The larger the stone the higher the carat weight. Large stones are obviously the most expensive because they are rare.

There are particular specialised terms used to define the quality of a diamond, such as 'royal' or 'radiant', although it is not necessary to be familiar with these when buying an engagement ring. If the jeweller refers to such terms, he should be asked to explain their meaning so that they are fully understood. The best stones are judged not only by weight and size but also by cut, colour, clarity and quality, so the biggest may not necessarily be the best. It is better to buy a small diamond of good quality than a large one of lesser quality.

Diamonds are not the only choice for engagement rings, any other precious or semi-precious or ornamental stones may be the perfect choice. The cost of rubies, emeralds and pearls can be as much as diamonds but sapphires, opals and amethysts are usually cheaper but equally beautiful. Some brides purposely choose not to have a diamond engagement ring and instead opt for a coloured stone such as their own birthstone.

Birthstones (or Month-stones)

Month	Stone	Meaning
January	Garnet	Constancy
February	Amethyst	Sincerity
March	Bloodstone	Courage
April	Diamond	Innocence or lasting love
May	Emerald	Success or hope
June	Pearl	Purity or health
July	Ruby	Love and contentment
August	Sardonyx	Married bliss
September	Sapphire	Wisdom or repentance
October	Opal	Hope
November	Topaz	Fidelity or cheerfulness
December	Turquoise	Harmony

Another idea (from Victorian times) is to choose a motto ring where the initial letters of the gem stones match the names or initials of the couple or sentiments, for example:

Jade)
Opal) Joe
Emeralds)

Topaz) T and C
Coral)

Amethyst) Always
Topaz) True

> **SUPERSTITION**
>
> *To wear an opal unless born in October, is considered bad luck.*
>
> *A fiancée's birthstone in an engagement ring is said to bring good luck.*

Stone Cuts

Cut	Top View	Side View
Rose		
Baguette		
Trap		
Antique Cushion		
Brilliant		
Fancy		
Cabochon		

Stone Colours

A coloured stone in the light should be intense, lively and clear, but not to the extent that it is transparent. When examining gems, the cut is important to their value and sometimes they may be poorly cut to maintain weight but this is, of course, at the expense of quality!

Agate	Banded in different colours
Amethyst	Transparent purple
Aquamarine	Pale blue-green
Beryl (Citrine)	Yellow
Bloodstone	Green with red flecks
Cameo	White image carved out of pink shell
Cornelian	Orange
Chalcedony	White
Chrysoberyl	Darkish green
Chrysolite	Olive green
Coral	Normally orange, but sometimes red or white
Emerald	Green
Garnet	Purple-red, can be green

Jade	Generally green, but can be yellow, pink or white
Jasper	Brown with coloured flecks
Jet	Black
Lapis Lazuli	Blue with gold flecks
Malachite	Banded green
Moonstone	Translucent white
Obsidian	Black
Onyx	Banded black
Opal	White, red or turquoise with rainbow flecks
Pearl	White or pale pink
Peridot	Greenish yellow
Rhodonite	Pale pink
Rose Quartz	Pink
Ruby	Red
Sapphire	Blue
Sardonyx	White onyx layers with yellow or orange-red sard
Spinel	Generally red, but can be brown, green or blue
Tiger's Eye	Banded brown
Topaz	Yellow, brown or pink
Tourmaline	Generally blue or pink, but can be red, brown or green
Turquoise	Turquoise
Zircon	Pale blue

The Setting

When choosing a setting it is wise to select one that will beautifully set off the stone or stones selected. The size of the hands and fingers will need to be taken into account; a wide heavy band would suit large hands but overwhelm small ones. Diamonds are usually set in 18 carat gold.

Stone Settings

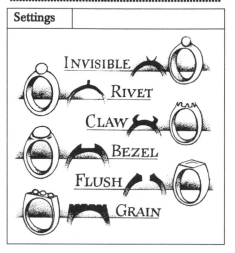

Settings	
INVISIBLE	
RIVET	
CLAW	
BEZEL	
FLUSH	
GRAIN	

Bands

Gold is the most popular metal for both engagement and wedding rings, and it is usually yellow, although white and red are also popular. Although red (often called rose) and white gold is more expensive, it does not keep its brilliance as long as yellow.

The amount of gold is measured in carats. Pure gold has 24 carats, but is generally too soft for jewellery, so it is alloyed with other metals to make it durable. The purest gold advised for rings is 22 carat, then 18 and finally 9. Men's rings are usually 9 carat gold as this is more durable.

Platinum is another precious metal and is a beautiful choice for wedding rings and is extremely durable. It is however considerably more expensive than gold.

Gold	% Purity	Carat	Description
Yellow	100	24	Purest, but very soft, heavy, very strong natural colour, very expensive and difficult to obtain.
	91.6	22	Soft, fairly heavy, strong colour, expensive and can be difficult to obtain.
	75	18	Serviceable and most practical.
	37.5	9	Harder, lighter in colour and more affordable.
White		18	
		9	
Platinum			White in colour. The most costly of all.

Manufacturer's Initials	A crown	Carat number	Assay Office (for Britain)	Alphabetically coded date stamp
		916 = 22 750 = 18 585 = 14 375 = 9	Leopard = London Anchor = Birmingham Rose = Sheffield Castle = Edinburgh	K = 1984 Q = 1990 W = 1996

Options to the more traditional gold band wedding ring for men include signet, claddagh or a tri-gold ring which is a traditional French wedding ring made of three different coloured gold bands twisted together. Options for women are virtually infinite.

Hallmarking

Under the Hallmarking Act of 1973, gold wedding rings must be sold hallmarked confirming their quality, although slender, delicate engagement rings may be exempt. The law also demands that traders of precious metals display a notice describing hallmarks.

The hallmark is made of five small symbols denoting when and where the item was made.

Insurance

Rings should be insured against loss (loss of a stone, for example), theft or damage and the jeweller should provide a valuation certificate for such purposes as this will be required by most insurance companies.

Rings can usually be added to household contents insurance but should be detailed separately as items of particular value and ones which are to be insured at all times, not just when they are in the house but when they are worn elsewhere.

Breaking Off the Engagement

Traditionally, if the woman breaks off the engagement, she should offer to return the ring to her fiancé. However, if the man breaks off the engagement, the woman has the right to keep her gift, but she may feel that she no longer wants to keep it.

Cleaning

The jeweller will be able to advise on caring for rings, i.e. cleaning and harmful substances to be avoided. Frequent checks for loose stones, home cleaning with an appropriate liquid detergent and lukewarm water or a commercial solution available from most jewellers every month and occasional professional cleaning will ensure maximum care. Pearls, opals, emeralds and turquoise should be cleaned with a dry cloth and paid special attention as they are more fragile; others should be soaked in warm water and detergent, scrubbed with a soft toothbrush and then rinsed and dried. Rings should be removed when doing chores such as housework and car cleaning as these activities are not good for any rings and diamonds can scratch many surfaces!

Gifts from the Bride and Groom

The Wedding party may consist of a chief bridesmaid or a maid/matron of honour, bridesmaids, flower girl, page boys, best man, ushers and both sets of parents. The reason for the couple purchasing gifts for the wedding party is to show appreciation for their participation and contribution to the day. Personal gifts, selected with care and thought, ensure that attendants and parents can reflect on the occasion in years to come. It is customary for the couple to pass on their gifts to the wedding party at either a pre-wedding party or at the reception.

Depending on the choice of gift, some items can be personalised with the couple's names or initials and the wedding date if desired. Jewellery is always a popular and special gift that may be treasured for many future years but there is no reason why gifts other than jewellery should not be given as tokens of thanks, for example: cameras, musical instruments, subscriptions to clubs. Here are some ideas to consider when shopping at jewellers.

INFILL/CHECK LIST

To the	Engagement		Wedding	
	Bride	Groom	Bride	Groom
Gift	Ring		Ring	Ring
Supplier Name Address Telephone				
Size Style Date ordered Details to be engraved Alterations Collection date				
Policy Exchange Return Refund Repair Replacement Guarantee				
Receipt should state: Material Gem quality Carat weight Cost				
Credit Interest £ Payment dates Balance due date				
Warranty Insurance				
Deposit due date				
Balance due date				
£				

Gifts for Each Other

Gifts to each other mark the special day and should reflect financial status: rings, pearls, pendants.

Gift for the Maid/Matron of Honour

Since the maid/matron of honour is the sole female attendant, she, like the best man should have a special gift.

Gift for the Chief Bridesmaid

If the chief bridesmaid is older than the other bridesmaids, she may like a special individual gift.

		GIFTS FROM THE BRIDE AND GROOM			
Chief Bridesmaid	Best man	Bridesmaids and Flower girl	Page boys	Ushers	Parents

Gifts for the Bridesmaids and Flower Girl

If the bridesmaids are of the same age gifts should be identical to prevent jealousy. Ideas will include: necklaces, lockets, pendants, crosses and chains; bracelets; brooches; rings; earrings; stick pins; compacts; framed wedding photographs; perfume; engraved glasses or goblets; figurines; jewellery which is complementary to the bridesmaids' dresses that may be worn on the wedding day.

Gifts for the Page Boys

The gifts should be identical to prevent jealousy. Boys might appreciate a high-tech watch or a signed football.

Gifts for the Best Man and Ushers

Ideas include: cufflinks, tie pins; watches; key rings; decanters; money clips; engraved pewter tankards. The best man's gift should be special as he will have contributed much to the success of the occasion.

Gifts for the Parents

Some couples present their parents with gifts as they leave home for the last time or at the reception to thank them for their love and care over the years and for the wedding.

Ideas: dish commemorating the day; engraved jewellery or glassware; wedding photographs in an ornamental frame; crystal decanters; engraved paper-weights; theatre or concert tickets.

Gift Wrapping

Price indications should be removed before wrapping the gifts. Receipts can be sealed in envelopes and passed to the young attendants' mothers in case of the need for exchange.

17

Wedding Gifts

With all the arrangements that wedding preparations entail, the bride can be forgiven for drawing a blank when asked what she would like as a wedding gift. Family and friends will all want to buy a gift that will please the bride and groom, and in order for them to do this, they will need some guidance. Consequently, this chapter is designed to provide the help and ideas needed.

Considerations

Although it is traditional for guests to give a gift, it must be said that they have no obligation to do so, nor should the bride and her family feel that every gift donor should be 'rewarded' with an invitation to the wedding.

The bride may feel that the idea of circulating a gift list is taking liberties but it is common practice today and it does give the guests some useful guidance without which there is a more than likely chance of gifts being duplicated. From the guests' point of view, they will not want to see half a dozen clones of their gift on a wedding day display!

The list may, of course, be held at home until guests ask for ideas but there will be the risk of duplication.

Another alternative is to place a list with a specialist shop or major department store where staff record purchases so that duplication is avoided.

The choice of gift is obviously the guest's decision, but everyone wants their gift to be well received, so most people like to consult the couple or a list before making a purchase and an organised approach will make life a lot easier.

Having explained the usefulness of a list, it is important that guests are allowed an element of choice, not only in terms of the all-important price, but also the style of the gift. Some people will be happy to purchase something practical, while others may prefer to choose an item of luxury or even something frivolous. The bride, on the other hand, wants to make the most of the generosity of her family and friends by asking them for things that she most needs.

Less expensive items should always be included so that guests do not feel 'blackmailed' into spending more than they can afford. Relatively expensive items may also be included since some people might like to 'club together' to buy a single gift. The list should include more items than expected, otherwise those who are last to receive the list or make an enquiry may be confronted with very little choice.

From the guests' point of view, if they are unsure of what to give, it is simply a matter of contacting the bride for her advice.

Gifts should be addressed to the bride's mother at her home or to the bride at her's even if the donor has never met the bride. Gifts should be sent in plenty of time before the wedding so that the bride may write thank-you letters before the event.

The wedding gifts may be displayed on the day for all to see, but such exhibitions seem to be very much less common these days. Gifts too large for display on the day should be represented by a card stating the nature of the gift and donor(s). In the case of money, the amount should not be disclosed.

Hopefully, most gifts will be received before the wedding day but many people will bring gifts with them and these should be handed to the best man. A table positioned behind the receiving line at the reception will avoid the juggling of parcels while the greeting of guests is under way. Perhaps some of the younger bridesmaids could help and ensure that labels remain with the gifts to which they relate. If at all possible the bride should try to find the time at least to glance at the gifts so that she can make some personal thank-yous at the reception.

The check lists at the end of this chapter list most of the items needed in a new home, especially in the first year or so, so that the bride can be selective in her choice of gift. The pages are organised in around-the-house sections which are comprehensive and easy to use allowing scope for written details, such as style and colours, and space to add personal extras, making an individual and complete check list for the bride-to-be.

Defining Lifestyle

Lifestyles differ and the bride should consider hers in relation to the items listed.

If there is a love for cooking, entertaining and a preference that someone else decorates the house, then this bride's list will be very different from that of the couple who are buying an old flat to renovate and who will be spending most of their time and money on the home. For working couples, time-saving devices can be important, especially in the kitchen where they may be vital aids for maximising capabilities and minimising labour.

It may also be worth stating priorities.

Even if an extensive wedding list is compiled, the bride and groom cannot expect to receive all of the items.

Making the List

It is good advice to start off with those items which will be most beneficial in early married life, particularly in the first year when stresses and tensions can be high. Additions to the home can be made later when there is more cash to spare, or when there is a change in needs. Most wedding lists concentrate on items for the home, but personal gifts can also be included as close friends might prefer this option.

The check lists provided indicate items for consideration; unwanted items may be deleted and new ones added. Items already purchased or promised should be ticked off so that the completed check list provides a clear and up-to-date picture of total needs.

To ensure plenty of choice, a wide range of items should be included. Any list needs to include more items than expected so that the last person to read it is not faced with the 'choice' of a colour television. A wide range of prices is also essential. For the more expensive items, people may want to club together to buy a gift. Lower priced gifts may be bought by acquaintances, or perhaps by relatives as 'extras'.

It will be useful to note the names of gift-donors on the master list as a reminder to send thank-you letters.

Home Contents Insurance

The lists will prove to be useful after the wedding for noting the actual replacement value of all furniture and property to ascertain the quote for a house contents insurance policy.

Shorter Wedding List

For the bride who feels that it would be intimidating to send such a comprehensive list to guests, the blank format at the end of this chapter may be used to create a shorter or alternative list.

Dispatch Options

It should be easy to keep track of gifts and avoid confusion.

Circulation

One master list can be sent with a letter of thanks and a stamped addressed envelope for return to anyone who asks to see it. The addressee should be asked to tick the item of their choice and either pass on or return the list as soon as possible. It is advisable to keep a note of the list-holder and date. This way of dealing with the list avoids the possibility of dup-licated gifts as only one person has possession of the list at any one time but the whole procedure does take time.

Distribution

Photocopies of the master list may be distributed to all who request a copy, and returned with a tick indicating choice of gift. Although this does create the possibility of duplicated gifts, it is a quicker method.

Shop List

Another option is to supply a department store with a list and advise people to visit the designated store to make their selections. This choice allows for large expensive items such as dinner services to be purchased by means of several affordable individual gifts. Those who ask to see the list can make their choice at the shop and the gift is duly ticked off the list. This is often a practical option when all or most of the shoppers live in one town.

Telephone

The bride can always hold on to the list and wait for people to enquire. She can then suggest a few options to suit their preferences and budget, but this option may cause embarrassment for some people.

Gift Receipt Record

The easiest way to monitor gifts is to make a note of them as they arrive by recording them on the guest/gift record as this will provide information such as addresses and numbers which are needed for the thank-you letters, notes or telephone calls. It may be an idea for the bride to write thank-yous immediately when she can enjoy writing a personal note, rather than being confronted with a large task after the wedding that can become a chore if left until a later date. Besides, family and friends will appreciate the politeness and thoughtfulness of a prompt personal response for their gifts. It is possible to buy pre-printed thank-you cards, but these may be considered rather impersonal.

Displaying Gifts

Most people like to see the couple's wedding gifts. A display can be arranged at the reception on the wedding day itself, or another day may be chosen if this is more convenient. Some people, however, feel that displaying gifts is an unnecessary practice that encourages comparison of value which can cause embarrassment and hurt feelings.

It is customary to display the wedding gifts in the bride's parents' home where they remain secure and safe. An arrangement in a spare room is preferable to disruption of the main living area. Each gift should have a card noting the name of the donor. It is sensible to display gifts in the home even if this means arranging for people to visit in order to see them.

If the gifts are displayed at the reception venue, it is advisable to obscure them from public view since they can be an advertisement of the contents of the newly-weds' home. In addition, it could be worth arranging temporary insurance cover. It is very awkward for the couple to handle gifts while they are in the receiving line welcoming guests. A solution would be to have a special table just inside the door and when the first few guests are asked to place their gifts on the table, others will then follow suit. Another solution is to have a table elsewhere, perhaps as part of the overall decoration, for example, near to the cake to create an effective display. The best man and/or chief bridesmaid can take charge of any gifts and re-fix labels to gifts when unwrapped.

Gifts should be arranged in groups so that all linen is together, all glass and so on, and each item labelled detailing the donor's name. Identical gifts or gifts very similar in nature should be tactfully positioned apart! An attempt should also be made to avoid embarrassing anyone by placing an inexpensive gift directly next to an extravagant one. Amounts of money should not be disclosed. In the case of a dinner service or sets of linen, it is quite proper to display only one place setting or one sheet and pillowcase. Gifts which have been damaged in the post should not be displayed unless they can be arranged in such a way that the damage is hidden from view.

Wherever the display, someone (usually the bride's mother) needs to be responsible for repacking the items after the reception and ensuring their safety until the honeymoon is over.

Exchanges and Returns

Although it is obvious that no guest should be told that their gift was not wanted, some shops will allow exchanges. In the unfortunate event of a gift arriving damaged, the bride should first ascertain whether it was insured by the shop or carrier. If at all possible it is better not to reveal the facts to the donor since they may feel obliged to buy a replacement.

Postponement or Cancellation of the Wedding

In either case, prospective guests must be informed as soon as possible and if the wedding is cancelled gifts must be returned immediately.

Gift Ideas

Kitchen

Many of the gifts on the list will find their home in the kitchen; there are plenty of useful essentials and numerous time-saving gadgets which a bride may be tempted to list but it is important to include only those items really needed. An item which merely sits in the kitchen cupboard and is never used is only a waste of space.

If there is a love of home cooking, then bakeware and storage jars make lovely gifts. On the other hand, it may be wise to concentrate on basics in the kitchen and include more in other rooms.

Dining Room

If the plan is to entertain regularly, a dinner service may figure high on the priority list. However, if kitchen meals or TV dinners are planned, much of the following list may need to be deleted.

Although many people automatically list a high quality dinner service and crystal glassware, they are really not essentials.

Sitting Room

The bride and groom might like to include leisure time items.

Hall, Stairs and Landing

There may be limited space available, but there are odds and ends which make excellent and useful gifts which may otherwise be forgotten.

Master Bedroom

Bedding is usually an essential on any wedding list. Two sets of sheets are plenty to start with.

Spare Bedroom

Unless the plan is to accommodate guests on a regular basis, fitting out the spare bedroom can definitely wait until a later date and should not feature high on the priority list. If friends want to stay, most will be only too happy to provide their own sleeping bag if a room is made available.

Bathroom

This is another room for which only the basics need to be considered. Towels are always useful and if the plan is to change the bathroom suite fairly quickly, it is a good idea to choose colours which will match both suites.

Garden, Garage and DIY

Many young couples start their married life in a flat, but others are lucky enough to have a small garden and may like a few basic garden tools and plants.

An experienced home handyman should be asked for his advice regarding the most useful tools that make up a starter tool-kit.

Home Safety and Security

Everyone wants a safe and secure home, protecting themselves as far as possible against accidents or intruders. Making a habit of following a few common sense safety rules can go a long way towards home safety.

Home safety and security are big industries today and there are many useful products on the market which can help to safeguard the home and property. The local police Crime Prevention Officer will be able to provide good advice to suit individual circumstances.

Personal Items

There is no reason why some personal items should not be included on the wedding list. Although most guests will probably choose gifts for the new home, close friends might prefer to buy something else to be personally enjoyed by the couple, such as sports equipment, books, money, travel tickets and insurance policies. When acknowledging a gift of money, it is courteous to indicate how the money will be spent.

INFILL/CHECK LIST							WEDDING GIFT LIST
	Guests' choices	Colour	Model/style Design	Make	Size	Qty	Available from

Kitchen
Crockery:
Plates — large
       — medium
       — small
Soup bowls
Vegetable dishes
Other serving dishes
Cereal/dessert bowls
Sugar bowl
Milk jug
Cream jug
Coffee cups and saucers
Tea cups and saucers
Butter dish
Mugs
Egg cups
 	
Cutlery:
Knives
Forks
Dessert spoons
Dessert forks
Soup spoons
Fish knives
Fish forks
Tea spoons
Coffee spoons
Measuring spoons
Serving spoons
Bread knife
Butter knives
Carving knife
Chopping knife
Steak knives
Salad servers
Ladle
 	
Apron
Baking tins and trays
Blender							

INFILL/CHECK LIST							WEDDING GIFT LIST
	Guests' choices	Colour	Model/style Design	Make	Size	Qty	Available from
Kitchen (cont)							
Bread basket							
Bread bin							
Bread board and knife							
Buckets/bowls, etc.							
Can opener							
Carving board							
Casserole dishes							
Cheese board and knife							
Coffee grinder							
Coffee percolator/maker							
Colander							
Cookery book							
Corkscrew							
Deep-fat fryer							
Dish drainer							
Dishwasher							
Dust pan and brush							
Fish poacher							
Flan dishes							
Flask							
Food processor							
Frying pans							
Freezer							
Garlic press							
Ice-cream maker							
Kettle							
Kitchen tools							
Knife rack							
Knife sharpener							
Microwave							
Microwave cookware							
Mixing bowls							
Oven							
Pedal bin							
Pepper mill							
Potato peeler							
Pressure cooker							
Rolling pin							
Salad bowls							
Salt and pepper set							
Sandwich toaster							
Saucepans							
Scales							
Sieve							
Slow cooker							
Souffle dishes							
Spice rack and jars							
Storage jars							
Storage tins							
Table cloths							
Table mats							
Tea strainer							
Tea towels							
Toaster							
Toast rack							
Trays							
Tumble dryer							

INFILL/CHECK LIST							WEDDING GIFT LIST
	Guests' choices	Colour	Model/style Design	Make	Size	Qty	Available from
Kitchen (cont)							
Washing machine							
Whisk							
Wok							
Wooden spoons							
Yoghurt maker							
Carpet sweeper							
Clothes dryer							
Iron							
Ironing board							
Spin dryer							
Vacuum cleaner							
Dining Room							
Dining table							
Dining chairs							
Dinner service							
Plates — large							
— medium							
— small							
Soup bowls							
Dessert bowls							
Vegetable dishes							
Meat plates							
Gravy boats							
Sauce pots							
Salt and pepper pots							
Coffee cups and saucers							
Coffee jug							
Sugar bowl							
Cream jug							
Glassware							
Drinking glasses							
Liqueur glasses							
Champagne glasses							
Wine glasses							
Decanters							
Jam pot							
Fruit bowl							
Ice bucket							
Place mats							
Table linen							
Table mats							
Waste bin							
Water jugs							
Wine cooler							
Wine corker							
Wine rack							
Sitting Room							
Bookcase							
Chairs							
CD player							
CD rack							
Coffee table							
Cushions							
Fireplace tools							

INFILL/CHECK LIST							WEDDING GIFT LIST
	Guests' choices	Colour	Model/style Design	Make	Size	Qty	Available from
Sitting Room (cont) Hi-fi Magazine rack Sofa Standard lamp Table lamp Television Video recorder Video cassettes							
Hall, Stairs and Landing Answering machine Linen basket/bin Mirror Pot plants Telephone Umbrella stand							
Master Bedroom Bed Bed linen Bedside table Bedspread Blanket box Blankets Duvet Duvet cover Electric blanket Lamp Mirror Pillow cases Pillows Radio alarm Sheets Tea-maker Vanity table Wardrobes							
Spare Bedroom Mattress							
Bathroom Bath mat Bath rack Bathroom cabinet Bathroom scales Bath sheets Bath towels Hand towels Mirror Waste bin							
Garage, Garden and DIY Barbecue set Electric drill Garden fork							

INFILL/CHECK LIST							WEDDING GIFT LIST
	Guests' choices	Colour	Model/style Design	Make	Size	Qty	Available from
Garage, Garden and DIY (cont)							
Garden furniture							
Garden spade							
Garden tools							
Hedge trimmer							
Lawn mower							
Paint							
Paint brushes							
Tool box							
Tools							
Washing line							
Wheelbarrow							
Work bench							
Home Safety and Security							
Door chains							
Door locks							
Home alarm							
Smoke detectors							
Window catches							
Window locks							
Personal items							
Books							
Calculator							
Camera							
Jewellery							
Ornaments							
Sports equipment							
Briefcase							
Personal organiser							
Miscellaneous							
Candlesticks							
Carpets							
Clocks							
Cushions							
Door mats							
House plants							
Lamps							
Luggage							
Photo album							
Pictures/prints							
Radio							
Rugs							
Vases							
Waste-paper baskets							

INFILL/CHECK LIST							WEDDING GIFT LIST
	Guests' choices	Colour	Model/style Design	Make	Size	Qty	Available from

18

Parties

P arties are a natural way of sharing with relatives and friends the happiness of a forthcoming or recent wedding.

Pre-wedding

Joint Families Social

Some couples host an evening or lunch-time party when both sets of parents are invited to meet and socialise. This is particularly favourable if the parents are not acquainted and, even if they are on familiar terms, it provides an opportunity to discuss the wedding arrangements or to set a mutually convenient date and time for future discourse.

Bride's and Groom's Friends and Colleagues

An evening party for friends and colleagues, to whom it has not been possible to send invitations, will provide them with an opportunity to convey their good wishes and also join in the celebrations in some small way.

The style of party should suit the couple's preferences and budget, as it is appropriate that they pay for this themselves or at least some part of the expense.

Engagement

Some couples like to announce their engagement officially and as a surprise at a party given by parents. The bride's mother issues the invitations. The bride's father makes the announcement at the celebration and toasts the happy couple

in response to which the prospective groom thanks the hosts for the party and proposes a toast to the health of both sets of parents.

Rehearsal Get-together

It makes a pleasant event to have a small dinner party for the wedding party and their partners after the rehearsal at the church to show appreciation for the hard work that they will be contributing to the special day. This is an ideal time for the couple to pass on their gifts to the attendants. An alternative is to dine the wedding party after the honeymoon when settled into the new home.

Showers

Showers are parties or talk sessions for the females which are usually held during the daytime and given by someone in honour of the bride-to-be. The bride-to-be is consulted about the arrangements and provides the organiser with a list of those people whom she would like invited in accordance with a maximum number deemed by the organiser. Although the shower is given by the organiser, she does not have to know those invitees whom the bride selects.

At the shower, small gifts are offered to the bride and these normally have appropriate themes, for example, 'kitchen shower', 'all-pink shower'.

Following the shower, the guests should

write to the organiser to thank her for the occasion.

Hen Night

It is traditional for the bride and groom to hold parties separately with their own friends of the same sex. The hen night is for the girls and most brides like to hold their party a week or so before the wedding to enjoy an evening out with the female members of the wedding party and friends.

It is the bride's decision as to how she would prefer to spend the evening – perhaps a meal in a smart restaurant or any way to relax among friends and to express gratitude for their help and support.

Stag Night

The stag night is for the boys who celebrate the groom's forthcoming marriage and commiserate on the loss of his single status. The party traditionally takes place on the eve of the wedding.

It is the groom's decision as to how he would prefer to spend the evening but it is the best man's responsibility to organise the celebration which should be one of his least arduous duties.

Although the best man should be allowed to enjoy the evening, he must remember his responsibility for ensuring that everyone returns home safely. On no account should anyone drive if they have had a drink. Transport arrangements need to be made before the event and the best man should ensure that all guests have made suitable arrangements. To economise, or to be sure, the guests could always walk if the venue is local. Even if a taxi is arranged for the groom, the best man must remain sufficiently sober to see him safely inside his house before returning home himself.

Although it is traditional for the groom to celebrate on the very last night of his bachelorhood, it is far more sensible to hold the party at least a few days or even a week before the wedding so that there is a suitable time lapse for recovery. The bride should try to persuade the groom that this is the sensible option.

The groom should inform the best man of the friends he would like to invite. The ushers usually attend as well as the bride's and the groom's brothers and close friends of the groom. Traditionally both the bride's and the groom's fathers are invited but generally they leave the celebrations before the young men.

A popular stag night is an inexpensive meal followed by a visit to a pub or pubs. Reservations for meals need to be made in advance especially if there will be a large group.

Traditionally, the groom pays for the stag night, but with current charges, it is more likely that all of those who attend will pay at least some of the expense. For example, the groom could pay for the meal and the guests contribute towards a 'kitty' for the drinks, or vice versa. The best man should let the guests know what they will be expected to pay in advance so that everyone is spared embarrassment on the night itself. The best man should also take charge of the money and ensure that there is a surplus by carrying some spare cash.

Post-wedding

Dinner Parties and Entertainment

It is traditional for the newly-weds to entertain both sets of parents, then the best man together with the bridesmaids and ushers during the following three months in the couple's new home.

It is thoughtful to dine those who were unable to attend on the wedding day and perhaps entertain any gift donors who were not included on the guest list.

INFILL/CHECK LIST	JOINT FAMILIES SOCIAL			
Date				
Time				
Number of guests				
Venue				
Address				
Telephone no.				
Date booked				
Transport arrangements				
Taxi firm				
Telephone no.				
£				

Guest's name	Address	Telephone no.	Transport

INFILL/CHECK LIST	BRIDE'S AND GROOM'S FRIENDS
Date	
Time	
Number of guests	
Venue	
Address	
Telephone no.	
Date booked	
Transport arrangements	
Taxi firm	
Telephone no.	
£	

Guest's name	Address	Telephone no.	Invited ✓	Reply ✓ or x	Transport

INFILL/CHECK LIST	ENGAGEMENT PARTY
Host/Hostess	
Date	
Time	
Number of guests	
Venue	
Address	
Telephone no.	
Date booked	
Transport arrangements	
Taxi firm	
Telephone no.	
£	
Decorations	
Menu	
Drinks	

Guest's name	Address	Telephone no.	Invited ✓	Reply ✓ or x	Transport	Gifts rec'd	Thank-you sent

INFILL/CHECK LIST	REHEARSAL GET-TOGETHER
Date	
Time	
Number of guests	
Venue	
Address	
Telephone no.	
Date booked	
Transport arrangements	
Taxi firm	
Telephone no.	
£	

Guest's name	Address	Telephone no.	Invited ✓	Reply ✓ or x	Transport

INFILL/CHECK LIST					SHOWER
Date					
Time					
Number of guests					
Venue					
Address					
Telephone no.					
Date booked					
Transport arrangements					
Taxi firm					
Telephone no.					
Organiser					

Guest's name	Address	Telephone no.	Invited ✓	Reply ✓ or x	Transport

INFILL/CHECK LIST		HEN NIGHT
Date		
Time		
Number of guests		
Venue		
Address		
Telephone no.		
Date booked		
Transport arrangements		
Taxi firm		
Telephone no.		
£		

Guest's name	Address	Telephone no.	Invited ✓	Reply ✓ or x	Transport

INFILL/CHECK LIST	STAG NIGHT
Date	
Time	
Number of guests	
Venue	
Address	
Telephone no.	
Date booked	
Transport arrangements	
Taxi firm	
Telephone no.	
£	

Guest's name	Address	Telephone no.	Invited ✓	Reply ✓ or x	Transport

INFILL/CHECK LIST	DINNER PARTY FOR PARENTS
Date	
Time	
Number of guests	
Venue	
Address	
Telephone no.	
Date booked	
Transport arrangements	
Taxi firm	
Telephone no.	

Menu

INFILL/CHECK LIST		DINNER PARTY FOR ATTENDANTS			
Date					
Time					
Number of guests					
Venue					
Address					
Telephone no.					
Date booked					
Transport arrangements					
Taxi firm					
Telephone no.					
Menu					

Guest's name	Address	Telephone no.	Invited ✓	Reply ✓ or x	Transport

The Day

Time	Timetable	Notes

Timetable

TRADITION AND SUPERSTITION
It is considered good luck if the bride is awakened by the song of a bird. Sunny weather is also a sign of good luck.
A bride should not see her groom on the day of the wedding until they meet at the ceremony.

Members of the wedding party may appreciate a timetable of the day's events.

By the time the day arrives everyone should be clear about their duties and when they need to be performed and, if preparations have been well organised in the preceding weeks, there is no reason why the whole procedure for the day should not be perfect.

A timetable for the day should be drawn up stating all the necessary details. This chapter may be used for this purpose. Times may be entered on the left and the right hand margin used for any notes. The blank form concluding this section may be reproduced and filled in if this programme of events is too detailed.

At Home

−2 hours

Going-away and honeymoon attire should be at the reception venue.

The bride will spend time preparing for the wedding, making up her hair and face and dressing into her bridal attire.

Time

Notes

SUPERSTITION

*The bride should not finish dressing until
the last minute.
It is good luck to find a spider in the dress
as the bride prepares for her wedding.
Bad luck will befall anyone who breaks
anything on the morning of the wedding.*

She transfers her engagement ring to her right hand.

Bridesmaids leave, allowing the bride's mother and father a few minutes alone with the bride.

Mother joins bridesmaids in the car, leaving father and daughter alone together for a few minutes.

Meanwhile the best man should be dressed and certain that he has the ring(s) in his waistcoat pocket and any other documentation, for example, money for marriage fees (if not previously paid), travel tickets, passports, hotel reservations, emergency taxi numbers and speech.

He collects buttonholes and service sheets and passes these onto the ushers.

The groom gives to the best man a sum of money to cover any out-of-pocket expenses that may be incurred during the course of the day, for example, tips.

TRADITION AND SUPERSTITION

*The groom should not see his bride on the
wedding day until he meets her at the
altar.*

At the Church

−40 mins

The ushers arrive at church ready to hand out service sheets and buttonholes and direct the congregation to the pews: bride's family and friends on the left-hand side of the aisle (facing the altar); the groom's on the right-hand side with close family members seated nearest the front.

−20 mins

The minister, organist and bell-ringers arrive.

The organ plays quietly, bell-ringing ensues until the ceremony starts.

Guests arrive.

−15 mins

The groom and best man arrive in good time and pose for any photographs.

The best man pays fees to the minis-

Time		Notes
	ter on behalf of the groom (if not dealt with beforehand).	
	The best man checks on the ushers.	
	The groom and best man stand or sit in the front pew to the right of the central aisle; the best man on the groom's right.	
	They sometimes wait in the vestry until a few minutes before the bride is due and then take up their positions.	
−10 mins	Most guests arrive.	
	Chief bridesmaid, bridesmaids, flower girl, page boys and the bride's mother arrive and gather in the church porch until and bride and her father arrive.	
−5 mins	The bride and her father arrive. The bride's chauffeur will usually ensure perfect timing of arrival at church.	
	Photographs may be taken.	
	The bride's mother or chief bridesmaid adjusts the bride's gown, train and veil. The bride checks that her engagement ring is on the right hand.	
−2 mins	The chief usher escorts the bride's mother to her seat in the front pew on the left of the aisle. She is the last guest to take her place before the ceremony starts and may either be escorted by the chief usher or a male member of her family. She keeps a seat vacant on her right for the bride's father when he has completed his part in the ceremony. When the bride's mother takes her seat, this is a signal to the congregation that the ceremony is about to start.	
	The organist changes tempo and begins to play the chosen processional music.	
−1 min	The ushers go to their pews at the rear.	
	The groom and best man rise and stand at the head of the aisle.	
	The congregation stands.	
	The bridesmaids and page boys form two columns at the main door through which the bride and her father pass, or line up behind the bride.	
	The flower girl positions herself ready to precede the bride and scatter petals or confetti (if allowed).	
	The minister may often greet the bride in the porch and then return to the altar to wait for the procession at the chancel steps or, in the case of a full choral service, he may greet the bride in the porch and the procession will be	

Time

Notes

led by the choir followed by the minister, the flower girl, the bride with her father and then other attendants. Alternatively, the choir may be seated.

The procession proceeds along the aisle with the bride on her father's right arm. The attendants follow in pairs, normally the youngest in front.

As soon as the bridal party enters the church, the groom and best man move from the front pew to the right of the chancel steps, with the best man at the groom's right and a pace behind him.

The groom and best man may turn to greet the bride as she walks slowly along the aisle or when she arrives at the chancel steps. This is the groom's first look at her bridal gown.

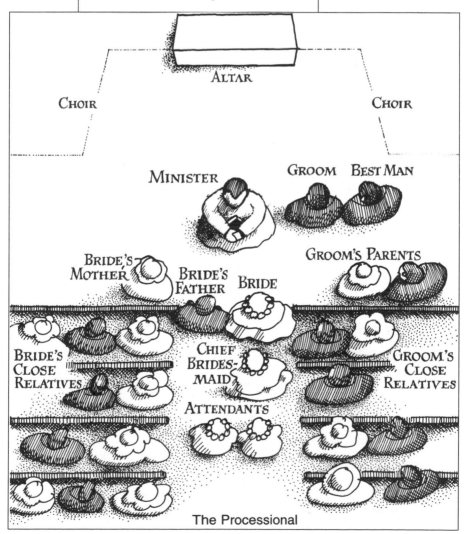

The Processional

Time   **Notes**

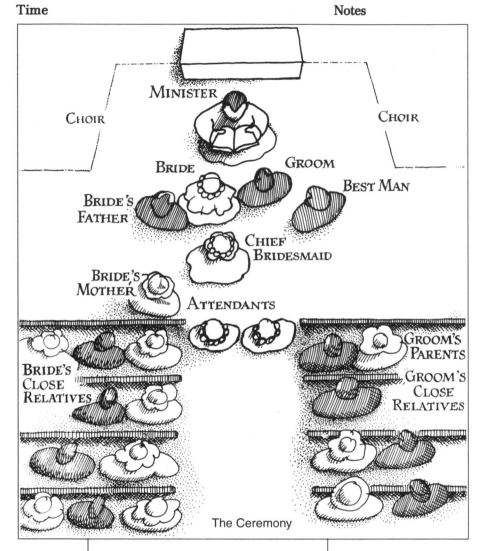

The Ceremony

At the chancel steps, the bride is led by her father to the groom's left. Her father moves to stand to her left and a pace behind her.

The best man and bridal attendants remain in their places.

Some brides wear their engagement ring on their wedding finger up to this point in the ceremony and choose this moment to change it to their right hand. Most will, however, have already made the switch earlier when dressing.

The bride may turn for the chief bridesmaid to lift the veil clear of her face (if she is wearing one), take her bouquet and gloves (if worn), though the bride may do this herself. The chief

Time

bridesmaid holds these until the bride has signed the register. If there is no bridesmaid the bouquet is handed to the bride's father who passes it to the bride's mother who returns it to the bride later in the vestry.

The minister issues a greeting and the service commences and lasts for about thirty minutes. The order and type of service varies but may open with a hymn and sometimes a prayer or bible reading before proceeding to the marriage itself. The precise details will, of course, have been decided long beforehand and the congregation can refer to their order of service sheets (if provided).

The minister emphasises the significance of marriage.

He asks if anyone knows of any impediment to the marriage and states that if so, he/she should make it known or 'forever hold his peace'.

He asks the couple to declare their intention to marry.

The minister asks the groom: 'Wilt thou have this woman to be thy wedded wife, to live together according to God's holy law in the state of matrimony? Wilt thou love her, comfort her, honour and keep her in sickness and in health and, forsaking all others, keep thee only unto her, so long as ye both shall live?' The groom answers: 'I will'.

The minister then asks similar questions of the bride to which she answers: 'I will'.

The minister asks 'Who giveth this woman to be married to this man?' The bride's father does not need to respond verbally but he may do so if he wishes or he may nod or step forward.

The bride's father takes the bride's right hand in his and presents it palm down to the minister. The minister places it in the right hand of the groom. Some couples choose to omit this 'giving away' part of the ceremony as its relevance dates back to the time when women were considered no more than man's 'property'.

The bride's father steps back to take his place in the pew beside the bride's mother (the responsibility for his daughter now passing to her future husband) or he may retreat later after the pronouncement.

Time

Notes

The minister offers the best man the open prayer book onto which he places the ring(s). The minister blesses the ring and offers it to the groom who places it on the third finger of the bride's left hand. The groom holds the ring in place.

The minister guides the bride and groom through the wedding vows, of which there are alternative versions.

The minister addresses the groom first, and then the bride. In turn they repeat the minister's words, which are delivered in short phrases: 'I [name] take thee [name] to be my wedded wife/husband, to have and to hold from this day forward, for better for worse, for richer for poorer, in sickness and in health, to love and to cherish, till death us do part, according to God's holy law, and thereto I give my troth'.

'With this ring I thee wed, with my body I thee honour and all my worldly goods with thee I share. In the name of the Father and of the Son and of the Holy Ghost'. If the couple are exchanging rings, the bride places a ring on the groom's hand. The bride repeats the minister's words.

The minister pronounces the couple man and wife and they are married in the eyes of the Church.

The bride's father steps back quietly to take his place in the pew beside the bride's mother (if not previously done).

The best man steps back slightly and to the right-hand side.

The bride and groom may kiss. (The kiss no longer has its original significance — the first kiss the couple exchanged!) The minister may also kiss the bride after the marriage if he knows the bride well.

The bride and groom kneel at the chancel steps while the congregation kneels in the pews for the blessing, prayers and maybe a hymn.

The minister may give a short sermon. There may also be hymns, prayers and singing to conclude the religious ceremony. If there is to be Holy Communion or a Nuptial Mass it will take place at this point.

The bride takes her husband's left arm, the bridal attendants take up her train as she leaves the chancel led by the minister. The best man picks up his

Time

and the groom's hats and gloves. The minister leads the bridal party into the vestry or to a side table for the signing of the register and certificate. The order of the procession: minister; bride with groom; chief bridesmaid with best man; bridesmaids with pages; bride's mother with groom's father; groom's mother with bride's father.

Notes

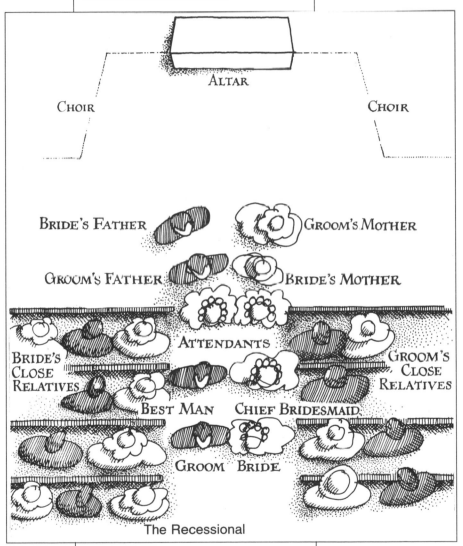

The Recessional

TRADITION

Ladies should always take the left arm of their escorts. When escorting a lady, the man should offer her his left arm so that his sword arm is free to protect her if necessary. Left-handed men ignore reality and abide by the custom.

Time

Notes

The marriage register and certificate will have been prepared beforehand by the minister.

The register is signed by:

- Minister
- Bride (using her maiden name probably for the last time if she chooses to take her husband's surname in future)
- Groom
- Two adult witnesses — usually the two fathers or the best man and chief bridesmaid (if she is of age) but the choice could be both mothers, or one representative from each family. It is advisable to choose the witnesses beforehand. When the register is signed the couple are legally married.

The minister hands the marriage certificate to the groom.

A few photographs will probably be allowed.

Meanwhile in the church, somebody could sing or the organist could play a particular piece, or perhaps a friend could play a flute or violin solo.

The bride's bouquet is returned to her. The groom, best man and ushers ensure that they have their hats and gloves. The groom offers his left arm to the bride whose veil is clear of her face.

The attendants take up the bride's train.

If the minister has asked that the fees be paid after the ceremony, it is the best man's responsibility to stay behind in the vestry to settle financial matters while the recessional takes place without him and the minister.

The bells peal and the music changes for the recessional from the church which follows in the same order as entry into the vestry.

The bride and groom should not be halted for congratulations as they proceed along the aisle and out of the church.

When the bridal party has left the church, others may follow from the altar — relatives first followed by friends.

After the Church

The wedding party may emerge to, and under, an archway of well-wishers or a reception in keeping with their jobs, hob-

Time

bies or interests, for example: a ceremony of swords for a military couple; an archway of rackets for tennis enthusiasts; school children for teachers; a football team (suitably dressed) and so on. Everyone can relax when they are outside the church.

Confetti and rice are showered upon the newly married couple, if this is allowed. (If not the ushers watch for confetti throwers and tactfully suggest that guests keep it for the reception.) Lucky symbols are given to the couple.

. . . .

TRADITION AND SUPERSTITION

Confetti, horseshoes and shoes are given to the couple as symbols of fertility. These are very ancient symbols believed to bring good luck.

The word 'confetti' is Italian for confectionery, or sweets, which is what was formerly used and symbolised wishes for lots of sweet experiences. In Britain, real flowers (or their petals) or rice were often used until the introduction of confetti. Rice and grain were used because of their symbolism with fertility. Sometimes the grain was in the form of small cakes which are the origin of our own wedding cakes.

Fruit and nuts are also other forms of confetti used in some cultures, again symbolising the wish for fruitfulness and richness.

Horseshoes must be stored upright 'to keep in the luck'. Shoes symbolise authority and at one time they were thrown at the newly married couples for luck! Today, shoes are normally tied to the vehicle in which the couple leave for honeymoon.

. . . .

The chief usher checks the church for any property left behind.

Photographs are taken outside the church building.

The best man organises the relevant guests to be included in the photographs.

The best man signals that it is time to leave for the reception.

The best man escorts the bride and groom to the first waiting car ensuring that they are the first to leave the church grounds. The second car is reserved for the bride's mother and groom's father who are followed by a third car carrying the bride's father and groom's mother. The bridesmaids, flower girl and page boys follow or travel with the couple's parents.

Time   **Notes**

When all members of the wedding party have departed, the other guests follow, making their way to the formal place for photographs or directly on to the reception venue.

The best man ensures that everyone has transport to the reception. He should have organised any necessary lifts beforehand but he should still double check that no one is left stranded. He may be the last to leave the church grounds after settling fees but needs to arrive reasonably early at the reception.

At the Reception

Although the newly-weds are first to leave for the reception, the bride's parents (as host and hostess) need to arrive first. At a very formal reception, the services of a toastmaster are usually employed who will announce the guests as they arrive and approach the receiving line. The receiving line ensures that every guest has the chance to meet the parents and thank the host and hostess for the wedding. The traditional order for the full receiving line is:

Time   **Notes**

9. Other attendants

8. Chief bridesmaid

7. Best man

6. Groom

5. Bride

4. Groom's father

3. Groom's mother

2. Bride's father

1. Bride's mother

The best man is not always included if he is the last to leave the church but if he does arrive in time he should be included between the groom and the chief bridesmaid.

Each guest is greeted by name or by politely asking the name. The bride and groom should introduce each other to the guests when necessary or convenient. Generally it is sufficient for each guest to make their identity obvious to the first in the receiving line. Officially, each member of the receiving line presents the guest to the next in the line with an appropriate remark, for example, 'Mrs Brown, meet Jane our chief bridesmaid'. The guests express their best wishes to the bride and congratulations to the groom. Men, and some women, shake hands and some will offer their cheek for a polite kiss. To avoid nose-jarring clashes, the rule is to offer the left cheek.

Today receiving lines tend to be more spontaneous and a faster-moving activity when exchanges in the line are particularly brief. After all, this is not the time to catch up on the news of the week.

At the end of the line, guests are offered a glass of wine or an aperitif and everyone circulates.

The best man, chief bridesmaid and ushers should be on hand to ensure the smooth passage of guests, help to intro-

Time

Notes

duce people to each other and ensure that they feel welcome. When introducing people to each other, men are introduced to women, for example, 'Andy, meet Carole', but if one person is clearly older than the other, the younger one is introduced to the other. A man stands up when being introduced to a woman.

Sometimes the guests are asked to sign a register.

A photo session after the greetings allows the guests to have a drink while the bride and groom relax for the photographs.

At a formal reception and at the agreed time, the toastmaster asks the guests to take their seats. At a more informal affair, the best man will prompt the bride and groom to take their seats. The processional order in which the guests enter the dining room is:

Bride's father with groom's mother
Bride's mother with groom's father
Best man with chief bridesmaid
Bridesmaids with flower girl
Page boys
Ushers
Guests.

The best man guides the guests to the seating plan and helps them to take their places as quickly and with as little fuss as possible. The ushers may also assist.

If a minister of religion is present, he must be invited to say grace and should have been approached in advance. If there is no minister present, grace may be said by the bride's father. It is not obligatory these days, but if said, the best man must first request and achieve silence. Suitable wording would be: 'For what we are about to receive, may the Lord make us truly thankful'.

If the meal is to be served, the toastmaster or the bride's father indicates to the waitresses when they should commence. For a buffet, it must be made clear whether people should collect their meal before taking their seats or go to the serving table a few at a time. The bride and groom are the first to be served or to serve themselves.

Time

Notes

For a sit-down meal, the speeches and toasts generally take place after the meal and before the cutting of the cake but sometimes the cake is cut first so that this can be served with coffee. For a buffet, the cake will be cut and the speeches made once the bride and groom have had time to greet all their guests.

It is important that everyone has a charged glass for the toasts; guests should not have to raise an empty glass and mime.

Someone acts as a toastmaster (if there is no professional present) to introduce the speakers. In most cases this is the best man. At the appropriate moment, (usually after the meal and before the cutting of the cake) the toastmaster should stand and ask for silence. The guests should be given a few minutes to quieten. The toastmaster then introduces the father of the bride or an old and close friend of the bride who gives a speech and proposes a toast to the health and happiness of the bride and groom. The groom speaks next and then the best man. Everyone stands to drink the toasts.

The cake-cutting ceremony usually comes next and will probably be photographed. The cake is then removed by the caterers so that it may be cut for the guests. This can be the signal for the guests to leave the tables in order to mingle. Bridesmaids, the bride and groom, or the caterers distribute slices of cake to the guests.

If the reception includes dancing, this will start after the cake has been cut, or the guests may move to another room

TRADITION

It is traditional for the bride and groom to make the first cut in the cake together ceremonially. The groom places his right hand over the right hand of his bride, her left hand is then placed on top, and she places the knife point at the centre of the bottom cake tier and slowly cuts the cake helped by the groom. They may cut a slice and share it between them.
Bridesmaids keep their slices and place them under their pillows that night in the belief that they will then dream of their own future husbands.

Time

Notes

for coffee and cake while the furniture is cleared from the dance floor. The bride and groom lead the dancing with a slow dance. If the bride's father cuts in to finish the dance, the groom should ask the bride's mother to finish the dance. After a few minutes of spot light, the best man and the chief bridesmaid join in followed by the parents of the bride and groom. Guests join in for the second dance. The bride should dance with all members of the wedding party and immediate family members of the opposite sex. The best man dances with all the ladies of the wedding party including the bride of course, and as many guests as possible. He generally socialises and rescues the bride and groom from anyone who monopolises them, allowing the couple to circulate as much as possible. The car is decorated under the supervision of the best man who ensures that no one interferes with the mechanics, does anything dangerous or causes damage. The best man packs the cleaning kit.

> **TRADITION**
> *The ancient tradition of attaching old boots to the going-away car stems from the time when the bride's father presented the groom with one of her slippers, giving the groom 'the upper hand' which 'entitled' him to thrash his wife should she displease him! The slipper was placed at the bed head on the husband's side to remind the wife who was boss. However, if the wife assumed the dominant role, neighbours transferred the power of the slipper to her and named her 'the old boot'!*

The best man reminds the bride and groom when it is time to change ready to leave. The bride, together with the chief bridesmaid, retires to change into her going-away outfit. The groom does likewise with his best man.

> **TRADITION AND SUPERSTITION**
> *A bride should remove and throw away every pin when removing her dress and veil or she will be unlucky.*

The best man drives the car to the front of the reception ensuring that luggage is packed and loaded. He hands over the car keys and documents to the

Time

Notes

groom. The bride and groom should find time to make a tour of the room, thanking guests for attending and thanking their parents specially.

The Couple's Departure

The best man or the bride's father announces that the couple are about to leave. The best man sometimes arranges an informal leave-taking line involving two lines of guests where male guests line up on one side and female guests on the other with the parents and other wedding party members last in line, nearest the door. The bride passes through thanking the men for attending and saying goodbye; the groom moves down the other line.

The groom may present his mother and mother-in-law with bouquets. The bride throws her bouquet backwards and over her shoulder towards the assembled females.

> **TRADITION AND SUPERSTITION**
> *It is said that the one who catches the bouquet can expect to be the next bride.*

Everyone goes outside to give their final send-offs as the couple leave for honeymoon.

> **SUPERSTITION**
> *The first one of the couple to make a purchase after the wedding is said to be the dominant partner!*

Guests' Departure

There is no set time for the guests to depart, through there is one firm rule that no one should leave before the bride and groom. The guests thank the host and hostess before leaving.

The host settles the reception account. The bride's mother collects the remains of the cake, her daughter's wedding clothes, cards and telemessages from the best man, and checks that nothing is left behind by female guests.

The best man collects the groom's wedding clothes and checks that nothing is left behind by male guests. He may also be expected to collect the wedding gifts and transport them to the

Time

bride's parents' or the newly-weds' home at some stage. He ensures that wedding cards and any telemessages are handed to the bride's mother for the bride when she returns from honeymoon.

The host, hostess and best man are the last to leave.

Notes

INFILL LIST	TIMETABLE

Time	Programme of Events

Double Weddings

If the brides are sisters, their family may escort each bride individually up the aisle. Alternatively, the brides may proceed up the aisle together. The grooms, with their best men, wait at the front of the church. The senior couple takes precedence in the ceremony, completing their vows first, and in the vestry by signing the register first.

The recessional (the walk along the aisle and out of the church) can be a complex manoeuvre and some couples prefer to allow the senior couple to complete their exit with their attendants before the second party starts its retreat. The alternative is for the senior couple to be followed immediately by the second couple with all attendants behind them: the chief bridesmaid and the best man of the first couple, followed by those of the second couple and so on. In the case of two sisters marrying, their mother walks with the father of the senior bride's groom and the girls' father walks with the mother of the senior bride's groom. The second party's parents are escorted by relations of the bride's or close friends.

The procession, recession and escorts are obviously a matter of individual preference. Decisions must be made tactfully and procedures thoroughly rehearsed so that there is no confusion and that everything runs smoothly on the day.

Other Wedding Ceremonies

Church of Scotland Ceremony

Weddings in Scotland can be solemnized at any time and in any place. The minister walks down the aisle to meet the bride and her father and leads the procession to the altar. The bride's father takes his place beside his wife before the service begins as there is no 'giving-away'.

The Church of Wales and Welsh Congregational Churches' Ceremonies

There are numerous speeches at the reception followed by Welsh folk dancing and reels.

Nonconformist Ceremonies

The ceremonies of many free churches (for example, Methodist, Baptist and United Reformed) are similar to Anglican ceremonies except that they may be somewhat simpler and will depend on the particular sect but must include the following declarations by the bride and groom:

'I do solemnly declare that I know not of any lawful impediment why I (full name) may not be joined in matrimony to (full name)'.

'I call upon these persons here present to witness that I (full name) do take thee (full name) to be my lawful wedded wife/ husband'.

As with most all marriages other than Anglican, the couple must obtain a Superintendent Registrar's Certificate or Certificate and Licence to marry and a registrar will need to be in attendance if the minister is not authorised to register marriages.

The Roman Catholic Ceremony

A Catholic wedding service is similar in content to the Church of England ceremony though the couple will require a licence to marry from the Superintendent Registrar. Where both parties are Roman Catholic, the ceremony usually forms part of a full Nuptial Mass though it can be conducted outside Mass and this is most likely if one of the couple is not Roman Catholic. The priest will almost certainly be authorised to register the marriage, in which case there is no need for a registrar to be present.

The elements of the service cover: the significance of marriage; declarations that there are no lawful reasons why the couple may not marry; promises of faithfulness to each other, and the couple's acceptance to bring up children within the Roman Catholic faith.

Once the bride has walked up the aisle the service begins with a hymn and a Bible reading, followed by a sermon. The priest then asks whether there is any impediment to the marriage and calls on the couple to give their consent 'according to the rite of our holy mother the Church' to which each responds 'I will'. The couple join right hands and call upon the congregation to witness the marriage and then they make their vows to cherish one another: 'Till death do us part'. Vows are exchanged. The priest confirms them in marriage and the best man hands over the ring(s) which are blessed and given or exchanged with the couple acknowledging them as a token of their love and fidelity. In addition to a ring, the groom gives gold and silver to the bride as tokens of his worldly goods. Once the rings are blessed, the groom places the ring first on the bride's thumb, then on three fingers in turn saying: 'In the name of the Father, the Son and the Holy Ghost. Amen.' There are bidding prayers and a nuptial blessing and possibly Holy Communion and Thanksgiving. Following a final blessing is the dismissal whereupon the bride and groom and the wedding party move into the sacristy to make the civil declaration and sign and witness the register. If there is to be a following Nuptial Mass, the bridesmaids take their places in a reserved pew at the front.

For the Nuptial Mass, the couple return to the sanctuary and kneel; the bride is assisted by the groom who supports her as she kneels and rises. If Holy Communion is to be received, those taking it move forward at the appropriate time, returning afterwards to their pews. When the Mass ends, the couple proceed down the aisle from the sanctuary followed by the chief bridesmaid and best man and then the other bridesmaids, page boys and parents before the rest of the guests.

Christian Scientists Ceremony

As Christian Scientist churches are not authorised for marriage, couples must marry in another church or in a register office.

Quakers (Religious Society of Friends) Ceremony

As long as the legal requirements are fulfilled, weddings between Quakers can take place at any time of day and at any venue such as a private house or hall but the usual place is the Meeting House normally attended by one or both par-

ties. It is customary for the couple to apply formally to the Meeting by letter. A small group of men and women may then be appointed to discuss with the couple the seriousness of the ceremony.

The Quaker tradition is very plain and the wedding usually reflects this. There is no procession, no music and no minister. The bride and groom sit at the front of the Meeting House facing the congregation, some of whom will be regular attenders at the Meeting and some will be wedding guests who may not be members of the Society of Friends. Those in attendance may stand and speak from time to time or they may keep silent. When the couple feel the moment is right, they rise and make their vows, holding hands. The Elders of the Meeting House will have agreed the vows beforehand. The couple then resume their seats and the Meeting continues as previously until two of the Elders shake hands which is a sign that the Meeting is over. The couple then sign the marriage certificate followed by two witnesses. The wording of the certificate is read aloud, then signed by all present and given to the couple to keep. The registering officer present then registers the marriage which is signed by the couple and their two witnesses.

The ring(s) may be given or exchanged at any time, perhaps after the vows or after the register is signed. The bride rarely wears traditional wedding attire; she wears her best clothes. Grooms do not wear morning suits, they wear grey suits with a buttonhole.

A reception may follow and it is customary for all those in attendance to be invited.

Jewish Ceremony

As with other marriages outside the Anglican faith, a civil licence must be obtained from the Superintendent Registrar and there are also several formalities that need to be agreed with the rabbi. The ceremony can take place at any time on any day — except on the Sabbath (from Sunset on Friday until Sunset on Saturday) and on certain festival days — and in any venue but it is usually solemnized in a synagogue. Wherever the ceremony venue, the secretary of the groom's synagogue must take down the necessary particulars. Most Jewish ministers are authorised to register marriages and so there is usually no need for the registrar to be present. However, if the minister is not authorised, either the registrar will attend the ceremony or there will be a civil wedding at a register office before the religious service. As with other ceremonies, the form of the service may vary depending on the synagogue.

The couple usually fast on their wedding day in repentance of past sins and offer prayers for their new life together. The bride wears a traditional white or ivory wedding dress with long sleeves and a veil.

The wedding ceremonies of the Orthodox, Conservative or Reformed synagogue differ slightly but it is customary for the ceremony to take place in the presence of a minyan (a quorum of at least ten adult males). In all cases, both men and women must wear some covering on their heads.

The Jewish ceremony takes place under a chuppah which is a canopy of silk or velvet supported by four poles and decorated with flowers.

· ·

TRADITION

The chuppah symbolises the nomadic nature of the Jewish people, the time when the Israelites dwelt in tents and represents the bridal chamber, the home the couple will make together and the importance of the couple's new home. Its fragility reminds the couple of their own weakness and of the need to nurture their union to ensure its continuance.

· ·

The groom arrives with his best man, his father and the bride's father and they are escorted from the synagogue door to take their places in front of the congregation near to the chuppah. In an Orthodox service, the men and women sit on opposite sides of the synagogue. The groom and best man stand under the chuppah and wait for the bride.

The bride arrives with her escort. The groom and the best man step under the chuppah while the two fathers walk back to greet the bride. The bride takes the arm of her father and proceeds up the aisle, the bridesmaids follow and behind them are the groom's parents and the bride's mother escorted by a male relative. The bride joins the groom under the canopy and stands on his right. The other escorts position themselves around the couple according to instructions previously agreed with the rabbi. The couple's parents may also stand under the chuppah, and the relations and friends may position themselves around or nearby. The rabbi welcomes and blesses the wedding party. There is then a psalm of thanksgiving and a short address. The rabbi gives the betrothal blessing which is recited over a cup of ritual wine.

The ceremony involves the couple exchanging vows, making promises and exchanging rings. The bride wears no other ornament, not even her engagement ring. The groom places the ring on the bride's right index finger and makes a declaration to which the bride is not required to reply. Her mute acceptance of the groom's ring and his vow are taken to constitute her side of the agreement, and the marriage is then complete. The bride may then transfer the wedding ring to the third finger of her left hand. The ketuba or marriage document is read aloud. The rabbi chants the Seven Benedictions, or these are sung, after which the bride and groom each sip wine twice from the same glass, symbolising that they will share all things. The groom then breaks the glass on the ground and crushes it under his heel. This may symbolise the destruction of the temple in Jerusalem, the warding off of evil spirits, the fragility of marriage without love or that they should share their pleasures and halve their troubles. These days, the glass is often enclosed in a bag for obvious safety reasons. The couple then sign a covenant, there is then a blessing and psalm of praise and finally, the couple sign the civil contract (if a civil marriage did not preceed the ceremony), and sign the register of the synagogue before their two witnesses. They then retreat to a private room to spend a few moments alone together when they may share a bowl of soup to break their fast.

The Buddhist Ceremony

Prior to the ceremony, the guests are greeted with chanting. The guests are ushered to their places by girls wearing white. A lay leader escorts the bride and groom to a holy cabinet containing a sacred scroll in front of which they kneel and perform the ceremony of Gong-yo, which involves reciting sutras and chanting. The couple sip three times from three bowls of increasing size to symbolise how their lives will grow and expand together. There may be an exchange of rings, after which the lay leader explains the significance of marriage. To conclude the ceremony, the guests cheer and clap. The bride will probably wear a dress with a veil and there will be a reception. Guests send gifts and attend the ceremony and reception wearing smart attire.

Greek Orthodox Ceremony

The Greek bride normally wears white. She may travel to church with her father and maid-of-honour. Depending on the couple's status there may be many best men and best women or bridesmaids. At the church door, a best man gives the bride her bouquet. The ceremony is called 'crowning', the priest places crowns on the heads of the couple. Guests are not required to cover their heads. At the reception, money is pinned on the bride.

Greek-Cypriot Ceremony

Instead of bridesmaids, the bride has female representatives from various families.

Ukrainian Ceremony

The bride and groom's headdress is a green wreath of myrtle and their hands are tied together. At the reception the couple are greeted by the bride's mother who offers them bread and salt.

Oriental Ceremony

The bride and groom at a traditional Japanese wedding both wear kimonos and the bride's face is made up chalk white. The bride is expected to wear up to five wedding dresses.

The Chinese decorate their wedding cars with a bridal doll.

The Hindu Ceremony

The reception venue is likely to be a hired hall as the wedding may last all day and there may be many guests. The bride wears a red silk sari, the groom is robed in white and guests wear their smartest attire — the women in gold-embroidered saris and the men may also wear bright colours. The ceremony is relatively informal and guests communicate among themselves while it is going on.

The bride's family will have arranged a 'sacred place' covered with a canopy of brocade or some other richly decorated material and many flowers in the middle of the hall.

The bride is the first to arrive and hides until the groom arrives with his relations and friends. As he enters, lights are waved over his head and grains of rice are thrown, symbolising riches and fertility. He then takes his place under the canopy. The bride is brought out to join him and relations and close friends may group around. Gifts may be sent or bought along to the wedding and given personally to bride and groom.

If a religious marriage is to take place in a building which is registered for the solemnization of marriages, couples should give notice of their intention to marry and comply with the civil preliminaries. It may be necessary for a registrar to attend to register the marriage. If a religious marriage is to take place in a building which is not registered, then a civil ceremony beforehand will be necessary.

The Muslim Ceremony

Muslim women may marry only Muslim men, yet Muslim men can marry Muslim, Christian or Jewish women.

The venue for a Muslim wedding is a mosque and is usually conducted by an imam. An Islam wedding is a contract and not a sacrament and therefore a lay Muslim male may officiate at the ceremony. The bride is dressed in red, the groom in a dark suit, and the guests in smart attire.

The women gather on one side of the mosque, the men on the other. There is a sermon followed by a reading from the Koran. The bride and groom give their consent to marry and they are pronounced man and wife. There is a further sermon followed by prayers. All guests are then given a sweetmeat, usually dried dates or figs before they leave.

The bride's parents host a reception to which relations and friends of the bride bring gifts. A week later the parents of the groom host a similar party at which his relations and friends donate their gifts.

If a religious marriage is to take place in a building which is registered for the solemnization of marriages, couples should give notice of their intention to marry and comply with the civil preliminaries. It may be necessary for a registrar to attend to register the marriage. If a religious marriage is to take place in a building which is not registered, then a civil ceremony beforehand will be necessary.

The Sikh Ceremony

Both partners must be Sikhs and are permitted to meet before the wedding if other people are present.

Sikh marriage ceremonies are similar to those for Hindus and Muslims in that many of their customs are similar. The ceremony may take place in the Sikh place of worship or in the bride's home and involves hymns and prayers.

The bride wears a red sari and a red headscarf or red trousers and tunic. In addition, she also wears a veil which is not lifted until she is married. The jewellery she wears is given by the groom's family.

The groom wears a scarf and his turban together with either traditional Eastern white attire or Western clothes.

Parties are held in the family homes and gifts are exchanged.

Afterwards

A lthough the newly-weds' departure from the reception usually concludes the wedding day's formal celebrations and marks the start of their honeymoon together, there are a number of 'loose ends' to be tied up before life returns to normality!

During the Honeymoon

Attire

The best man and chief bridesmaid return hired attire if appropriate, return any deposits to the couple and pass on any bills for cleaning.

Photographs/Video

The bride's mother will be dealing with photograph orders while the couple are on honeymoon. If the photographs are a disaster, they can be re-taken at a photographer's studio, the reception venue or at home after the honeymoon.

Press Report

Details of the press report following the wedding are contained in Chapter 11.

Cake

Small slices of cake are sent by the bride's mother to those who were unable to attend on the day.

Security

The best man or the parents of the bride should check on the security of the couple's home whilst they are away on their honeymoon.

Honeymooners' Return

Expenses

The husband reimburses the best man any out-of-pocket expenses incurred at the wedding.

> **TRADITION AND SUPERSTITION**
> *The husband should carry his wife over the threshold of their new home in order to bring good fortune in their future life. This may stem from the days when grooms captured their reluctant brides. It is also said that it prevents the bride from stepping into the new home 'left foot first' which is considered to be unlucky for the couple.*

Thank-you Notes

From the Bride

Upon return from honeymoon, there will probably be extra thank-yous to write for gifts that arrived on the wedding day. The bride should send notes to all gift donors and acknowledgement notes to message senders. When acknowledging a gift of money, it is courteous to indicate how the money will be spent. There may also be people to whom a special thank-you is appropriate, for instance both sets of parents for their support up to and during the wedding and the attendants for their help. These should be handwritten and sent promptly upon return from honeymoon.

The bride's mother should express her thanks to the helpers. It may also be appropriate to thank formally those service providers who excelled on the wedding day.

To the Bride's Parents

It is customary for guests to write brief thank-you notes/letters to the bride's parents (or host(s) of the wedding).

Documentation

Name Change

Although it is traditional and the most popular choice, there is no legal requirement for the bride to change her surname when she marries. She can retain her maiden name entirely in which case there is no need to change any documents or she may use both. For example she can continue to use her maiden name for professional purposes and use her married name socially. She may hyphenate the two names. In which case, both partners should use the same name and it is worth considering that for identification purposes it may be necessary to substantiate both names depending on the circumstances. This can create confusion especially in financial and legal matters and will undoubtedly result in lots of 'red tape'. This is perhaps why most brides decide to take their husband's surname as their own as it does make life simpler.

Organisations should be informed in writing. A written or typed 'skeleton' let-ter can be photocopied and then filled in with the relevant information for each specific addressee.

Finances

Advice concerning finances may be found in Chapter 1.

Wills

As marriage automatically renders any previous wills invalid, it is important to make new provisions.

Making a will will ensure that property and other assets are divided as desired after death. Once there is a property and a family, an estate may be complicated and valuable. When making specific bequests, they should be written in a way to protect the spouse and children should the value of the estate drop. It is wise to choose a reputable solicitor and obtain an estimate in advance of the expected costs.

Banks and Building Societies

Joint arrangements may need consideration.

Pensions

If not involved in a work's pension scheme, it is prudent to take out an affordable saving plan spread over a stated number of years.

SAMPLE SKELETON LETTER STATING NAME CHANGE

(Sender's address
and telephone number)

(Date)
(Addressee)

Dear Sir/Madam

Account no./Policy no./Pay no./NI no./Ref no.

I wish to inform you that following my marriage on . . ., my name changed/I will be changing my name from . . . to . . . .

I should be grateful if you would amend your records accordingly. Please inform me if you need any additional information, specimen signatures, copy marriage certificate, etc.

Yours faithfully

INFILL LIST	DOCUMENTATION
	Date done
Employer	
Inland Revenue	
Department of Health	
Department of Social Security (if necessary)	
Electoral Roll	
Utilities	
Bank	
Credit Card Companies	
Building Societies	
Post Office (Savings Account)	
Premium Bond Office	
Insurance Companies and agents	
DVLC	
Passport office	
Doctor	
Dentist	
Clubs	
Associations	
Mail-order catalogues	
Relatives	
Distant friends	
Others	

Insurance: Life, Buildings and Home Contents

The wedding-gift list will provide a useful guide when assessing the contents and value of possessions for home contents insurance. After the wedding and when established in a new home, an assessment should be made. Mail order catalogues may be a useful guide to prices. A note should be made of the date and subsequent additions also dated. Lists should be updated frequently. This method ensures easy assessment of value for insurance purposes and any claims if property is stolen or damaged at any time.

Entertaining

It is traditional for the newly-weds to entertain both sets of parents, then the best man and bridesmaids in the couple's new home during the three months following the wedding.

Memorabilia

Photographs/Video

Naturally there will be photographs and/or a video which will record the best moments of the wedding and the reception.

Keepsake Books

Books with pre-printed layouts may be bought and added to or alternatively a large scrap book or blank photograph album may be suitable. Ideas for inserts include: fabric samples, dried flowers from the bouquet, sample stationery, telemessages, cards and gift list.

Guest Book

A guest book at the reception for guests to sign their names can provide a pleasurable memento.

Preserving the Wedding Dress and Veil

Details are included in Chapter 13.

Flower Collages

It is possible to have flowers preserved by making a collage from the dried blooms. A silk replica is another option.

Starting a Family

Parents are often very keen to become grandparents and the couple need to be prepared for the inevitable hints and comments. If plans have not already been made during the engagement, now is the time for serious discussion and agreement about starting a family, or not starting a family. Modern contraceptive methods allow couples much more freedom of choice today.

Happy Anniversaries

Most people like to remember their wedding day by celebrating their wedding anniversaries. It is a good time to recall all the good things about marriage past and present, to take stock of the relationship and to prepare for the years ahead. The husband sometimes gives his wife an eternity ring on the birth of their first child or at another significant event such as a special anniversary.

Traditionally, certain materials are associated with particular years of marriage; the idea being that they will replace the wedding gifts which may have worn out.

TRADITION

1 Cotton
2 Paper
3 Leather or Straw
4 Silk or Flowers
5 Wood
6 Iron or sugar
7 Wool or copper
8 Bronze
9 Pottery
10 Tin
11 Steel
12 Silk and fine linen
13 Lace
14 Ivory
15 Crystal
20 China
*25 Silver
30 Pearl
35 Coral
40 Ruby
45 Sapphire
*50 Gold
55 Emerald
*60 Diamond
75 Second diamond
*Main anniversaries/celebrations

21

Second Marriages

Second marraiges are generally more informal and quieter celebrations than first marriages, especially if both partners are divorced, but they are still a time to celebrate a joyous occasion.

Engagement

Children from a previous marriage should be the first to hear the news as the changes affect them most; they need to know directly, not indirectly from a grandparent or other relative.

Legal Requirements

The law of England and Wales recognises a divorced person as single as long as they can produce a Decree Absolute.

There is no limit to the number of times a person (in the UK) may marry provided that their former spouse is dead or their Decree Absolute has been granted.

No person who is already married to a living spouse should marry someone else; if they do so, the second marriage is invalid. No person who is going through divorce proceedings may marry until the Decree Absolute has been granted.

All persons who have been previously married should produce documentary evidence of the death of the former spouse or of the dissolution or annulment of the marriage. Photocopied documents are not acceptable without certification. All relevant certificates or licences must be handed to the minister or registrar before the ceremony.

Ceremony

A Superintendent Registrar is duty bound to perform a marriage ceremony for divorced persons so long as the Decree Absolute has been granted and all other legal requirements have been met.

Widows and widowers are quite free to marry in a church; the ceremony is exactly the same as for first marriages.

The Church of England forbids the re-marriage of a divorcee during the lifetime of a previous partner and consequently a minister may legally refuse to marry in church anyone whose previous partner is still living irrespective of whether the person concerned is the injured party. Also, he/she cannot be compelled to permit the re-marriage to take place in his/her church nor can he/she be compelled to conduct a service for anyone who has re-married under civil law. Therefore, no marriage service can be performed in a Church of England church where either the bride or groom has a previous partner still living, unless the clergyman is prepared to ignore the church authorities. There are, however, a few Church of England ministers who are prepared to consider individual circumstances and may be prepared to perform the ceremony with the permission of their bishop but this is the exception rather than the rule. If a minister is prepared to ignore ecclesiastical authority or manages to obtain the permission of his bishop and agrees to conduct a marriage ceremony for a divorcee, he/she may discourage the presence of attendants, flowers, bell-ringers and choir.

The question of divorcees marrying in church is currently under consideration by the General Synod of the Church of England but still remains highly contentious. The majority of Church of England ministers share the view of the Roman Catholic faith and would not permit a bride and groom to make vows "...until death us do part" for a second time! The marriage of divorcees will therefore, almost certainly, be a civil ceremony in a register office. Most ministers are prepared to conduct a service of blessing after a civil marriage and this can be a satisfactory compromise solution.

Service of Blessing

Ecclesiastical authority permits a minister to conduct a service of blessing following a civil wedding, though this must not resemble a marriage ceremony and there are no legal formalities. It is a simple service, usually including hymns, prayers, a bible reading and a blessing but not an exchange of vows. It can take place at any time after the civil ceremony but often the couple, their parents, and a few close friends (acting as best man and matron or maid of honour) attend church before joining the guests at the reception. The service of blessing may be held in a church or at the reception venue.

Free Churches

Many of the churches of Free Church denominations have been registered by a Superintendent Registrar of Marriages as buildings in which marriages may be solemnized. Ministers of the United Reformed Church, the Baptist, Methodist and other Protestant churches take advantage of their right to become registered as 'authorised' persons to conduct the service and to act as the registrar under the civil law. Those who do not possess this authority may conduct a marriage ceremony but a Superintendent Registrar, or his deputy, must be present to record the wedding, or a separate civil ceremony must be conducted by a Superintendent Registrar in his office. Wherever the marriage venue, the register must be signed by the bridal couple and witnessed by two others. The Free Churches are traditionally more liberal and normally allow a divorced person, whose ex-spouse is still living, to re-marry in church but if the couple are strangers to Methodist or Baptist Churches for example, their chances depend on convincing the minister that there are extremely sincere reasons for wanting to re-marry in church and that they are not interested only in the aes-

thetics of the setting! Although Free Churches generally view a marriage as binding for life, each minister has discretion to consider the re-marriage of a divorced person, considering each individual case in the light of its own merits. Some ministers may adamantly refuse to marry a divorced person, others will sympathise with the injured party and others consider that everyone is entitled to another chance.

The Society of Friends

Although the Society of Friends retains its belief in the sanctity and life-long nature of marriage, Quakers may be sympathetic of divorcees who wish to re-marry in a Friends' Meeting as long as all the circumstances are taken into account and the monthly Meeting is satisfied that the person seeking their permission is well known to them and associated with the Meeting. It may be possible for the matter to be investigated discreetly by a group of Friends so that the monthly Meeting might be advised by them without the need to broadcast all the details in public. Any decision made by the church involved is made on the merits of each case.

Roman Catholic Church

The re-marriage of a divorced person, whose ex-spouse is still living, is strictly forbidden. There are, however, some circumstances where the previous marriage is not recognised by the Church and is therefore deemed invalid, as in the case of a civil marriage, or where the Catholic authority's Marriage Tribunal has declared a previous marriage to be null and void, which can be a complicated and lengthy process. In such cases, the Church will be prepared to marry that person provided that he/she has the legal right in civil law (by being divorced by the State from their original partner).

Jewish Faith

A Jewish divorcee wishing to re-marry and have her second wedding recognised under Jewish law requires a Get (a certificate of divorce which is issued if the husband agrees to the divorce). Further information may be obtained from the

Chief Rabbi via the local Rabbi or synagogue office secretary.

Finance

It would be inappropriate to expect either set of parents to take on financial responsibility. Generally, the couple pay for their own wedding especially since their parents probably contributed to their first. However, if parents do offer to pay, their generosity need not be refused. If a first-time bride is marrying a widower or divorcee, her parents usually contribute and host the reception in the usual way.

Reception

Although ceremonies tend to be comparatively simple and informal, there is no reason to restrict the reception afterwards; the traditional reception is perfectly acceptable but, conversely, there is no necessity to provide a meal and entertainment as the main purpose of a wedding reception is to allow guests to congratulate the newlyweds, join in the toasts to their health and happiness, witness the cutting of the cake and wish them well as they leave for their honeymoon.

Children from a previous marriage should have special duties so that they feel important.

Speeches at a woman's second marriage are subtly different as the tone needs to be a little more serious.

Honeymoon

The honeymoon is an opportunity to confirm the new relationship together and should be taken.

Duties

If facilities in the church or register office allow, the couple may be attended by a full wedding party.

Older children from a previous marriage may serve as bridesmaids and ushers. A widow may want her teenage son as best man if the groom agrees. Traditionally, however, a widow would not be attended by bridesmaids but by a matron or maid of honour who waits at the chancel steps to relieve the bride of her bouquet or posy. A matron of honour is a married lady attendant; a maid of honour is an unmarried lady attendant. It is possible to have both in which case the maid of honour takes precedence by holding the bride's bouquet or posy and serving as a witness. She acts as the bride's adviser, messenger and general assistant with duties of a chief bridesmaid and she is the equivalent of the groom's best man.

It is essential that children from a previous marriage are part of the proceedings so that they do not feel excluded in any way. If there are to be no attendants and the marriage is to take place in church, children may read special verses or lessons if the minister agrees. The feelings of a former spouse must be sought at the planning stage before suggestions are made to the children.

As for a first wedding, there is no obligation to 'give the bride away'. A giver-away at a bride's second marriage may still be her father but it is more usual for a close friend to perform this role. The bride could choose a son or a brother. Alternatively, the 'giving-away' ceremony may be omitted from the service altogether where the bride walks the aisle alone or with her groom.

The toast to the bride and groom may still be made by the bride's father but this is fairly unusual as he is not giving his daughter away in marriage this time; it will normally be made by a male friend, perhaps the husband of the bride's friend who sent out the invitations for her, or by the best man if there is one. There are normally only two speeches: the proposal of the couple's health and the groom's response.

Guest List

It is obviously insensitive to invite a former spouse unless the relationship is still very good. However, children from a previous marriage must be invited and if they are expected to perform the roles of attendants, the agreement of the former partner should be obtained.

A widow or widower who remains close to their late partner's family may wish to invite them to the wedding providing this will not cause any ill-feeling. They may choose to decline the invitation but should not be offended by an invitation.

Announcements and Printing

Press Announcements

An older couple's announcement would normally exclude parents' names and would instead elaborate on the ceremony, professions and future plans.

There is no requirement to state whether it is a first or second marriage and it is acceptable to announce the news after, rather than before, the event.

A widow uses her former husband's name (for example Mrs Sam South); a divorcee uses her own first name (for example Mrs Nel South); an alternative is to exclude titles and use only first names.

Invitations

If the wedding is small and informal or if there is little advance notice, a personal letter, handwritten card or telephone call is sufficient and acceptable. Facsimile transmissions should not be used for sending wedding invitations.

For the more formal occasion, invitations are normally sent out by a friend of the bride but if the bride's parents are hosting the reception, then they would send them out or they may be sent by the bride and groom. The bride's surname is not normally included. For a widow re-marrying in church, her parents may issue the invitations just as they would for a daughter who is single, though they would use her married name. Invitations may be worded to include children.

The bride may wish to invite only close family to the register office and additional guests to a reception afterwards.

Attire

For all second-time brides, whether divorced, widowed or older, her dress is often simpler in style and more restrained than the traditional regalia. She would not normally wear a veil and though it is usual for women to wear some form of headdress in church, this is not obligatory in the Church of England, the Roman Catholic Church and some of the Free Churches. Some people believe that all second-time brides should not wear a full traditional white gown and veil because they are symbols of virginity and innocence traditionally reserved for maidenhood. Something extra special could include a well-cut suit or long silk dress, usually in pastel colours with a corsage or simple bouquet or posy. Although the ceremony is exactly the same for a widow, tradition calls for less formality and this is also reflected in dress and suggests the omission of the bridal gown and veil.

Women over the age of forty generally look better in something other than a wedding gown, such as formal evening wear, dressy suits or dinner/cocktail outfits and although any of these choices may be pure white, off-white or pastel shades tend to be more flattering. A small bouquet and a hat or headdress of flowers usually replaces the veil.

The marriage of a widower is much less restricted than for a widow. However, it is still commonly less formal than a first wedding.

If the bride is a widow, tradition calls for less formality and suggests the omission of a full white wedding gown and veil and that the groom should wear a dark lounge suit rather than the formal attire usual for a bride's first wedding. At a formal evening reception, the groom wears a bow tie; for daytime his choices can vary from formal wear to a blazer and slacks.

The best man and the rest of the male members of the wedding party should follow the degree of formality set by the groom.

At a service of blessing, the wedding party's attire should be discussed with the minister.

Flowers

Popular alternatives to the traditional large elaborate bouquets include small bouquet, posies and single flowers. A corsage is appropriate for a simple ceremony where the bride wears a suit or a dress.

Rings

A woman who plans to re-marry following her divorce should not wear her new engagement ring until the divorce is final. Any woman who has been wearing an engagement ring from her previous marriage, should remove it and not wear it again when she becomes re-engaged. The former ring could be passed onto a son so that he may give it to his future bride or the stones may be reset and used as another form of jewellery for the bride or for a daughter.

A wedding ring from a previous marriage may be worn until the day of the second wedding at which time it should be removed and not worn again.

Wedding Gifts

Traditional wedding gifts of household items may be inappropriate but relatives and friends may still want to buy something special. A list of more unusual items may be produced or it is permissible to include 'No gifts please' on the invitations.

Parties

An engagement party for an older couple who have grown children could be given by the bride's and/or the groom's children.

If the bride has long-standing friends who attended her first shower, the bride should reject the offer of another shower to which invitees would feel obliged to donate a gift.

22

Information on the Internet

Weddings take an awful lot of planning and involve a lot of different purchases, so it's handy to know that there are sites that specialise in helping you to arrange things. Some of those below offer planning services, others have links to wedding resources of all kinds, while others offer unusual or one-off wedding items. There are also some sites on marriage – mostly giving advice and guidance on how to make it work after that first big day. After all, as one of these sites puts it, 'A wedding is a day … a marriage is a lifetime.' For details of marriage ceremonies in faiths other than those included here, consult the sites listed under *Religion.*

Confetti

www.confetti.co.uk
This Internet service has been designed to make your wedding experience enjoyable and stress free by giving you all the information and advice you want, and when you want it. It aims to meet the needs of everyone involved in the wedding.

Hitched

www.hitched.co.uk
Another all-encompassing site with sections for everyone involved and an enviable selection of suitable jokes and tips for speeches. It has links to hundreds of wedding and reception venues throughout the UK, plus a handy diary planner facility to make sure you get everything done on time. You can even buy stag and hen night 'accessories' in its online shop.

Weddings and Brides UK

www.weddings-and-brides.co.uk
Weddings and Brides UK have pulled together all essential wedding information and put it into one place. You will even find out what the potential pitfalls are at this site. For example, is your wedding car reliable and is there a back up available if your car breaks down? It also has details of products and services for weddings and honeymoons. This site is a must for anyone planning a wedding.

WeddingChannel.com

www.weddingchannel.com
Weddings are often one of the most stressful, complex and expensive endeavours people undertake. Wedding-Channel is aimed at helping both men and women through the process of planning a wedding and starting a new home. This is a comprehensive and very useful wedding-related site.

Wedding Guide UK

www.weddingguide.co.uk
This site offers information and advice to anyone planning a wedding. It has a comprehensive product and service section giving details of hen and stag activities, marquee hire and wedding insurance – right through to where you can buy all your bridal wear.

Weddingbells

www.weddingbells.com
This is the web site of the American magazine with the same name. It is published twice a year, with many of the articles being free for you to browse on the web site. Here you can find out information for the best man, parents of the bride and groom, guidance on stag and hen parties and lots more. Also available are lots of difference speeches and information about the wedding ceremony.

Church of England Weddings

www.cofe.anglican.org/lifechanges/ wedding.html
This site details the legal requirements and fees.

Register Office Weddings

www.registerofficeweddings.com
Use this site to locate the one closest to you, and find all the information you need on procedures including how to book, how much notice is required, how much it will cost, etc. There is also a handy search facility allowing you to locate wedding services in your area, but this does not yet cover all areas of the UK.

Hindi Weddings

www.lalwani.demon.co.uk/sonney/wedding.htm
If you are invited to, or are participating in, a Hindi marriage ceremony, it is wise to know what to expect beforehand. This simple one-page guide will help.

Jewish Weddings

www.jewish.org.pl/english/edu/JewFAQ/marriage.htm
This simple text-only guide to Jewish weddings and marriage will tell you all you need to know. It is part of a huge site giving information on all aspects of Judaism but has a most comprehensive guide to Jewish weddings.

Weddings Abroad

www.weddings-abroad.com
If you fancy getting away from it all for your wedding rather than just for the honeymoon, visit this site. The company that runs it arranges in excess of 4,000 weddings each year for couples wishing to marry outside their country of residence, and boasts some of the most beautiful and exquisite places to marry in the world.

Web Wedding

www.webwedding.co.uk
If you want ideas for your wedding, this is the place to browse. It has an impressive database of over 10,000 wedding suppliers – for everything from the dress to the honeymoon – with some special offers and competitions as well. There are also links to online wedding stores.

Wedding Rings UK

www.wedding-ringsuk.com
This Birmingham-based company offers discounted handmade wedding rings in a range of styles and price ranges. You can purchase over the net, and if you don't know your size they will send you a gadget to tell you before despatching your order. All items are delivered by secure courier.

Marriage Encounter

www.marriage-encounter.freeserve.co.uk
This service, offered by the Anglican Church, helps married couples to get the most out of their marriage, their commitment to one another and learn to improve their relationship. It is open to all married couples, whatever their faith, and consists of a weekend learning break in which you can explore and share your feelings, hopes, joys, fears and disappointments while learning to improve communication and deepen your relationship. Apart from a registration fee, there is no charge and accommodation and food are provided. It is not recommended as an alternative to counselling for couples with serious problems.

Marriage Care

www.marriagecare.org.uk
This site gives information on marriage in the UK, marriage preparation classes run by the Catholic Church, and gives advice on how to maintain a healthy, happy marriage. You can download their marriage preparation guide or find details of courses in your area at this site.

2-in-2-1

www.2-in-2-1.com
This American site gives information on shaping and maintaining your marriage, as well as offering the usual wedding services. Its marriage clinic covers all sorts of marital problems and issues, and it also has links to many other marriage research sites.

~ *Index* ~